ASTOR

ASTOR

THE RISE AND FALL OF AN AMERICAN FORTUNE

Anderson Cooper

and Katherine Howe

HARPER

An Imprint of HarperCollins*Publishers*

HarperCollins books may be purchased for educational, business, or sales promotional use. For information, please email the Special Markets Department at SPsales@harpercollins.com.

FIRST EDITION

Insert art credits: Page 1, top, DcoetzeeBot/Wikimedia Commons; page 1, bottom, John Wesley Jarvis/ Wikimedia Commons; page 2, top, John Jacob Astor (1763–1848) ca 1840, unidentified artist, watercolor on ivory, 4 3/4 x 3 1/2 in, gift of Mrs. George K. Livermore, New-York Historical Society, 1974.33; page 2, bottom, National Trust, Cliveden/Wikimedia Commons; page 3, top left, Peter Paul Skeolan, photographer Daniel John Pound, London Joint Stock Newspaper Co./DCOW/EUB/Alamy Stock Photo; page 3, top right, National Portrait Gallery, Smithsonian Institution, Frederick Hill Meserve Collection; page 3, bottom, The Miriam and Ira D. Wallach Division of Art, Prints and Photographs, Picture Collection, New York Public Library, "Astor Place Opera-House riots" New York Public Library Digital Collections; page 4, Carolus-Duran/Sepia Times/Universal Images Group/Getty Images; page 5, top, Library of Congress/ Corbis/VCG/Getty Images; page 5, bottom, Museum of the City of New York, X2013.139.91B; page 6, top left; GL Archive/Alamy Stock Photo; page 6, top right, Archive PL/Alamy Stock Photo; page 6, bottom, Caroline Astor Residence, 1893, Mina Rees Library, CUNY Graduate Center Archives and Special Collections, The City University of New York; page 7, Frank M. Ingalls/New York Historical Society/ Getty Images; page 8, top, Prisma by Dukas Presseagentur GmbH/Alamy Stock Photo; page 8, bottom, The Print Collector/Getty Images; page 9, top, Museum of the City of New York, 90.44.1.785; Page 9, bottom right, Wikimedia Commons/Library of Congress; page 10, top, Collection Philippe Clement/Arterra Picture Library/Alamy Stock Photo; page 10, bottom left, Division of Work and Industry, National Museum of American History, Smithsonian Institution; page 10, bottom right, Everett Collection Inc/Alamy Stock Photo; page 11, top, Museum of the City of New York, 93.1.1.4915; page 11, bottom, Jacob A. (Jacob August) Riis (1849–1914), Museum of the City of New York, 2008.1.15; page 12, top, Frederic Lewis/Archive Photos/ Getty Images; page 12, bottom, Los Angeles Times Photographic Archive, Library Special Collections, Charles E. Young Research Library, UCLA; page 13, top, Everett Collection Inc/Alamy Stock Photo; page 13, bottom, Bettmann/Getty Images; page 14, top, Ron Galella/Getty Images; page 14, bottom, AP Photo/ Mary Altaffer; page 15, Chester Higgins Jr/*New York Times*/Redux; page 16, Popperfoto /Getty Images.

Endpaper credit: John Jacob Astor's house on Fifth Avenue and Sixty-Fifth Street, New York, ca 1900. Photograph by the Museum of the City of New York/Byron Collection/Getty Images.

Designed by Nancy Singer

Library of Congress Cataloging-in-Publication Data

Names: Cooper, Anderson, author. | Howe, Katherine, author.
Title: Astor : the rise and fall of an American fortune / Anderson
    Cooper and Katherine Howe.
Other titles: Astor, the rise and fall of an American fortune
Description: First edition. | New York : HarperCollins Publishers, 2023. | Includes bibliographical references and index.
Identifiers: LCCN 2023021875 | ISBN 9780062964700 (hardcover) | ISBN
    9780062964670 (ebook)
Subjects: LCSH: Astor family. | Astor, John Jacob, 1763-1848—Family. |
    Astor, Brooke—Family. | Upper class—United States--Biography. | New York
    (N.Y.) —Biography.
Classification: LCC CT274.A86 C667 2023 | DDC 974.7/1—
    dc23/eng/20230517
LC record available at https://lccn.loc.gov/2023021875

23 24 25 26 27 LBC 5 4 3 2 1

For Sebastian and Wyatt
—A. C.

For my mother
—K. H.

CONTENTS

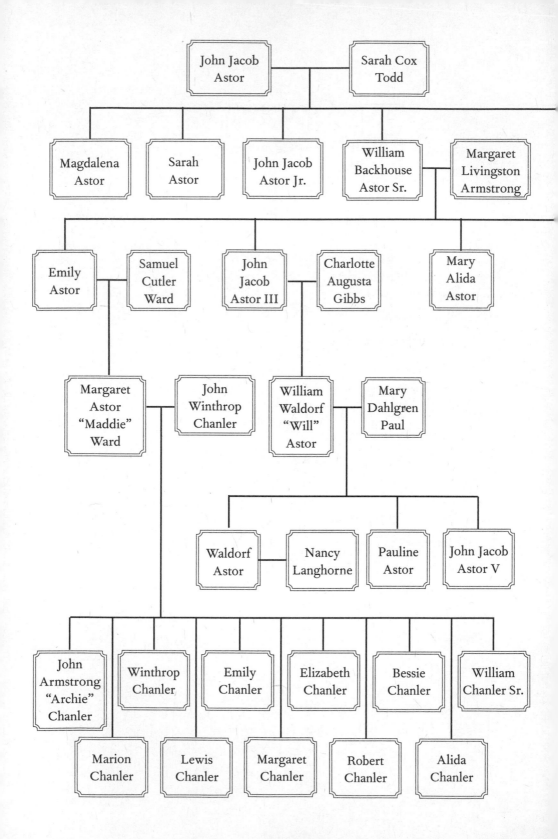

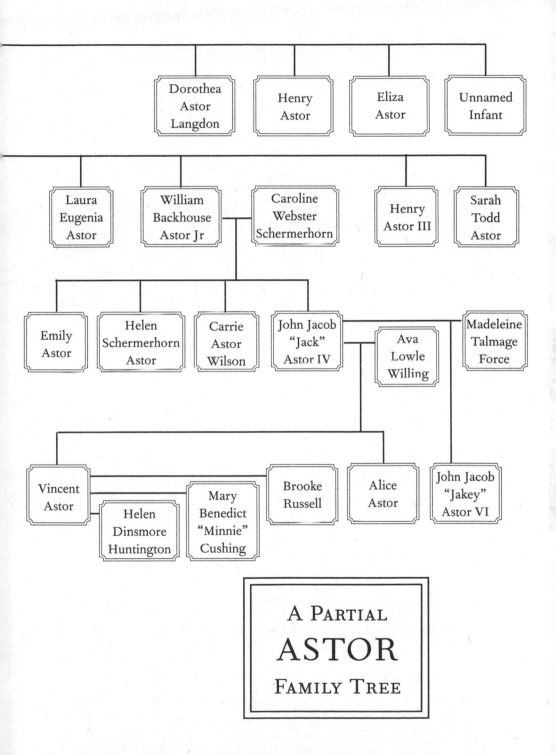

A PARTIAL
ASTOR
FAMILY TREE

ASTOR

INTRODUCTION

After Mrs. Astor there was chaos.

—Frederick Townsend Martin

My first thought when I met Brooke Astor was, *Who is this very small lady in a very big fur coat?* I was thirteen, and it wasn't the first time I'd asked myself such a question upon being introduced to someone by my mom, Gloria Vanderbilt. I knew the name "Astor" only because of the Astor Place subway stop in the East Village and the barbershop nearby called Astor Hair, where the cool kids from my school liked to go. I didn't know "Astor" was the name of a family whose fortune began with beaver fur; that the pearls Brooke Astor was wearing around her neck and the gold glinting on her earlobes, the lustrous coat over her shoulders, even the food she was about to put into her mouth, would have been paid for—if you traced it back far enough—by the bloody business of removing fur pelts from dead beavers, otters, and other small animals. I'm pretty sure the fur she was wearing that day was sable.

It was 1981, and I was eating lunch at Mortimer's on Manhattan's Upper East Side with my mom and Carter, my brother, when Mrs. Astor swept in. My dad had died three years before, and my mom often took us to places she would otherwise have gone with him: Broadway plays, Elaine's for a late-night dinner, the Café Carlyle to hear Bobby Short sing Cole Porter. I enjoyed hanging out with my mother. It was like having a front-row seat to a never-ending performance filled with fascinating and often odd characters you actually got to interact with. And she didn't take that world too seriously—that was part of the fun of going out with her. We'd all make mental notes of things people said or did and then giggle about it together afterward. I was probably the only thirteen-year-old in New York who did imitations of society figures like Jerry Zipkin and Nan Kempner to make his mom laugh.

We were having chicken paillards and burgers at Mortimer's that day, but the food was beside the point. Mortimer's, on the corner of Seventy-Fifth and Lexington, was to New York society what Delmonico's or Sherry's had been a century before, that is, once society ladies allowed themselves to be seen eating in restaurants. The original Mrs. Astor, Caroline Astor, who defined and dominated New York society during the Gilded Age, didn't eat in a restaurant until almost the end of her life, in 1908, when she finally bent to the liberalizing changes of the twentieth century and set foot in Sherry's, when it was on Fifth Avenue and Thirty-Seventh Street.[1] Her coming was an "event" that lit up the gossip pages all over the city.[2] Less than eighty years later, Mortimer's was the scene of many such "events." It was *the* "see-and-be-seen" watering hole for the boldest of boldface names on Manhattan's Upper East Side. "Mortimer's is the best show in New York. If you can get a table," Dominick Dunne wrote in *Vanity Fair*, before cautioning, "But don't count on getting a table."

Mrs. Astor, of course, had no such concerns. Her table was waiting for her, right next to ours. Before taking her seat that day in 1981, she paused by our table and said something like "Hello, Gloria. Nice to see you. What handsome young men you have here"—that sort of thing.

Carter and I stood and took turns shaking her gloved hand. We'd had a lot of practice being well-behaved young men, making good impressions when out with our mother. The conversation was brief, which was probably for the best. I could tell right away my mom didn't like Mrs. Astor.

Later, when I asked her why not, she said, "She just never grabbed me"—which was classic Gloria. My mom rarely said bad things about people, but when she did, she had a lexicon all her own. "Dreadful" was her harshest criticism, usually reserved for someone who was very pushy or rich and money-obsessed. "Vincent Astor was dreadful," she later informed me, speaking about Brooke's third husband, whose name and fortune Brooke had inherited after five and a half often miserable years of marriage. I've since learned, while researching this book, that nearly everyone who knew Vincent described him similarly.

So, when my mom said that Brooke Astor "just never grabbed her," I knew exactly what she meant. I suppose someone walking down Lexington Avenue that afternoon and looking through Mortimer's expansive picture window might have been intrigued to see Gloria Vanderbilt, then fifty-seven years old, and seventy-nine-year-old Brooke Astor, the last two exemplars of Gilded Age New York, dining shoulder to shoulder. Had iPhones existed then, a passerby might even have snapped a picture and posted it on Instagram. #Iconic. Their reasonable assumption would have been that these high-profile women had much in common beyond glittering last names: elegant fashions, powerful friends, and well-appointed homes. My mom had in fact lived for several years in the same penthouse apartment at 10 Gracie Square that Mrs. Astor had once lived in, but in most ways, the two women could not have been more different. Despite the name "Vanderbilt" (which she used only in professional settings) and all that came with it, Gloria had little interest in the social world in which Brooke Astor lived, ruled, and reveled.

Though my mother also found herself in serious financial straits at times, she would never have married a man like Vincent Astor for his money, as Brooke had. My mom did not attend gala benefits or play canasta or gossip with other ladies and gentlemen who lunched. She could have chosen that life; she was expected to—but she didn't. She rejected it early on, driven by a relentless desire to prove her worth, to make something of herself by herself. She was at heart an artist, a painter and writer, and she preferred to surround herself with creative people, people who were *making* things.

My mom's longtime friend Ben Brantley, who closely followed the comings and goings of New York society as a writer at *W Magazine* before becoming the theater critic for the *New York Times*, recently remarked to me, "I think there was a vestigial part of Gloria that felt they disapproved of her as a maverick. Gloria was instinctively repelled by anything that smacked of hierarchy, with its codes of judgment." I think he's right. Like Caroline Astor and Alva Vanderbilt a century before, Brooke and Gloria looked alike only if you didn't know either of them very well.

I saw Brooke Astor a number of times in the ensuing years, and briefly chatted with her once or twice, but our last, fleeting interaction was the most profound—for me, at least. It happened at Mortimer's, only, this time, I was waiting tables in its newly opened sidewalk café the summer before my senior year in high school.

I was, it should be noted, a terrible waiter. I was totally inexperienced, intimidated by the cooks, and unable to figure out a system to take care of several tables at once. I'd make an individual trip to get a diner more sugar or a new fork, instead of covering multiple tasks per trip. As a result, I was always running around and, yet, always late to respond to a diner's request. I also sweated profusely in the summer heat, which no one likes to see in a waiter. It got so bad that I started suggesting customers might want to sit at tables I wasn't responsible for. Nevertheless, looking back, I see that it was one of the most valuable work experiences of my life.

I never had to serve Mrs. Astor, which was lucky for both of us. She was not an outdoor café kind of customer. She sat inside with all the other regulars. But one harried afternoon, I ran into her as I was hurrying to the kitchen to place an order and she was returning from the ladies' room.

"Hello, Mrs. Astor," I said.

She glanced at me for a split second, then kept walking. Now, keep in mind that every time she had met me before, I'd been with my mom and wearing a blazer and that, on this day, I was in my waiter's uniform of white shirt and dark pants. So, it didn't surprise me that she didn't recognize me. What did surprise me, however, was the look she gave me—or, more accurately, the lack of one. She gazed right through me. She may have slightly, almost imperceptibly turned up one corner of her mouth as though to smile when she heard her name, but when her eyes met mine, she must have decided in an instant that there was no need to smile, and she never broke her stride.

Perhaps she was having a bad day or had a lot on her mind, or it's possible she didn't hear me, but she wasn't the only customer who looked at me that way that summer. I received the same aloof nonrecognition from many other prominent people, including some I'd already met while sitting with my mom at the same conspicuous tables where they were sitting, on full display as part of the greatest social show in New York City. I was not naïve. I had long been aware of the privileges that being Gloria Vanderbilt's son afforded me, but seeing it play out as I did that summer waiting tables—that was a valuable education.

Just as Ebenezer Scrooge was given the chance to get perspective on his life with the Ghosts of Christmas Past, Present, and Future, I had been given a chance at perspective by Glenn Bernbaum, Mortimer's mercurial owner, who allowed me to work there despite my complete lack of experience. I got to see what my future might look like from the other side of the table, and I didn't like what I saw. It got me thinking about what kind of person I wanted to be. What side of the table did I want to be on, if I even wanted to be at that table at all?

That summer, Brooke Astor was still very much the doyenne of Upper East Side society, beloved for giving to New York City charities tens of millions of dollars of the fortune she'd been handed when Vincent Astor dropped dead of a heart attack in 1959. In so doing, she had reinvented herself as a major philanthropist and redefined the name "Astor." She may not have been one by birth, but by 1981, she was the most famous Astor in the world.

Brooke liked to portray the founding of the Astor fortune as a uniquely American, heroic tale of grit, pluck, and determination. In her version, it was the story of a man, John Jacob Astor (Vincent's great-great-grandfather), who came here with nothing, carved an empire out of the wilderness, and then helped to build a great American city. And that is one version, from one side of the table, as it were.

John Jacob Astor did boldly venture into the wilderness, and he came to dominate the North American fur trade as no one ever had. The *New York Herald* called him "a self-invented moneymaking machine."[3] By 1834, his American Fur Company was the largest business enterprise in the United States.[4] And when he died in 1848, he was the richest man in America, having shrewdly plowed his fur profits into New York real estate, which became the enduring source of his family's phenomenal wealth. For generations to come, Astor men owned New York. Literally.

But, today, nearly all of that real estate and money and power is gone—as is the world of New York high society that Brooke Astor and the original Mrs. Astor worked so hard to dominate. So, what happened? How does one of America's greatest fortunes disappear? It's a question I first became interested in while researching my own family's history for my previous book, *Vanderbilt*, which I also cowrote with Katherine Howe.

Growing up, I knew little about the Vanderbilt dynasty. My mom rarely talked about her tumultuous childhood or the fractious family she was born into in 1924, and my parents made sure I understood early on that there was no inheritance waiting for me when I turned twenty-one. But when my mom died in 2019, I began going through boxes of files and documents she had stored away and found letters from her aunt Gertrude Vanderbilt Whitney and her father, Reginald Vanderbilt, whom she never knew. Their voices became real to me.

I have two sons of my own now, Wyatt and Sebastian, and I wrote *Vanderbilt* because I wanted to be able to answer their questions about their ancestors one day. The Vanderbilts were the original new-money arrivistes. They burst onto the scene in the late 1800s and used their wealth to buy prestige and respectability. Their millions bought palatial houses, astonishing yachts, cars in the hundreds, and jewels both magnificent and rare. But the Vanderbilt dynasty crumbled underneath the weight of all that splendor. It was the greatest American fortune ever squandered.

In researching the Gilded Age society the Vanderbilts spent tens of millions of dollars to break into, I became fascinated with the family who had codified and defined that world: the Astors. John Jacob Astor, like "the Commodore," Cornelius Vanderbilt, possessed a genius for making money that bordered on the pathological. And that pathology would go on to infect each successive generation in different ways.

Both families seemed to think their money would last forever, an infinity of wealth and access, power and privilege. Both were wrong.

Looking at Brooke Astor sitting in Mortimer's in 1981—a delicate, well-groomed woman about to enjoy a delicate, well-groomed lunch—I could never have suspected the very real brutality that lay at the heart of the Astor fortune—a fortune that was ruthlessly wrung out of the skin and gravel of New York City, transformed into palaces and hotels and diamonds, lavished upon art museums and libraries, squandered on yachts and parties, and, finally, frittered away in a blur of betrayal, legal fees, and infighting.

This is the Astor story told from both sides of the table—the Astors as they imagined themselves to be and the Astors as they were seen by others. It is the story of an American fortune—the fantasy and the reality. From one man's vision inscribed in the American landscape, it becomes a story of one family's name broken free of the people it once belonged to, reclaimed and redefined and made into part of the fabric of American life in unsuspecting ways. The name "Astor" came to mean many different things to many kinds of people: sumptuous wealth, glamour, and social prominence, but also greed, miserliness, and rapaciousness.

But it began with one young German immigrant, John Jacob Astor, the son of a butcher. It began—as great fortunes often do—with blood.

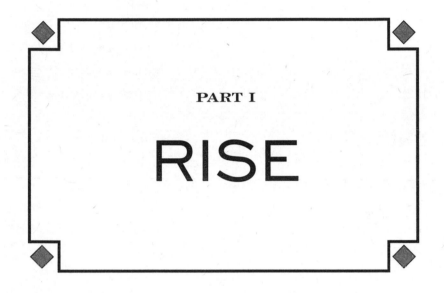

PART I

RISE

1

NEW YORK

1784

He who has the most whiskey generally
carries off the most furs.

—*Colonel Josiah Snelling*

Tricking a beaver into resting one tender paw in just the right place took skill and cunning, and John Jacob Astor employed both when kindling his fortune to life.

Beavers can weigh as much as sixty pounds, and they live along rivers and in ponds in dense lodges they make themselves. They are the only animals (apart from humans) to take an active role in reshaping the landscape to suit their needs. The lodges have multiple entrances and exits under the surface of the water, part of a complex network built for hiding and making quick escapes, designed to hold teeming masses of warm, breathing life, not unlike a hotel or tenement house.

The traps used to catch them in the years of the blossoming North American fur trade in the late eighteenth and early nineteenth centuries were made of steel, forged by blacksmiths into two semicircular jaws, occasionally toothed, connected by a spring. The traps could cost as much as six dollars each, which was a chunk of change at the time—more than a hundred dollars in today's currency.[1] Clanking, they were carried in sacks by trappers, slung over the flank of a mule or chucked into the bottom of a canoe paddled up the Missouri River and portaged overland. When the traps were pried open, the jaws were held under extreme tension by a trigger, called a "dog," which was released when a beaver's paw pressed the metal pan at the center, causing the jaws to clamp shut with a sharp, metallic snap and hold the startled animal fast.[2]

Trappers positioned the yawning steel jaws in a few inches of water, on the shore of a pond or river.[3] Attached to each trap, a forged metal chain of several feet would be held by a wooden stake driven into the silty mud deeper in the water. The trapper would then take a twig, splintered at one end and perhaps with a few leaves or pine needles still clinging to it, and dip it into the "medicine" he carried in a small bottle made of animal horn.[4] The "medicine," a musky aroma designed to lure a passing beaver in for a sniff, would be the trapper's own proprietary blend of castoreum (the yellowish, waxy substance beavers exude from sacs at the base of their tails to scent-mark their territory) and other additions of his own devising—camphor, maybe, or juniper oil or other arcane ingredients.[5] Trappers guarded their medicine recipes with a tenacity known only, perhaps, by the Coca-Cola Company a hundred years later. Once the twig was dipped into the secret scent, the trapper would place it in the mud along the water's edge, dangling it at beaver nose height, only a foot or so away from death.

If the trap clamped on a paw only, the desperate beaver could still get free—if it was able to gnaw its own limb off through the bone. But if the trap hit higher on the animal's leg, sinking its teeth into a haunch, the glossy-furred creature, panic visible in its small, dark eyes, would try to flee to deeper water. It wouldn't get far. When the beaver reached the end of the chain's length, its flight would stop with a jerk. Normally, a beaver can hold its breath underwater for some fifteen minutes, thanks to valves that close off its throat, ears, and nostrils. But a terrified, ensnared animal would inevitably exhaust itself, thrashing and gasping, and be dragged under the water by the weight of the trap and the chain.[6]

Steel traps are quick and sharp—nothing escapes them unscathed—hence the "mind like a steel trap" idiom that likely originated in the wildernesses of the fur trade. And so it was with the mind of John Jacob Astor, whose riches originated in that same wilderness and who grew to become one of the wealthiest men in American history.[7]

He was born Johann Jakob Astor, in Walldorf, Germany, in 1763. At the time, his father's trade, butchering, was not about selling; it was about killing. Butchers were predators, in a manner of speaking, making their living by slitting throats and letting blood and by rendering animal muscle and sinew into cuts of salable meat. Trappers were predators, too. Both the trade Astor was trained for and the one he embraced after his arrival in New York relied on the ability to render living flesh and skin into money.

It's hard to conceive, in a society as wrapped in polyester as ours, how important fur was to European and Indigenous societies in North America and Canada in the seventeenth and eighteenth centuries. Mink and sea otter pelts might have commanded higher prices, but the backbone of the fur trade was beaver. Their fur was used to make warm felt hats in Europe and, later, men's top hats. Small barbs on the underfur made for tight matting when the fur was felted, so hats made with beaver fur held their shape for much longer.[8] In fact, beaver fur was in such demand that by the time trade was beginning to open in the American wilderness, the animals had been hunted to extinction in Europe. A beaver fur obtained from an Indigenous trapper for a handful of goods, like a pint of liquor or a pocketful of cheap glass beads, could be sold in Europe at a 600 to 900 percent markup.[9]

With a sharp knife, an experienced trapper could rough-skin a beaver in minutes. It took only another ten minutes or so to "flesh" the hide before it was ready to dry. He would start by cutting the beaver's legs at the joints and snapping them off. Next, he would carve around the base of the flat tail and twist it until the bone snapped. The next cut was the longest: a quick slice from the vent at the base, past the castor scent gland, straight up to the animal's lower lip. From the bottom of the long ventral cut, the trapper would work the outer two inches of the pelt, peeling it back from the carcass, trimming off meat and fat as he went. The hide was the money, and the trapper would be careful not to poke holes through the money. The fur around the animal's face peeled off last.[10]

Beaver pelts came in two grades: castor sec, which were skins scraped clean by Indigenous women and stretched on a frame to dry; and castor gras, or "greasy beaver," which were pelts worn next to human skin for as long as a year—a service for which Indigenous people charged a premium—to render them soft, pliable, and more easily worked.[11] When John Jacob Astor arrived in New York, beaver pelt was the common currency on the frontier. One gun cost about ten beaver skins. Eight skins for a thick blanket. Three for an axe. Two skins for a half pint of Caribbean rum or a pound of glass beads, which were easier to use for clothing decoration than the traditional hammered and dyed porcupine quills. A fine petticoat cost five.[12]

John Jacob Astor knew nothing about the fur trade, though, when he set out for America. His formal schooling had stopped when he was fourteen, after which he had learned butchering from his father.[13]

His older brothers left home first—George lit out for England, and Henry for New York—which made it easier for John Jacob when he decided to leave home at sixteen. He stopped in London to work with George selling flutes and pianos for their uncle's company, Astor and Broadwood. It was during this time that he likely Anglicized his name from "Johann Jakob" and, discovering that he had an ear for languages, picked up some rudimentary English.

After four years in England, he decided to cross the Atlantic in November 1783, bringing with him flutes to sell or trade in America.[14] He paid five pounds for his passage in steerage and meals of salt beef and biscuits. Baltimore would be his first port of call, but New York City was his goal.

The voyage was miserable, plagued by bad weather and stormy seas. At times he thought the ship might founder. When they finally arrived in the Chesapeake Bay, which had frozen over after a hard winter, the ship became locked in ice along with several other vessels.[15] Astor spent three months aboard it, waiting for the ice to thaw, before deciding to climb down with fellow passengers and walk to Baltimore on foot across the frozen bay, his sack of flutes on his back.[16] It was March 1784, and John Jacob Astor was twenty-one years old.

As one of his many biographers put it, at that moment, "America as a land of opportunity had not yet become a cliché."[17] Astor himself might arguably serve as one of the authors of that cliché. Over the course of his long voyage, the young fortune hunter befriended a fellow German traveler who worked trading furs and learned that there was serious money to be made in the buying and selling of pelts and that it didn't require much capital up-front.[18] What it did require was the gumption to voyage into the wilderness.

When John Jacob finally arrived in New York, his brother Henry was already there and had successfully established himself as a butcher.[19] John Jacob briefly worked selling cakes and cookies in the streets, but he also started skulking around the wharves, looking out for anyone who had happened into a fur or two in the course of his travels and who wanted to trade. To learn more about the business, Astor got a job with a fur trader named Robert Browne, "beating the dust and bugs out of furs and then packing them into bales."[20] For this unglamorous work, he was paid two dollars a week plus meals. One biographer has noted that working in a fur warehouse would have been "repulsive to anyone not used to the bad smells, blood, and mess of a butcher shop."[21] For Astor, it just smelled like home. Within about a year, he had amassed a sizable quantity of furs, enough to make a trip back to London to sell them worthwhile.[22]

By the late 1780s, Manhattan newspapers would report on "Jacob Astor" having imported "an elegant assortment of Piano Fortes" to the United States, while also mentioning that he was willing to buy all kinds of furs for cash.[23] When he wanted to expand his idiosyncratic import-export business, he found himself in need of more capital and approached his brother Henry for a loan of two hundred dollars, a big sum in the 1780s, to be sure. Henry offered him one hundred as a gift—provided John Jacob never ask him for money again.[24]

Now, at the age of twenty-three, John Jacob was ready to commit himself to the fur trade, and he set forth into the wilderness, heading to Albany on foot. The journey was grueling, muddy, cold, and often uncharted, but John Jacob was sturdily built and hardy, unfazed by the rigors awaiting him. He stood at about five feet, nine inches tall and had "small, piercing eyes beneath heavy eyebrows."[25] He had to sleep where he could find shelter, sometimes in a settler's cabin, sometimes outside. He traded cloth, tobacco, liquor, and bright jewelry with

Indigenous people in exchange for glossy pelts of beaver, otter, and muskrat.

The pelts themselves were smelly, heavy, and revolting to handle. Most American businessmen vastly preferred to outsource the actual labor of trading for furs to intermediaries, who would barter with Indigenous peoples on their behalf. But insulation from the unpleasant truths of skin and fur and weather and risk chipped away at profit, and profit was all John Jacob cared about. He had no qualms about getting his hands dirty.[26] His ear for languages helped, and he was able to learn enough Seneca, Mohawk, and Oneida to personally negotiate and close advantageous deals.[27]

When he returned to the city, he roomed at a boardinghouse run by a widow named Mrs. Todd, who had a daughter named Sarah.[28] The choice of a partner can make or break someone's fortunes, and John Jacob and Sarah chose wisely when they sized each other up. Both were accustomed to hard work, and Sarah proved to have a good eye for the quality of furs. Together, they forged an alliance that would become nothing less than a juggernaut.

Sarah Todd also brought a decent-size dowry of three hundred dollars to their union, enough for John Jacob to open a storefront of his own, selling pianos and flutes he procured through his connections in England and furs from his growing networks. Sarah urged him to get to know the other fur traders who hung out at the merchants' coffeehouses on Water Street, and she supported him when he left their growing, busy household full of children for months at a time to sail up the Hudson River to trade in the interior of the northeastern United States and Canada.[29] His success was due as much to her industry as to his.

Sarah would end up bearing eight children, five of whom lived to adulthood. Their first son, John Jacob II, was developmentally disabled, though the precise nature of his condition is hard to tell from contemporary accounts. It was said he had wild mood swings and was unable to learn. So, as John Jacob Sr.'s fortunes grew, he focused his dynastic attention and ambition on his second son, William Backhouse Astor, who was born in 1792.

Around that time, the international scene was shifting in Astor's favor. In the 1780s, London had still imposed strict restrictions on importing and exporting furs. Any pelts obtained in British territory, specifically the frontier outposts in Canada, had to be shipped first to London, taxed, and then shipped back to New York to be sold.[30] John Jacob had been undaunted, doing business with Canadian trappers and fur companies anyway because the promise of profit in New York, even with that added expense, was too great for him to ignore. Then, in 1794, the United States negotiated a treaty with Great Britain to permit furs to be exported directly from Canada to New York.

By the time of this monumental shift in Astor's business profitability, John Jacob was successful enough that he could outsource the hard work of trading, leveraging his established networks in Canada, New York, and London so that he could work largely as a merchant. No more did he have to venture into the wilderness to negotiate. By 1798, he was thirty-five years old and worth $250,000. By way of comparison, a family in Manhattan could live comfortably for a year on about $750.[31] Inflation can be difficult to calculate, as it's dependent on several factors (including periods of deflation in the occasional intervening years), but one estimate suggests that Astor's burgeoning fortune at the end of the eighteenth century translates to about $4 million in today's money.[32] Four million is nothing to sniff at, but it would not necessarily merit an entry in a history book two centuries later, either.

How, Astor wondered, could he increase his control of the fur trade now that a substantial and costly step had been eliminated? The British East India Company controlled trade with China, but Astor managed to strike an agreement with that monopoly to permit his fur company to use British East India ports, the only American fur merchant who was able to do so.[33]

Before long, Astor was sending all his finest furs to China and bringing back silks, spices, and tea to unload at a huge profit in an increasingly flush New York City, a place hungry for the luxuries that could finally be afforded in the consumer revolution. Sea otter pelts were in such high demand there that the animal's numbers in North America started to dwindle, largely thanks to trappers in Astor's employ. John Jacob had a shrewd eye for any profit-making opportunity and a sharp enough mind to take full advantage of those opportunities he recognized. For instance, his pelt-filled ships had to stop in Hawaii to take on food and fresh water as they made the long passage south from New York, around Cape Horn, the southernmost point of the Americas, and across the Pacific Ocean to China. If they had to stop in Hawaii anyway, he reasoned, why not buy up cheap sandalwood there and trade it in China, too? As a result of this simple insight, Astor wound up essentially having a monopoly on sandalwood for almost two decades.

In the years leading up to the War of 1812, Astor had to contend with American forces blockading their own country's ports in order to restrict trade with France and Great Britain. Seeking a scheme to get around the blockade and its restrictions, Astor sought approval from Thomas Jefferson to have a ship called the *Beaver* bring a worker from China home to attend a family funeral. It just so happened that this passenger voyage also contained a huge load of Astor furs.[34] Furthermore, when the *Beaver* returned the worker to the United States after the funeral, with a cargo of tea, silk, sandalwood, and spices, she was the first ship allowed entry into New York City ports in more than a year. One historian estimates that that single voyage netted Astor two hundred thousand dollars in profit.[35]

John Jacob Astor was beginning to understand the true extent of his power to remake the world into a machine for lining his pockets with gold.

2

ASTORIA

1810

*Take the American Fur Company in the aggregate, and
they are the greatest scoundrels the world has ever seen.*

—Zachary Taylor, independent fur trader[1]

At the dawning of the nineteenth century, John Jacob Astor looked westward with avaricious eyes at a rapidly expanding New World. As he saw it, the vast forested interior of North America west of the Missouri was an unknown land, teeming with animals just waiting to be skinned. In 1803, President Thomas Jefferson commissioned an expedition to explore and map the wilderness that had been added to U.S. territory by that year's Louisiana Purchase, and Second Lieutenant William Clark set out from Camp Dubois in Illinois the following year, rendezvousing with his friend Captain Meriwether Lewis at Saint Charles, Missouri. Their expedition voyaged up the Missouri River, across the Continental Divide, finally arriving at the Columbia River and then down to reach the shores of the Pacific Ocean on the West Coast of North America in 1805. When Clark returned to the East

Coast in 1806, he brought with him rough maps of the landscape and tales of a wilderness rich with animals.

Astor dreamed of the wealth he would amass trading with China if all those furs fell under his control and if he established a trading post on the Pacific coast at the mouth of the Columbia River, instead of having to sail all the way around Cape Horn. He began to dream of empire.

Before the idea of Manifest Destiny took hold, it was not a universally held belief that the United States should expand all the way to the Pacific Ocean. Astor imagined a different destiny. Instead of the continental United States of America as we know it today, stretching from the Atlantic to the Pacific and from the Great Lakes to the Rio Grande, with disparate states uneasily hanging together by threads of common narrative, flashes of common culture, and gossamer political truces, he imagined two separate countries. The first would be a United States beginning on the Atlantic coast with the thirteen original colonies and ending at the Mississippi or, at the farthest, the Continental Divide. On the West Coast, there would be another, shadow country, founded along similar principles but centered on a bustling city at the mouth of the Columbia River on the Pacific Ocean, with settlements reaching deep into the forests and mountains of what is now California and Idaho and Wyoming. In Astor's vision, St. Louis, at the top of the Mississippi River, and New Orleans, where the Mississippi meets the Gulf of Mexico, would serve as the two major points of commerce and cultural exchange between the United States to the east and this parallel country to the west.

But just as the United States centered its first cultural exchanges and trade with Europe and the Caribbean and Africa—in an epic crisscrossing of the Atlantic Ocean by goods and migration, both forced and at will—this parallel country along the West Coast would have centered its trading relationships with China, Japan, and Russia. This country of John Jacob Astor's imagination might have been a Pacific Rim power from its inception, rich with furs, initially, and then with porcelain, spices, satins, and more from trading around the Pacific, with no middlemen and no need to round the Horn. He would have named this country for its founder, and mastermind: himself. He would have called it Astoria.

In the spring of 1808, to begin his project of empire, John Jacob Astor created the American Fur Company, capitalized with stock valued at one million dollars. He intended to organize trading in New York State and westward to the trading posts along the Missouri River.[2] Though he pretended that the company was funded by a variety of investors, the truth was that the American Fur Company was largely John Jacob Astor's personal enterprise.

President Thomas Jefferson agreed with Astor's vision for a trading hub on the Pacific coast, though his ambition lay less in personal enrichment than in political consolidation. Jefferson sent Astor the following missive: "I learn with great satisfaction the disposition of our merchants to form into companies for undertaking the Indian trade within our own territories. . . . In order to get the whole of this business passed into the hands of our own citizens . . . every reasonable patronage . . . in the power of the Executive will be afforded."[3]

In 1810, Astor formed a subsidiary of the American Fur Company, which he called the Pacific Fur Company, to establish trading posts along the Missouri and Columbia Rivers. He foresaw a whole network of trading posts and supply chains veining through the wilderness, every one of them under his control, every one of them an engine for enormous financial gains. He would buy the best furs at the most advantageous prices and would also sell supplies to the traders, trappers, and Indigenous peoples who did the real, bloody work. This network of trading posts would connect cities on the East Coast with a permanent outpost on the West Coast, founded at his instigation and expense, which would serve as the gateway to trade across the Pacific. Settlers would flow into the wilderness along these arteries of Astor-controlled forts, relying on Astor-controlled supplies and Astor-controlled relationships with the people who already lived there. All that remained was to establish the anchor settlement on the West Coast.

He knew time was short. His chief Canadian rival, the North West Company, was moving aggressively to control fur trapping in the same territory. Hoping to sidestep them, he offered them a percentage of the Pacific Fur Company, but without success.[4] Whichever was the first company to establish a fort at the mouth of the Columbia River would win.

Astor's plan was simple. The Pacific Fur Company, with backing from the U.S. government, would sponsor two expeditions. One, consisting of hardened *voyageurs*, experienced trappers, and wilderness experts, would travel overland roughly along the route already mapped by Lewis and Clark. At the same time, another group, consisting of moneymen, suppliers, and company leadership, would set out by sea. The sea voyage would transport around the Horn the clerks, trading supplies, and arms required to make the fort an ongoing business concern, to rendezvous at the mouth of the Columbia River with the overland party. When the two forces joined, they would construct Fort Astoria, planting the Astor flag on the West Coast. Astor's personnel included several Canadians who had worked for the North West Company and were considered by Astor the most talented trappers around. In order to reassure anyone with doubts that this was an American enterprise, he put an American merchant, Wilson Price Hunt, in charge of the overland expedition, envisioning him as the agent in command of the western outpost. Then Astor personally put up four hundred thousand dollars for expenses. By 1810, the undertaking was ready to begin.[5]

The overseas expedition set out in a ninety-four-foot ship called *Tonquin*, which was new and fast, and armed with ten guns. A square-rigger, she carried a crew of twenty-one sailors, plus the thirty-three Pacific Fur Company employees, four of whom were partners in the enterprise: Alexander McKay, Duncan McDougall, David Stuart, and Stuart's young nephew Robert.[6] The ship was under the command of Navy lieutenant Jonathan Thorn. Thorn had a naval officer's commitment to discipline, which probably seemed like a good idea at the time. "He was a strict disciplinarian," Gabriel Fanchère, a French Canadian clerk on the voyage, wrote of their captain, "of a quick and passionate temper, accustomed to exact obedience . . . taking counsel of nobody, and following Mr. Astor's instructions to the letter."[7] "To prevent any misunderstandings," Astor cautioned Thorn in a letter, "will require your particular good management."[8] Unfortunately, good sailing and good management are not necessarily the same skill set.

The ship set sail from New York Harbor on September 8, 1810. Only hours later, Thorn already had his hands full with unruly passengers. He wanted to establish naval order on board and decreed that lights out would occur at eight o'clock. The sailors on board obeyed. Not so the Scottish fur traders, who lingered over their pipes, feeling themselves partners in the enterprise, passengers rather than workers on board a ship. Nor the French Canadian *voyageurs*, accustomed to keeping their own counsel on when they slept and when they rose. Nor the Canadian clerks, who had been personally hired by Astor for their brains rather than their brawn.[9] Furthermore, space was at a premium in the overcrowded vessel. Several of the lower-ranking company employees had been berthed in the cramped quarters at the front of the ship, with the common sailors, and Thorn had made clear they were expected to help those sailors with their duties.

Grumblings over these arrangements commenced almost immediately, with the fur company employees feeling they had effectively chartered this boat and, so, ought to have a say in how she was run, and with Thorn feeling that while they were on board his ship, they ought to obey his command. Alexander McKay, a forty-year-old partner in the American Fur Company, was secure in his authority, having traipsed across the continent back in 1793 with famed Canadian explorer Alexander Mackenzie, and he took matters into his own hands to speak on behalf of the passengers. "We will defend ourselves rather than suffer such treatment," he informed the captain.

Thorn stared furiously at the imperious Scot and countered, "I will blow out the brains of the first man who dares disobey my orders aboard my own ship."[10]

That was the first night. The worst was yet to come.

By the winter of 1810, the *Tonquin* was approaching the Horn, and on December 4, nearly three months since they'd set sail, the ship put in at the Falkland Islands for resupply. Some of the passengers went ashore to explore and stretch their legs—a ship, according to Samuel Johnson, being akin to a prison, with the added risk of drowning—while the crew took on a load of fresh water. Time and tide wait for no man, and Thorn had instructed everyone to return to the ship immediately after the signal gun was fired. Perhaps ignorant of the importance of wind and tide in determining departure times for sailing vessels, or perhaps just stubborn and enjoying the surreal land sickness that takes hold in bodies after long stretches at sea, the fur company contingent all ignored the signal gun. They returned hours late, giddy and unheeding. Thorn was apoplectic.

A few days later, on December 7, the *Tonquin* stopped at a different island in the Falkland chain, needing to undertake some maintenance before attempting the arduous passage around the Horn and into the Pacific. The ship lay at anchor for four days as the sailors got to work hammering and mending and splicing while the partners and clerks loafed in a tent on an island nearby, idling their days away shooting at penguins and combing the landscape for rotting wooden headstones.[11] By December 11, the repair work was done, and Thorn gave the order to fire the gun summoning everyone back on board the ship.

Before long, all the fur company employees had assembled on the beach near the small launch that was to return them to the *Tonquin*, but two important people were missing: the partners Alexander McKay, who had nearly been shot challenging Thorn's authority on their first night at sea, and David Stuart.

Everyone waited.

McKay and Stuart did not appear, and a fed-up Thorn gave the order for the *Tonquin* to weigh anchor, and by the time McKay and Stuart arrived back with the others at the beach, she was disappearing toward the horizon. The passengers on board pleaded with Thorn to return for the men left behind, and one even threatened him with a gun. Thorn refused. Panicking, the abandoned clerks and partners clambered into the launch and rowed hard for the *Tonquin*, pursuing the vanishing ship through the brutal Antarctic chop for more than three hours.

Good thing for them there was a wind shift slowing the *Tonquin* down. Were it not for that serendipitous turn of events, the men in the launch would have been rowing to their almost certain death in the falling temperatures of a December Antarctic night. Instead, they climbed, shaken and shaking, back on board the *Tonquin* and continued their voyage to the unknown wilderness of the western coast of North America.[12]

The expedition finally arrived, with all their still-brewing resentments, at the mouth of the Columbia River on March 22, 1811. They had been at sea for half a year. But the miserable company's travails were far from over.

The Columbia dumps into the Pacific behind a deadly wall of sand-bars, making for high waves, froth and churn that obscure the bottom, and unpredictable currents. They couldn't just drop anchor and row to shore—they had to find a safe path through the invisible network of sandbars, with deadly surf breaking over their backs. Thorn tasked the first mate to take four men, three of whom were Canadian trappers who were largely useless in an open whaleboat, to identify a safe path through the crashing breakers. The mate worried that this was a death wish.

"If you are afraid of water, you should have remained in Boston!" Thorn bellowed. "Do not be a coward! Put off!"[13]

Sobbing, the first mate said to his fellow sailors and passengers, "My uncle was drowned here not many years ago, and I am now going to lay my bones with his. Farewell, my friends! We will perhaps meet again in the next world."[14]

They pushed off, and within minutes, the treacherous currents and breakers had the whaleboat in their grip. She rose, fell, rose again on the rolling backs of the waves, the men's oars as thin and useless as matchsticks against the powerful rage of the water. They made it fewer than one hundred yards away from the *Tonquin* before the ocean swallowed them whole, never to be seen again.

Three more sailors were sent, and they, too, gave their lives before a safe path was finally found. The *Tonquin* dropped anchor in Baker Bay, the sea portion of their journey finally coming to an end near midnight on March 24, 1811.

The partners bushwhacked up and down the coast for weeks, hunting for the best location to erect Fort Astoria. They settled on Point George (now called Smith Point), on the south shore of the river, but it took two months for them to clear one measly acre.[15] As they started their grueling work, groups of Chinook and Clatsop people drifted out from the forest, bearing furs and food to sell or trade, or just wanting to keep an eye on the proceedings.

In June, Thorn readied to take the *Tonquin* up the Columbia on a trading expedition. That was, after all, the whole point of the enterprise. He brought McKay along as supercargo—a representative of the company's interests—along with an interpreter named Lamazu. They anchored in Clayoquot Sound, an inlet on Vancouver Island. Once the ship was settled, a group of Indigenous people paddled out, bringing furs to trade. Then, at one point, their chief was hassling Thorn, driving a hard bargain for some particularly fine furs. Thorn, being Thorn, lost his temper and smacked the respected leader in the face with an otter pelt. The chief and his people withdrew, simmering with rage.

Some days passed before they returned.

One calm and peaceful morning, dozens of canoes laden heavily with packets of furs pressed smoothly through the waters of the sound and drew up alongside the *Tonquin*. The crew were excited by the prospect of so many furs and invited the chief and his people on board in waves until the deck was crowded. John Jacob Astor had specifically warned Thorn not to allow more than a handful of Indigenous people on the deck of the ship at any one time, but Thorn was confident in himself and his firepower. Too much so. The crowd of visitors on deck grew denser until, finally, even Thorn became nervous about how outnumbered he and his crew were. He abruptly ordered all the Indigenous people to vacate the ship and for the crew to make ready to weigh anchor and set sail.

That's when the chief gave the signal. Knives and war clubs instantly appeared from deep inside bundles of fur. The Pacific Fur

Company people had already traded their knives away, and their guns were stashed belowdecks.[16] They were defenseless.

Alexander McKay was the first to fall, clubbed over the head and thrown overboard, landing hard in a canoe full of women, who then beat him to death with paddles and cooking utensils.[17] Thorn defended himself as best he could with a pocketknife, taking down two men before he was stabbed to death. In minutes, only five crew members remained, one of whom was gravely wounded. They ran down to the gun deck and managed to fire a cannon back at their attackers, who then fled in canoes back to shore.

That night, the four surviving and terrified fur traders escaped in a whaleboat under cover of darkness, leaving behind their fatally injured compatriot. The next morning, the raiders returned. Finding the ship abandoned, they boarded the *Tonquin* in triumph, climbing up the rigging and exploring between the decks. As they did so, the remaining crew member ignited the gunpowder in the ship's magazine.

The *Tonquin* blew apart in a roaring fireball of splinters, shattered bodies, and a rain of blood. Eventually, the four escapees in the whaleboat were captured and tortured to death. The only survivor of the misadventure of the *Tonquin* was Lamazu, the interpreter.

John Jacob Astor heard the news when he was about to go to the theater in New York City. Onlookers were surprised when he didn't turn on his heel and go home but, instead, sat down to enjoy the performance. "What would you have me do?" Astor reportedly said. "Would you have me stay at home and weep for what I cannot help?"[18]

The overland party had it almost as bad. The trip to the West Coast took them two years, and at one point, they were so starved that they devoured their horses. Finally, in 1812, the survivors drifted into Fort Astoria, the first group arriving in January, followed by two subsequent bands in February and the last stragglers in May.[19] The handful of remaining members of the sea journey welcomed them into their armed camp, which was complete with fur bales and a turnip garden. They built a small schooner, named *Dolly*, in honor of Astor's daughter Dorothea, and established trading posts at what would become Boise, Salem, and Spokane.[20]

Astor's ability to exert his will over the world, however, met its match in June 1812, when Thomas Jefferson's successor, President James Madison, declared war on Great Britain. The British captured Fort Astoria, and the Pacific Fur Company liquidated its fur holdings to Astor's hated Canadian rivals, the North West Fur Company, for pennies on the dollar. The death knell of Astoria was rung without much fanfare in 1814. That November, the *New-York Gazette and General Advertiser* announced, "The firm of the Pacific Fur Company is dissolved."[21]

Ultimately, the Treaty of Ghent, signed on Christmas Eve 1814, returned the land that would have been Astoria to the United States. Astor didn't want to relinquish his dream of a fur-rich country of his own, but ultimately, the dream proved untenable, in part because of then—Secretary of War James Monroe's refusal to grant Astor military protection for his private enterprise. However troubled, Astoria's brief existence lent credence to the United States' claim on the Oregon Territory. Oregon finally became a U.S. state in 1859.[22]

Undeterred, and eager to seek revenge on the Canadian North West Company, Astor turned his attention to the American Fur Company he'd established in 1808. The company began occupying posts along the Canadian border that had been vacated by British traders, but Astor wanted more.[23] He gave lip service to the company's stated goal—to the United States government, anyway—of maintaining good trading relationships with Indigenous people to smooth the path of settlement in the West. But, in truth, his aim was single-minded: he wanted to make money. And he wanted to do it without competition from Canada or the U.S. government. Under Presidents Washington and Jefferson, the federal government had established trading posts to protect Indigenous populations. According to historian Virginia Cowles, these posts "sold their goods only a fraction above cost prices, rigorously banned alcohol and gave the Indians fair returns for their furs."[24] Astor was determined to undermine the government posts. His employees spread rumors about them and aggressively competed against them by cutting their own prices, if necessary. But, according to Cowles, alcohol was "their most effective weapon."[25]

As government trading posts faltered in the face of Astor's onslaught, the American Fur Company expanded westward, monopolizing trade along the Mississippi and Missouri Rivers with a pitiless willingness to supply liquor at hugely inflated prices to addicted Indigenous people.[26] American Fur Company whiskey sold for anywhere from twenty-five to fifty dollars a gallon in the first decade of the nineteenth century—the exact same price as a handle of Jim Beam in 2023, two hundred years later.[27]

"The neighborhood of the trading houses where whiskey is sold presents a disgusting scene of drunkenness," Colonel Josiah Snelling, commander of a U.S. garrison at Detroit, wrote to the secretary of war. "It is the fruitful source of all our difficulties and of nearly all the murders committed in the Indian country."[28] Historian Kenneth Porter wrote that the use of alcohol in trading led to "hostility between the natives and the border settlements, disease, poverty, starvation and death. But it also left, here and there, fur traders with weighty packs of furs and well-filled pocket books, the fruits of the ruin which their greed and their kegs of rum had brought upon the natives."[29]

The American Fur Company's use of debt was also notorious. At one time, Astor bragged that the Winnebago, Sac, and Fox tribes collectively owed him $50,000, at a time when a standard shipment of beaver pelts went for $180.[30] Astor sought to profit not just from the sale and trading of furs, but also from the goods sold to the traders to use to barter with Indigenous people. Traders were forced to rely on stores run by the American Fur Company, typically paying such astronomical prices that their own profit margins were razor-thin. In order to make enough money to sustain themselves, they were incentivized to take advantage of their Indigenous trading partners. "To cheat them more completely," a trader's son wrote, "he brings to his aid ardent Spirits . . . which have sent more to the grave . . . than all the wars they have waged with the whites, or among themselves, even sickness and disease added to it."[31]

The white workmen, often French Canadians, who did the heavy labor for the agents and traders in Astor's company were supposed to be paid $250 for three years' work. But three years is a long time in the wilderness. Often, they didn't get what they were promised. Often, they died. The traders themselves were kept so deep in debt to the company for their supplies that they would occasionally murder their workers when the time came to pay them.[32]

By 1830, the American Fur Company was one of the most profitable businesses in the country. But Astor saw the future and decided, in 1834, to get out of the fur business for good, having netted an estimated two million dollars for himself. It was time for him to remake a different landscape entirely—the landscape of Manhattan. His dream of empire was about to be realized right outside his door.

John Jacob had begun investing in Manhattan real estate early on. His general strategy was to identify land that looked worthless and pick it up for cheap. In this way, his empire grew, as he accumulated dozens of lots on lower Broadway for only two hundred to three hundred dollars.[33] Rather than improve the lots or manage businesses on them himself, Astor would rent the land out, giving each tenant a long-term lease, often twenty-one years. The tenant would build a house on Astor land at his own expense. When the lease ran out, Astor could buy the house and rent it out again for considerably more money. Cognizant of the importance of shipping to a growing New York City, he worked hard to secure waterfront rights. The more money John Jacob Astor acquired, the more power he consolidated. The more power he held, the more money he had at his disposal. The more money he had, the more land he devoured, until Manhattan was, in a way, a new Astoria.

As his fortunes increased, John Jacob used his surplus capital to buy up undeveloped property and vacant lots beyond the threshold of settlement on Manhattan Island. Some sources credit his brother Henry for this idea. Others point to Sarah, whose family had been in Manhattan already for decades by the time of her marriage and who had seen firsthand how quickly New York was expanding. Before long, the Astors would hold in their portfolio a sparsely populated rural section of Manhattan that had once belonged to Aaron Burr. In 1803, Burr was vice president of the United States, but he was deep in debt. He asked John Jacob for a loan, securing it with 241 lots of his personal property in Manhattan. Burr did the same again when he had to flee after killing Alexander Hamilton in a duel. The land that was signed over to John Jacob was called then, as it is now, Greenwich Village, where I have lived for more than ten years.

Later, Astor would also come to own Eden Farm, a rolling, grassy expanse that belonged to a whiskey distiller, located well north of the city limits. When Medcef Eden fell into debt, the distiller went looking for a loan from John Jacob, and before long, the farm belonged to the Astor family. It is almost impossible to imagine serene farmland lying underneath the present-day urban overload of Times Square, but that spot was once Eden Farm.[34] Only fifty years after John Jacob's death, that parcel alone, stretching along Broadway from Forty-Second to

Forty-Sixth Street, would be worth twenty million dollars.[35] Near the end of his life, Astor would be quoted as saying, "Could I begin to live again, knowing what I now know and had money to invest, I would buy every foot of land on the island of Manhattan."[36] Even John Jacob Astor lived with regret.

At the age of seventy, sensing New York's growing prominence on the world stage, Astor entered the hotel business. He started planning the Park Hotel, which would later be called Astor House. He wanted to build on an entire city block, but as sometimes happens today, there was a lone holdout—a Mr. Coster, who refused to move. John Jacob offered the stubborn householder sixty thousand dollars for his property, roughly double the actual value of the land. No dice. Workmen began demolition on the buildings around Coster's until only his house was left. The workers weren't sure how to proceed.

"Just start tearing down the house anyhow," Astor said. "And— by the way—you might begin by taking away the steps."[37]

When it was finally completed, the stately Astor House hotel stood six stories high, boasting three hundred bedrooms and seventeen bathrooms. A single room cost two dollars a day, including meals of stewed kidney in champagne sauce, corned leg of pork, roast loin of veal, boiled chicken, and "perfect soft vanilla custard."[38] Upon opening in 1836, the Astor House was the hot spot of its day, attracting politicians and public figures, including Edgar Allan Poe, Jefferson Davis, Abraham Lincoln, Henry Clay, and frontiersman Davy Crockett.

But even men with the power to remake the world around them grow old. As he reached the age when men typically start reflecting on the sweep of their lives, John Jacob Astor mounted an otter skin on the wall of his town house, north of Vesey Street.[39] It was a fine house but modest, as was the country estate he had built over Hell Gate, a narrow tidal strait that would be engulfed by the onward march of the city in only a few years (and is now part of Carl Schurz Park, in the Yorkville section of Manhattan). "Usually at twilight he would painfully make his way out to the terrace of his home, supported by two servants, and watch the night boat going down the East River."[40]

In his later years, Astor's wealth began to exert a warping influence, shifting the contours of his mind just as age and time etched themselves onto his body. He refused to let anyone know the true extent of his wealth, or even tip his hand about his business intentions. The more money he accumulated, the more bitterly he complained about any expenditure and the more he tried to trim the wages he paid his employees. One historian notes that Astor "never rewarded long and faithful service, and even failed to honor promises which would not have cost him more than a few dollars."[41]

But despite his famous parsimony, people would congregate around his front door, hoping to catch a glimpse of the richest man America had ever seen. Poet Walt Whitman remembered standing outside Astor's house as a child, watching as he came doddering out. He described him later as "a bent feeble but stoutly built old man, bearded, swathed in rich furs, with a great ermine cap on his head, led and assisted, almost carried down the steps of the high front stoop (a dozen friends and servants, emulous, carefully holding and guiding him) and then lifted and tucked in a gorgeous sleigh, evelop'd in other furs, for a ride. The sleigh was drawn by as fine a team of horses as I ever saw."[42]

As the 1840s wore on, diarist Philip Hone painted a grim picture of the ravages of age on John Jacob Astor. "Mr. Astor . . . presented a painful example of the insufficiency of wealth to prolong the life of man. . . . He sat at the dinner table with his head down upon his breast, saying very little, and in a voice almost unintelligible, the saliva dropping down from his mouth, and a servant behind him to guide the victuals which he was eating, and to watch him as an infant is watched . . . there are some people, no doubt, who think he had lived long enough."[43]

By 1847, Astor's digestion was so fragile that he was fed by a wet-nurse, and a team of servants would toss him about in a blanket to aid his stalling circulation.[44] But his bodily weakness didn't extend to his business. It was rumored Astor still knew to the penny what rent was owed on his properties at any given time. A biography of Astor published in 1865 describes an argument he had with an agent who had let slide some rent that was in arrears for a particular tenant.

"She can't pay it now," the rent collector reportedly said to the dying man. "She has had misfortunes and we must give her time."

"I tell you she can pay it and she will pay it," Astor shouted. "You don't know the right way to work with her."

Distraught, the agent took the matter up with Astor's son William. Presumably wishing to spare his father further agitation, William gave the agent the requisite amount, with instructions to present the money to John Jacob as if it had been paid by the tenant.

"I told you she would pay it if you went the right way to work with her," the old man crowed.[45]

John Jacob Astor finally died at the age of eighty-five on March 29, 1848. One historian characterized the many different sides of his character thusly: "Brilliant, bold, daring, vigorous, possessed of financial genius . . . this is how he was viewed by most of the people of his time. Cold, calculating, crafty, unscrupulous, unprincipled, grasping . . . this is the image held by those who competed with him in the fur trade, export-import, or real estate. Warm, loving, sentimental, charming, vital, magnetic . . . this is how he was known to his friends and family. Crude, vulgar, ill-mannered . . . this is the opinion held by members of society of his day."[46]

John Jacob Astor died perched atop a veritable mountain of wealth, money squeezed out of the landscape by his own hands and his calculating mind. His only charitable interest was the Astor Library, which would become the New York Public Library, which he'd been encouraged to found by a former schoolteacher named Joseph Green Cogswell, who read aloud to Astor as his eyesight failed in his old age. In his will, Astor left the library $400,000 (roughly $13 million in 2021 money), only a meager percentage of the overall value of his unfathomable estate.

"This German butcher's son," one historian mused, "took a handful of flutes and $25, parlaying them into a fortune so vast that upon his death in 1848 estimates of the value of his estate ranged all the way from $8 million to $150 million. The numbers awed the minds of those days."[47] By comparison, the richest man in the city of Boston died the same year with an estate of $2 million. The generally accepted estimate of Astor's fortune at his death is $25 million in 1848 money, roughly one fifteenth of all personal wealth extant in America at that time and the equivalent of about $650 million today.[48]

3

MASSACRE OPERA HOUSE

1849

Excepting on occasions of religious ceremonial,
nowhere is greater dignity of manner
required than in a box at the opera.

—Emily Post

"There are no legends about William Backhouse Astor," one historian has written, but this hardly seems fair.[1] We are talking about a man who, upon the death of his father, John Jacob Astor, became the richest man in America. A man who—as his father once was—would be universally hailed as the "Landlord of New York," a man who endowed what is now the New York Public Library, an institution that is arguably a signal achievement of American public life, where any city resident can obtain a library card and, thus, access to an honest-to-God Gutenberg Bible. How can William Backhouse Astor have been anything but legendary?

"He sat in his office as if it were a prison to which his father had condemned him for life," said one of his friends by way of explanation.[2]

From the moment of his birth in Lower Manhattan on a crisp September day in 1792, the path of William's life had been laid out. John Jacob was still a fur trader then, with a sharp-eyed wife as intent on growing his business interests as he was. From childhood, William was given to understand that the hopes of the Astor family would rest upon his perhaps initially reluctant, but ultimately capable shoulders. When William was just a toddler, my great-great-great-grandfather, Cornelius Vanderbilt, was born across New York Harbor on a farm in Staten Island. In time, these two men would come to control almost every manner of getting to, and living in, New York City.

But first, William had to get through his adolescence in the shadow of his indomitable father. Every spare moment away from his schoolwork, William spent working in his father's storefront office. In his mid-teens, he went to Columbia College, where he proved both sociable and bookish. But even if William was finding some path for himself at Columbia, his father—with the shrewd demandingness of a butcher's son who hadn't himself had the benefit of a university education—didn't believe American universities were rigorous enough. So, he shipped William off to Germany when he was sixteen to study at the University of Göttingen.

William would later look back on his time in Europe as the salad days of his life. He was free there. Free from his father's wide and long shadow. Free to read as widely and deeply as he wanted. Free from the American Fur Company and its stinking pelts and endless notes and bills and ledgers. From Göttingen, William moved on to the Heidelberg University, where he immersed himself in history and philosophy and chose for his tutor a graduate student of classical archaeology. The two traveled together, roving through Italy, and were talking of wandering as far as India when the organizing influence of

William's life, his father, reached out his moneyed hand and dragged him across the Atlantic and back to New York.

The War of 1812 had broken out, and John Jacob Astor couldn't sell or ship his furs because the U.S. Navy was enforcing a blockade against trade with France and Great Britain. But John Jacob heard that a French general needed to get back to Europe posthaste and kindly offered him passage on his ship the *Hannibal*, which also happened to be packed with tens of thousands of furs. With the general on board, the ship had a legitimate reason to pass through the blockade.

When the *Hannibal* finally arrived back in New York, she had unloaded all her furs at considerable profit and now bore a reluctant passenger, William Astor.[3] His dreams of exploring the archaeological relics of the Orient dissipated like so much sea mist as the *Hannibal* sailed smoothly into New York Harbor, ferrying him back to the life his father had chosen for him, a life he would lead until his death.

To celebrate William's return to the fold, his father made him his official partner, renaming the company John Jacob Astor and Son. Once installed for good in the Astor family office, William applied himself to his dogged and unexciting management of their growing family affairs. "Perhaps, as has been said, he was a prisoner in the office," one historian remarked of him, "but prisoners sometimes grow fond of their cells."[4] After his brief flirtation with the life of the mind, the splendors of ancient history, of language and of literature, William "found it impossible," another historian wrote, "to disengage from a scholarly mode of thinking, and the fact that he applied it to the mundane details of the fur trade and the real estate business made him intensely boring."[5]

He wasn't much to look at, either. One society observer called him "the richest and least attractive young man of his time."[6] William had the Astor nose, somewhat long and downturned without being entirely beaklike, and small eyes. Though he was taller than his father, and muscular, he had a scholar's slouch. Where his father struck everyone who knew him as an energetic and vital man, someone whose daring wilderness exploits only served to burnish his reputation for decisiveness and shrewdness in business, William was just the opposite: He was shy. He moved slowly. He didn't show emotion as a rule and, so, gave an impression of coldness.[7] He spent his days poring over figures and balance sheets, rent rolls and property maps. It was a dull life, of dollars and cents and reams upon reams of paper.

Before long, it came time for William to marry. Despite his looks and lack of charm, he did possess that single characteristic that guarantees access to as glittering an array of social butterflies as any man can possibly imagine in New York: money. One visiting Englishman characterized the husband hunters of William's day as "the most heartless worldly b[itche]s that can be imagined," which would not shock anyone who is a regular reader of gossip columns or a viewer of reality television today.[8] Suffice it to say, the marriage market in 1818 wasn't all that different.

Fortunately for William, in late May of that year, he married a woman almost as dull and unprepossessing as he was. Her name was Margaret Alida Rebecca Armstrong, of the New York Armstrongs. She had all the Knickerbocker—that is, original Dutch—family connections that John Jacob dreamed of for the man he viewed as his only son. Her mother was a Livingston. Her grandfather was General John A. Armstrong, who had fought in the French and Indian War and served as a brigadier general in the American Revolution. Her father, John Jr., enjoyed a distinguished military record of his own and had been secretary of war under James Madison.

Margaret and William met when she was eighteen years old, while he was on fur trade business in Albany.[9] She was a country girl, plain in looks and certain in morals. She didn't mind that William was parsimonious and hated to spend money on himself, so much so that he often had a shabby appearance.

Margaret's father was unfazed when John Jacob mildly suggested she renounce her dower rights—her entitlement to one third of the fortune William would one day inherit—in exchange for a cash settlement on the day of their wedding. Armstrong, "having more class than money to support it," as one historian has put it, delightedly agreed.[10] (This would all work out fine for Margaret, but it set a precedent that other Astor wives would come to rue in the bitterest of terms.)

John Jacob chose a house for the newlywed couple at the corner of Broadway and White Streets, on an elegant block with painted brick homes and a flagstone sidewalk rigorously swept by servants. There, the young couple settled down into a well-appointed domesticity. "William set his life into a pattern," one historian noted, "and followed it until four days before his death at the age of eighty-three."[11] First, he would get up early and write letters, then eat breakfast precisely at nine. Nothing too heavy. Then he would walk to the Astor family office, arriving at exactly ten. He would work all day, in a manner that more than one observer characterized as little different from that of any other office clerk. "William was really no better than a head clerk—a very good clerk, and a trusted one—but an underling, nonetheless," one of his friends recalled.[12] This marginal status remained true even at the American Fur Company, of which William was now president.

Case in point: William didn't approve of supplying liquor to Indigenous people with whom the company traded for pelts, in part because of his religious convictions. He and his wife went to church every Sunday. We don't know if he was a teetotaler, but the temperance movement was gaining steam around this time, and William was certainly more restrained in his habits than subsequent members of his family. John Jacob, though, made clear to his son that religion and business didn't mix. And so, William caved, as he did on all things.

His father had reportedly once remarked, "William will never make money, but he will never lose any either."[13] But his father was wrong. William's plodding stewardship was enormously successful. Perhaps because he was good at eliminating waste and careful about expenses. Or perhaps he was just lucky, living in New York with money to invest in real estate just as the city started to boom. In 1826, for instance, he spent $25,000 to buy a sizable plot of bad farmland, one that stretched from Thirty-Second to Thirty-Fourth Streets, between Fifth and Madison Avenues. His children would build mansions on the site, and then the first Waldorf-Astoria hotel. Today the land is home to the Empire State Building, some of the most iconic real estate in the world.

Through one lens, William's life appears mundane, with year after year of stifling regularity, but it's also possible that this avoidance of risk, this embrace of routine, meant something else entirely: that William was happy. "John Jacob," a historian wrote, "had made sure that William would be required to do nothing, and that is precisely what he did."[14] But he did nothing exceptionally well. Perhaps what observers took for coldness was more like shyness or diffidence.

Regardless, William knew that Margaret, whom he called Peachy because of her complexion, harbored the trembling heart of a romantic. When their first child was born, Margaret named her Emily, after Emily St. Aubert, the heroine of the gothic novel *The Mysteries of Udolpho*, who faces supernatural terrors in a grand crumbling castle and must contend with the romantic overtures of a dastardly Italian count.[15] The couple doted on Emily, and soon their house began to fill with children, one arriving every other year. They had their final child, a girl they named Sarah, in honor of William's formidable mother, in 1832, but she died shortly thereafter. Then, in 1833, John Jacob's brother Henry also died. Henry, the butcher who arrived in New York ahead of John Jacob, had never had any children of his own, and he named William the primary beneficiary of his substantial estate, which numbered about half a million dollars, roughly akin to $15.5 million today.

This material change in their already comfortable circumstances caused William and Margaret to pick up stakes. All of fashionable New York was moving northward, looking for better sanitation and more space between themselves and the increasing number of downtown tenements (many of them built on Astor-owned land) teeming with the poor. A potter's field full of yellow fever victims was leveled to make a grand, shady park called Washington Square.

On nearby Lafayette Place, in a secluded enclave between Broadway and the Bowery owned by his father, William built a marble-colonnaded redbrick mansion, which Margaret staffed with servants in livery. Not far from them was the newly built LaGrange Terrace, nine Greek Revival row houses on Astor land that offered indoor plumbing and central heat, modern amenities that attracted other fashionable and rich New Yorkers. Even William's sister Dorothea Langdon, who had fallen out with the family for eloping without John Jacob's permission, returned to the fold. She moved into an elegant mansion on the corner of Lafayette and Art Streets, the latter of which soon came to be called by the name it still bears today: Astor Place. "On Sundays," one historian writes, "New Yorkers used to drive down Lafayette Place to stare at the mansions and wait for the Astors to come out."[16]

To escape the stifling summers and increasingly crowded Manhattan streets, William purchased Margaret's father's estate in the Catskills, which General Armstrong could no longer afford to maintain on his own. Margaret renamed it Rokeby. William added a library wing to the rambling old farmhouse and liked to pass his evenings in the country reading his favorite German encyclopedias and lexicons by the fire.

Meanwhile, the city around them was changing. In 1825 alone, when William and Margaret were still young marrieds, five hundred new businesses opened in New York, including twelve different banks and ten insurance companies. More than three thousand houses were built. In 1812, when William was dreaming away his youth in Europe, the idea of lights lining New York City streets seemed crazy, but by 1825, many streets had been piped for gaslight, and only ten years after that, Manhattan was already beginning to look like the city that never sleeps. Robert Fulton invented the steamboat—the first engine of the Vanderbilt fortune, which was then being built downtown—and steam ferries began to ply the waters around Brooklyn, Manhattan, and Jersey City, even as some rowboats still loitered on Wall Street offering to carry passengers across the river for ten cents a head.[17]

By 1832, the year before William and Margaret moved to Lafayette Place, the New York and Harlem Railroad company began operating horsecars between Prince and Fourteenth Streets. By 1834, trolley cars stretched north for another seventy blocks.[18] In one year, more than 1,300 sailing ships entered New York Harbor, and in May 1837, the month William and Margaret celebrated their nineteenth wedding anniversary, a staggering 5,700 immigrants arrived in New York.[19] Important for William: all those immigrants had to live somewhere.

By the 1840s, the Astors were able to charge $175 a year in rent for a single lot—up from $50 a year only two decades earlier.[20] The Astor method, instigated by John Jacob and refined into a science by William, lay in buying up as many lots of land as possible and renting them out to sub-landlords on long-term leases. The sub-landlord would be responsible for building a house or apartments on the lot and doing any other improvements and would collect rent from the tenants. The trick was that with the addition of a building to a lot (or two buildings, as many downtown lots would be overcrowded with a residence in front and another in the rear, with privies, or outhouses, in between), the rent the sub-landlords owed the Astors skyrocketed, just like in the game of Monopoly, shooting up to anywhere from $600 to $1,400 a year. And when a sub-landlord's lease ended, the property reverted to Astor ownership.

This meant that the surest way for the sub-landlord to turn a profit in this punishing system was to squeeze as many people as possible into the buildings, with each tenant paying as high a rent as the buildings could command. Of course, because ownership would revert when a lease ran out, there was no incentive for the sub-landlord to do any maintenance or repairs on the building. In fact, run-down buildings were often considerably more profitable than newer ones, as they attracted the poorest tenants, who were willing to pay for use of even a sliver of space in a room.

Then, in 1845, across the ocean, a fungus-like organism, *Phytophthora infestans*, began to spread, destroying successive potato crops in Ireland. Over the next seven years, the Great Hunger, as it was known, led to the deaths of as many as a million people and the emigration of a million more. The waves of immigration into the United States became torrents, as revolutions ripping across Europe in 1848 sent thousands upon thousands of Germans to safer shores as well. By 1850, almost half of New York City's residents had been born abroad.[21] Everyone who arrived had to find a place to live, and the tenements grew denser. Formerly large single-family houses in fashionable districts were carved into warrens of rooms rented to boarders.

An itinerant cartoonist named Thomas Butler Gunn, writing a humorous "Physiology" of New York boardinghouses in 1857, described these accommodations memorably: "Their spacious rooms have been divided and subdivided into so many apartments, that the place resembles a penitentiary, a hive, or a barrack. Ours . . . was eight feet by six. It was just possible to open the door to sufficient width to obtain ingress, the bed partially blockading it, and upon this we could recline, poke the fire in the stove, and touch three sides of the room with perfect facility."[22] With every tenant added to the rent rolls of every tenement, and with every partition and shared bed in every boardinghouse on their considerable and wide-ranging properties, the Astors got richer. And richer. And richer still.

William could shrug off any sense of personal responsibility for the squalor in which these tenants, most of them desperately poor recent immigrants, were forced to live as the fault of the sub-landlords. "He saw the tenements not as a source of tragedy," wrote a historian, "but only as a source of income."[23] And anyway, hadn't his own father come to New York as an immigrant, with next to nothing? In his heart, Christian though he was, William truly believed that if a man was poor, it was because he was lazy and lacked the gumption to make himself rich. The other biggest slumlord in the city at that time was Trinity Church, whose leaders also had no qualms about profiting from the desperation of immigrants.

In 1848, when John Jacob Astor died, the family held the funeral in William and Margaret's living room on Lafayette Place, on Saturday, April 8.[24] "The coffin was placed in the hall," a newspaper reported the following Monday, "and the doors thrown open, that every one might have an opportunity to see him, and thousands rushed in, until the hall was crowded almost to suffocation. The coffin was covered with rich black velvet, and bound with bullion fringe, over which was a velvet pall of beautiful workmanship; over the face a square of plate glass had been set, that all might have a look upon the remains of the richest man in the country."

One wonders how William felt, as thousands of friends, colleagues, associates, politicians, would-be politicians, Tammany Hall functionaries, gangsters, and curious strangers traipsed with muddy feet through the fine hall of his mansion. Did he appreciate that so many of New York's teeming masses wanted to see his father's waxen visage through the plateglass window on his coffin? What did they hope to learn from reading the seams in his lifeless face?

Finally, at four o'clock, the procession left for the crypt. Many society gentlemen served as pallbearers, including writer Washington Irving and the diarist Philip Hone, and the family followed behind. The cortege wended its slow way up Broadway, for more than eight miles. Finally, it arrived at the Trinity Church Cemetery in Upper Manhattan, where the patriarch of this unspeakable fortune was slid into his final resting place in the family vault. "Tho' there has been some uncertainty as to the precise amount of Mr. Astor's wealth," the *Cleveland Plain Dealer* remarked the following Monday, "there can be no doubt that of all the property he had accumulated he did not take one particle with him."

William may have taken his father's place as the richest man America had ever seen, but his days continued much as they always had. He got up in the morning, attended to his correspondence, had a light breakfast, and walked to the Astor family office on Prince Street. He was taking his sons John Jacob III and William Backhouse II into the business with him, but they were still young; William Junior was only twenty in 1849.

Of course, not every day was exactly the same. In March 1849, several disquieting letters arrived that would temporarily derange William Senior's schedule.[25] They alleged that his father, John Jacob, had committed heinous crimes some thirty years before, having schemed with the letter writer's father to make "spurious coin" in the fur trade. The letters threatened that the house in Lafayette Place would be burned to the ground, and William and his entire family murdered, unless Astor paid the writer $50,000 (about $1.8 million today). If William accepted his terms, the extortionist said, he should place an ad to that effect in the *New York Herald*. The letters were signed "E. K. Baswood," a name that meant nothing to William, who determined that his next stop should be George W. Matsell, the city's chief of police. Together they hatched a plan.

William took out an ad in the *Herald* as instructed, stating that the money could be had if a letter were sent addressed to "A.R.D." at the *Herald* office. When the answer came, the villain informed Astor that he would arrive at his home to retrieve the cash at ten in the morning on March 13, and instructed that the money must be conveyed in denominations of fifties and five hundreds, adding that "it was useless to attempt to find out the writer, as everything had been so arranged as to render it impossible."

A police officer named Bowyer assembled a package of worthless bills and took it to William at his Lafayette Place mansion. The officer told the anxious millionaire to deliver the package to anyone who asked for it. Several policemen then hid behind fences and in doorways around Lafayette Place and waited.

At the appointed hour, a fellow named Franklin D. Bragg skulked up to Astor's door. He collected the package—whether from a servant or William himself, the newspaper doesn't say—and left, unconscious of the police officers tailing him. They tracked Bragg to a corner downtown, where he ducked into a storefront and was wrapping the package in newspaper when the cops burst in and arrested him.

Bragg, it turned out, was just the bag man. He was supposed to leave the money with a barkeep at the United States Hotel, which had stood at Fulton and Water Streets since 1831, only two blocks away.[26] So, the police followed him into the hotel bar and waited until another man, by the name of Isaac A. Biggs, arrived asking for the barman. Biggs collected the package, unaware that anything was amiss, and left. When he climbed onto a stagecoach, the police clambered onto the roof, and the coach rocked and clattered its way to the corner of Broadway and Canal Street. There, Biggs disembarked, looking around to make sure he was in the clear, and then ducked into an exchange office on Mercer Street. That's when the cops nabbed him red-handed, trying to trade in the bills for ones that couldn't be traced.

Biggs insisted he was just the fall guy, but the police weren't buying it. Franklin Bragg, it turned out, was Biggs's brother-in-law. And Biggs was described in the paper as "well known to the authorities."

Viewed from this perspective, perhaps William's risk aversion looks like a rational response to a world grown unrecognizable, even explosive, around him. The years 1848 and 1849 ushered in a moment of intense and often violent conflict between rich and poor, eruptions of resentment growing more threatening with each passing month. Revolutions were convulsing Europe, beginning with the French Revolution of February 1848, but class violence was also bubbling forth closer to home, and in William's case, it was about to get closer still.

Attending theater was not part of William's routine. And he certainly had his hands full in 1849, assuming control of all his father's wealth and interests while training up his sons. So he probably didn't pay much attention to the announcement that the celebrated British tragedian William Charles Macready would be performing the lead role in *Macbeth* at the Astor Opera House on May 10, 1849.

Though it bore his surname, the Astor Opera House was not named for William or even for his father. Already, the name "Astor" had begun to decouple from the family that carried it. The theater was named for its location, Astor Place, the former Art Street at the northern end of Lafayette Place where William and so many other Astors had made their elegant homes. (If you have ever been to the Astor Place Starbucks, you have stood in the very spot where the Astor Opera House used to be.) But the opera house's very existence was a sign of the rarified environment in which elite New Yorkers were beginning to live.

The building was almost brand-new, neoclassical in style, its columns echoing those of the nearby LeGrange Terrace. It was designed as a haven for the "Uppertens," a name coined in 1844 to mean the richest ten thousand residents of New York City, but that soon became a catchall for upper-class people all over the country, not unlike the way we use "one percent" today. A theater impresario named Edward Fry conceived of the opera house as a specialty venue to showcase Italian opera, and when he first opened its exclusive doors in the fall of 1847, it was for a performance of Giuseppe Verdi's *Ernani*.

European tastes were a marker of class and social status, and so, calling the theater an opera house—for Italian opera specifically— sent a message to the people of New York. And that message was: *This is probably not for you.* The opera house offered amenities that would appeal to a moneyed elite: elegantly upholstered seats available by subscription only, together with two tiers of boxes. The cheap seats, benches, were tucked upstairs in a "cockloft" that could only be reached by climbing a narrow staircase. The theater went even further by enforcing a dress code, mandating evening dress, kid gloves, and, most infamously, a clean-shaven face.

Social observer N. T. Hubbard recalled that "each subscriber [paid] $300 a year in advance, which entitled him to three seats for the season."[27] Three hundred dollars then is a little less than ten thousand dollars today, an unthinkable amount to most people living in New York City in the 1840s. As it turned out, Edward Fry overestimated the upper ten's appetite for Italian opera. According to Hubbard, subscribers were also sometimes assessed as much as $250 to pay for performers' salaries and keep the opera house going. But even that was not enough, and eventually Fry began hosting "legitimate" dramatic plays, balls, and the occasional vaudeville act at the venue, to make ends meet.

On May 10, 1849, the night Macready's *Macbeth* opened at the Astor Opera House, a few blocks away, at the more popular and raucous Broadway Theatre, the famous American actor Edwin Forrest was also appearing as *Macbeth*. In a daguerreotype taken by Matthew Brady, who would later become famous for his photographs of soldiers killed in the Civil War, Forrest appears as a handsome rake, with chiseled features, thick sideburns, and a lush mop of dark hair rising from his brow, like the hero of a Regency romance. Forrest was around forty-five years old and was among the first generation of homegrown American theatrical superstars. He was especially popular with the working people in the Five Points neighborhood, native-born Americans and the recent Irish immigrants who were enraged at the English. Everyone knew his story: Born poor and obscure, Forrest had scratched and clawed his way to fame and fortune. His rivalry with William Macready had been the stuff of gossip and breathless reportage for several years.

Macready was Forrest's exact opposite: Already seventy, he was an elder statesman of the stage, refined and cultured. Though he himself had been born in Ireland, his presentation and style were more European—classier, as it were—which made him the favorite of the elite in both America and Great Britain. Each man quickly came to assume symbolic importance much more profound and dangerous than might be suspected by a slightly idiosyncratic reading of *Macbeth*.

Presumably, William Astor was as indifferent to Forrest's scheduled appearance as he was to Macready's. But many of William's associates, including the chief of police, were more than aware of the two competing Shakespeare productions being staged blocks apart in Manhattan that night. In fact, they were terrified.

Before we get to what happened next, it's worth pausing to mention what theater and, specifically, Shakespeare meant to regular people in the nineteenth century. Today we think of Shakespeare as highbrow entertainment, not all that different from opera—unless it's made hip and modern by cool young movie stars in dazzling modern-day settings. But in the 1840s, Shakespeare belonged to the common people, who worked punishing hours for very little pay and lived with very little privacy. Theaters were one of the few refuges for public gathering and recreation. They were a place to be sociable, to be entertained, to get out of one's life and have fun, to drink and carouse and sometimes to have sex in the balcony or throw rotted cabbages at the actors and boo and hiss when the show was bad. Cheap tickets were considered a public right. Shakespeare belonged to all.

The Astor Opera House stood at the intersection of two great thoroughfares in Lower Manhattan: Broadway and the Bowery. Broadway was the main artery of plush New York City. It was wide and elegant and well lit. The Bowery was something else. It was a working-class district lined with vaudeville theaters and saloons and coffeehouses and cathouses. It has been said that Bowery is the only street in New York City that has never had a church on it. It gave its name to the

Bowery B'hoys, one of the notorious nativist, anti-immigrant, anti-Catholic gangs of mechanics, tradesmen, and volunteer firefighters who would brawl in the streets over the right to put out fires. The Astor Opera House, with its fancy programming and snooty pretensions and ridiculously high prices, stood like a rebuke in the face of the working people on the Bowery, who felt that theater was theirs by rights.

The rivalry between Forrest and Macready had been running hot for several years already when the *Boston Mail* of October 30, 1848, reported that Macready was playing the Howard Athenaeum, with no seats cheaper than a dollar a ticket.

A dollar a ticket! Who does Macready think he is? Edwin Forrest would never put on such airs!

In 1849, Macready had a successful tour of theaters in the South, and he was booked into the Astor Opera House for Monday night, May 7. Forrest was already booked at the Broadway Theatre, and clearly the producers smelled a publicity bonanza. "The announcement of this engagement was the signal for an outbreak of long-smothered indignation," a contemporary account published by H. M. Ranney describes. "It was determined that Mr. Forrest should be avenged, and that Macready should not be permitted to play before a New York audience."[28] The causes were given as hostile feeling against England and Englishmen "handed down to us from the Revolution, and kept fresh by the insults and abuse of British writers on American manners," the imagined professional injuries against Forrest at Macready's hands "increased by the fact of Macready playing at the aristocratic, kid-glove Opera House."[29]

On the evening of May 7, shortly after William Astor would have arrived home from a presumably orthodox Monday at the office, Macready's engagement as Macbeth at the Astor Opera House began. Trouble did not erupt spontaneously. A man named Isaiah Rynders

had purchased fifty tickets and handed them out to his friends in saloons and coffeehouses, intending to heckle Macready off the stage.
Other gang leaders handed out money to buy allegiance to Forrest
against Macready. The chief of police would later estimate that as many
as five hundred people were in the audience expressly to disrupt the
performance.[30]

"The night came," Ranney describes, "the house was crowded,
and there was an ominous looking gallery. The curtain rose, and some
of the actors, who were popular favorites, were received with obstrep-
erous applause; but when Macready appeared upon the stage, in the
character of Macbeth, he was assailed by a storm of hisses, yells, and
a clamor that defies description."[31] He stood his ground, but nobody
could hear a thing. "It was a dumb show," Ranney wrote—"dumb"
meaning a performance when the actors give up trying to make themselves heard over the din and, instead, mouth their lines and exagger-
ate their gestures. (The fact that there was already both a name and a
method for dealing with this level of disruption should give a sense of
how common theater riots were.)

The Forrest partisans hurled pennies, rotten eggs, and, eventually,
chairs from the upper gallery onto the stage. Some had even smuggled
in papers of gunpowder to throw into the gas chandelier, which would
have caused firecracker-like explosions, smoke, and showers of sparks.
As many members of the audience were ladies, the police finally decided to stop the performance. The next day, everyone took stock of
what had happened. What should Macready do about his remaining
performances? His friends in New York and the Astor Opera House
producers encouraged him to keep the engagement. "Finally, a number
of influential citizens, men of wealth and standing, with Washington
Irving at their head, wrote a formal request to Mr. Macready that he

should play out his engagement, and pledging themselves that the public should sustain him," Ranney wrote. This letter supporting him was published in newspapers all over the city on May 9, along with an announcement that Macready would resume his role as Macbeth the following evening, Thursday, May 10.[32]

William Astor's name did not appear on this letter, but those of many other prominent men of his acquaintance did. Washington Irving, who was William's neighbor on Lafayette Place, may have thought he was taking a stand in the name of freedom of artistic expression, but no stronger signal of Macready as a symbol of the Europe-aligned ascendant elite could possibly have been imagined unless the letter had also been signed by William Astor himself.

The announcement caused outrage. The producers were told that if they reopened the Astor Opera House for Macready, they would be giving the signal for a riot. The city was responsible for issuing theaters licenses to operate—couldn't it also revoke those licenses in the interest of public safety? Mayor Caleb Woodhull thought so. He tried to force the Astor Opera House to stay closed. The lessees argued they had the right to go on and recoup their investment, and insisted city authorities had to help. "The fatal decision was made," the Ranney account concluded, "which made New York, for a few hours afterward, one wide scene of horror."[33]

Thursday morning, May 10, dawned. Forrest's friends gathered their forces, handing out tickets. Overnight, handbills had sprouted upon walls and lampposts all over town, summoning "WORKING MEN" to descend on the "English ARISTOCRATIC Opera House."

Meanwhile, city authorities met in the mayor's office. The city recorder; chief of police George Matsell, who had freed William Astor from his extortion plot earlier that spring; the sheriff; a major-general;

and a brigadier-general all assembled to consult on how to protect the opera house so that Macready could go on. Mayor Woodhull begged the producers not to open that night. They refused.

The august men in the mayor's office realized they had no choice but to back the opening. Chief Matsell, despite having nine hundred police officers on his payroll, feared this would not be enough. The decision was made to call in the military. "The nature and extent of the approaching riot was well understood by the authorities, and still no means were used to prevent it. It seems to have been their policy to let it gather, and come to a head, when, one would suppose, it might easily have been scattered," Ranney wrote.[34] Soon, the city was alit with news of the coming demonstration. But the mayor didn't issue any kind of warning proclamation.

Chief Matsell stationed two hundred policemen outside the Astor Opera House. He also stashed a further detachment in Mrs. Dorothea Langdon's stables on Lafayette Place, at the corner of Astor Place opposite the opera house, and yet another detachment in a nearby yard. General Charles W. Sandford, meanwhile, ordered companies mustered from several different military regiments. Nobody really thought this was about Forrest and Macready anymore. "Macready was a subordinate personage," Ranney admits. "It was the rich against the poor—the aristocracy against the people."[35]

As curtain time approached, hordes of people streamed from all over the city, converging on Astor Place, curious to see what might occur. A crush of demand for tickets caused the opera house to sell out almost instantly. One wonders if William Astor noticed the hundreds of excited men around him on Broadway as he walked home from his office. Did he know that a band of armed police lay in wait in his sister's stables? Was the yard where the other police were stationed Astor's own? We don't know, but given his reliance on the police in

March, it is possible he knew. Once the seats were filled, the doors and windows of the opera house were barricaded.[36]

By the time the curtain rose, the crowds outside were already trying to force their way in and were being held back by police. Ranney describes what happened next:

> The entrance of Mr. Macready in the third scene was the signal for a storm of cheers, groans, hisses, and yells: The whole audience rose, and the greatest part, who were friendly to Macready, cheered and waved their hats and handkerchiefs; but when these cheers were spent, the noise had not subsided. A large body in the parquette, and another in the amphitheater hissed and groaned; and the contest was kept up until a placard was displayed on the stage, on which was written—"The friends of order will remain quiet." The friends of disorder, however, kept up their noise through the first act, when the recorder and chief of police decided to quell the tumult; and in a few moments the noisiest of the rioters were arrested, and conveyed to a room in the basement, and the play went on in comparative quietness.[37]

Meanwhile, outside, all hell was breaking loose. Somewhere between ten and fifteen thousand people had descended on Astor Place, and as arrests were made inside, the crowd outside started throwing recently dug-up paving stones at the theater. "The stones crashed against the windows, and in some instances broke through the barricades," Ranney reported.[38]

Then the sound of horse hooves clattering on cobblestones echoed through the streets, and everywhere were shouts of "The military! The military are coming!" When the troops appeared, the mob erupted in rage and turned from attacking the opera house to throwing stones at the advancing cavalry. Horses reared, tossing their riders into the fury of the mob and scattering away into the streets of downtown Manhattan.[39] And then came the infantry, bayonets gleaming in the gaslight, marching in formation down the city sidewalks. But as the troops set up to defend the opera house, the mob regrouped, showering them with stones and knocking down soldiers.[40] An attempt at a bayonet charge was thwarted by the denseness of the crowd, and some soldiers had their muskets taken from them by angry rioters. "At last the awful word was given to fire—there was a gleam of sulfurous light, a sharp quick rattle, and here and there in the crowd a man sank upon the pavement with a deep groan or a death rattle."[41]

"I was standing on the corner of Mrs. Langdon's house when the first firing took place," a young boatman, Thomas Belvin, recalled later. "A man fell; I laughed, and so did others, as we thought that it was only blank cartridges to scare them; I heard a man say, 'My God, look at this; he's shot'; . . . I heard no notice given to disperse. . . . After this I . . . ran down to the church on the corner of 4th street. . . . I don't know how long I stood there, I was so frightened."[42]

A second, more furious volley of musket fire lit up the night, as the mob screamed for vengeance. "The ground was covered with killed and wounded—the pavement was stained with blood," Ranney continued. "A panic seized the multitude, which broke and scattered in every direction. In the darkness of the night yells of rage, screams of agony, and dying groans were mingled together. Groups of men took up the wounded and the dead, and conveyed them to the neighboring apothecary shops, station-houses, and the hospital."[43]

A young attorney named Stephens W. Gaines was standing near Belvin, observing the mayhem from atop a stack of boards at the corner of Astor Place and Lafayette Place from around eight thirty until the last muskets were fired. He saw the troops riding down Broadway on horseback, passing the opera house and setting up their position on Fourth Avenue (later Park Avenue). He tried to leave, but it was too crowded to move. Then the infantry passed right in front of Mrs. Langdon's house.

Gaines gave this account of what he saw: "I saw the fire from the discharge of the muskets as it left the barrels. . . . I was still standing on the board, when the last discharge took place up Astor Place towards the Bowery. . . . A man fell upon the sidewalk in front of us; . . . On picking him up, a wound was discovered in his back, by the blood running. . . . On examining the body, we found a wound in the lower part of his stomach; . . . After leaving him, I learned that others had been shot; I have been informed that he has since died."[44]

"The scene which followed the firing of the military, beggars all description," says Ranney.

The wounded, the dying, and the dead, were scattered in every direction. There were groans of agony, cries for help, and oaths of vengeance. The dead and the wounded were borne to the drug stores at the corners of Eighth street and Broadway, and Third Avenue, and others in the vicinity, and surgeons were summoned to attend them. Some were conveyed by the police to the Fifteenth Ward Station House, and a few carried to the City Hospital. Some of the dead and wounded were laid out upon the billiard tables of Vauxhall Saloon, a large crowd gathered around, and speeches were made by excited orators.[45]

When the play was over, the audience streamed out through the Eighth Street entrance under military cover. Macready, meanwhile, fled in disguise as an officer, mounting a horse and hightailing it out of the city and on to Boston, from whence he sailed for Europe.

"We looked over the scene that misty midnight," wrote Ranney. "The military, resting from their work of death, in stern silence were grimly guarding the Opera House. Its interior was a rendezvous and a hospital for the wounded military and police. . . . It was an evening of dread—and it became a night of horror, which on the morrow, when the awful tragedy became more widely known, settled down upon the city like a funeral pall."[46]

In the end, twenty-two people were killed, with at least thirty more hurt, in some cases maimed for the rest of their lives. One of the dead was a young newlywed Wall Street broker named George W. Gedney, who was standing at the railing outside Dorothea Langdon's mansion. At the first volley, a musket ball pierced his skull, spilling his brains over the mansion's stoop. Like most of the people killed that night, Gedney was a spectator rather than a rioter. One man was shot to death stepping out of a car of the Harlem Railroad. Bridget Fagan was walking along Bowery with her husband when a musket ball shattered her femur. She was carried to a hospital, where her leg was amputated at the hip. She died anyway.

The violence continued for a further day, with the mob clashing in the streets with the police and the military, advancing and retreating, until the final standoff at around nine in the evening over a barricade on Ninth Street and Bowery. The police stormed the barricade in the hot, red light of bonfires, finally rounding up the most die-hard resistors. Around thirty people were arrested, and the last of the rioters scattered into the dark. By midnight, an uneasy order was restored to that quarter of the city.

The Astor Place Riot, as it came to be known, was the deadliest riot in New York City history up until that point. And it took place quite literally in William Astor's sister's front yard. Was William home that night? Or was he off at Rokeby, enjoying a nice evening of reading by the fire? His sister was home, we know, because the mob tried to break down her front door and demand aid for the wounded, which never came. After that night, the theater was, for the rest of its short and undistinguished life, called the "Massacre Opera House," located on "DisAster Place." The name "Astor" had come to stand for something new: In some quarters of New York, it had come to mean injustice.

"Society," concluded H. M. Ranney, "but an unjust distribution of the avails of industry, enables a few men to become rich, and consigns a great mass to hopeless poverty, with all its deprivations and degradations. . . . We are all responsible, all guilty; for we make a part of a society that has permitted thousands of its members to grow up in poverty and ignorance, and exposed to the temptations of vice and crime. This mob is but a symptom of our social condition, and it points out a disease to which we should lose no time in applying a proper remedy."[47]

And here we are, 174 years later. Long lines snaking out the door of the Astor Place Starbucks, where we are all still waiting.

4

840 FIFTH AVENUE

1908

She was, in every sense, society's queen.

—Ward McAllister

A hackney cab rattled up the brick cobbles of Fifth Avenue one morning in late summer 1908, its still-new green-and-red carriage body sporting lanterns on either side, its driver dressed in a rented uniform designed to make him look as trustworthy and honorable as a West Point cadet.[1] The fifty-cent-per-mile rate was exorbitant, especially given what she was being paid, but it was worth it.

Rebecca Insley couldn't afford to arrive at her destination rumpled. She peered out the window at the passing marble façades of the houses lining the avenue, their windows blank with silks, their doors closed to all but the most exclusive company. Today, she was finally being invited inside.

The cab threaded its way through deepening traffic dappled with leafy green shade cast by the trees in Central Park, past the palaces of

New York City's moneyed aristocracy. Every year, fashionable New York moved farther north.

Rebecca could admit, if pressed, that she had mixed feelings about society. Something in her stolid midwestern nature rebelled against such extravagance at the same time that she appreciated the fineness of its taste and the strange mystery of its power. But despite her misgivings, she had always admired the woman she was scheduled to meet. And the more she learned about her—her shrewdness, her interest in art and ideas and current affairs, her towering reputation—the more appreciative she became.

For that reason, Rebecca was the perfect writer for this assignment. The daughter of a notable Indianapolis doctor and sister of a successful businessman, she had spent some years living in Europe and acquiring Continental polish before alighting in New York, five years earlier, determined to make her mark as a writer. She was in her mid-thirties but passed for younger.[2] Her manners were impeccable.[3] And the *Delineator* was a thoroughly respectable publication—with none of the sordid gossip of *Town Topics* and not as middlebrow as *Harper's Weekly*. The *Delineator* was a trusted news source for women interested in keeping up appearances, with current fiction, of-the-moment Butterick patterns, and articles of interest on politics and home economics.[4] Rebecca's elusive interview subject, who hadn't deigned to speak to the press in more than two decades, wouldn't have considered anything less.

The cab pulled up to the corner of Sixty-Fifth Street and rolled to a stop.[5] Rebecca climbed out, careful to keep her skirts clear of the gutter, and looked up at the imposing wedding cake that was 840 Fifth Avenue. Like most of the ancestral homes of "old" New York, the building was almost brand-new. Its smooth marble, grand mansarded roofs, elegantly not-quite-Gothic arched windows, and ornate twin balconies—the only real clue that this massive castle was actually two buildings in one—had been designed by Richard Morris Hunt, favorite architect of New York's richest families. It had taken two long years to complete, finally opening its exclusive doors in 1896, when the woman Rebecca had come to interview was already a widow and in her mid-sixties. Before that, the home's occupant had reigned over New York society from an elegant brownstone on East Thirty-Fourth Street, and had spent a charmed girlhood in the then-tony enclave of Bond Street, just off Lafayette Place. But Rebecca's subject's infancy had been passed in a proper home near Bowling Green, all the way at the southernmost tip of Manhattan. Fashion in New York City had then followed her northward over the long years of her life, until she finally settled here, on Fifth Avenue, in a would-be ancient French château that was all of twelve years old.

Rebecca approached the imposing front door, shaded under an awning thoughtfully designed to keep the rain off guests in the heated crush of entry for a ball, and knocked. No balls had taken place here for some time. Menus were still meticulously discussed, flowers decided upon, guest lists pored over and pruned and reshuffled and pruned again. But the orders for flowers were never delivered to Klunder, the preferred supplier of the city's most elegant hostesses. The extravagant entertainments that used to bring Rebecca's subject attention, acclaim, and power now took place only in the halls of memory.[6] The chatelaine of this house had suffered a severe nervous breakdown in 1906. Society still feared her, but she was seen only on her afternoon carriage rides through Central Park, attended by medical assistants, where she greeted admirers who existed mostly in her own mind.

The door was opened by a distinguished man in rich blue livery. This was probably Thomas Hade, who had run the eminent lady's household since the most glittering years of her reign, in 1876, when Rebecca herself was just a baby back in Indiana. She was expected, having made her arrangements with Maria de Barril, the grande dame's social secretary, known around New York and Newport as much for her taste in lush ostrich feather hats and smart dresses as for the elegant handwriting with which she used to address the coveted invitations to her employer's entertainments.[7]

Hade ushered Rebecca inside. The rest of the household staff was also outfitted in livery: green coats, white knee breeches, black stockings, shoes with gold buckles, and red whipcord vests studded with brass buttons stamped in an invented coat of arms.[8] Years later, a social observer would note the following about this household: "The livery of their footmen was a close copy of that familiar at Windsor Castle, and their linen was marked with emblems of royalty. At the opera they wore tiaras, and when they dined the plates were in keeping with imperial pretensions, at least so far as money could buy the outward signs of sovereignty. Indeed, the daughter of Queen Victoria in her Potsdam palace could have made no such display of money."[9] Even Rebecca's European finish would have left her unprepared for the world into which she was about to set foot.

She passed through the domed entry vestibule and into a long, lavish hallway lined with dour busts of Stuyvesants and Livingstons and other ghosts of old New York. Then stepped into a great hall covered in marble, from the end of which soared a cantilevered staircase lit by a massive crystal chandelier and softly glowing gas lamps. There, making her way slowly down the steps, a wrinkled hand heavy with jewels gripping the banister for support, came Rebecca's elusive subject: Mrs. Astor.

There were several women in New York who could, theoretically, have gone by that name. But only one of them did. Caroline Webster

Schermerhorn Astor was still, even in her relatively diminished state, the only Mrs. Astor who mattered.

Mrs. Astor would not be rushed, though Rebecca thought that the grand lady seemed much sturdier than might be expected of a woman approaching eighty. She was buttoned into a rather severe black day dress, and her smallish figure had gone somewhat stout—but Rebecca would never say so in print. Mrs. Astor held herself with the regality and self-assurance of her position, her soft waves of hair kept artfully black by a skilled hairdresser and topped with a capacious black hat swathed in gentle folds of black veiling. These days, Mrs. Astor was never seen without a veil, which had an elegantly softening effect on the lines etched into her face by age and, Rebecca knew, worry. But today, underneath the veil, Mrs. Astor was smiling.

Rebecca knew she must tread carefully. Mrs. Astor's trust had not been easily won. The great lady seemed under the impression that there had been a turn toward decency and dignity in journalism, and Rebecca had no wish to disabuse her of this impression. Mrs. Astor exercised complete control over how she was presented in the press, never allowing herself to be photographed unless she was in a studio, never granting interviews for any reason. If her rival Alva Belmont, formerly Vanderbilt, had had a genius for courting and manipulating the press, Mrs. Astor had a talent for circumspection. The night the Metropolitan Opera opened in 1883, presenting an audacious challenge by new money to the iron exclusivity of the eighteen hereditary patron boxes at the old guard's Academy of Music, of which Mrs. Astor was the standard-bearer, the lady herself had arranged to be out of town.

"As far as I was concerned," Mrs. Astor began as they settled next to each other in the elegantly appointed reception room, the press had never been "unkind, but rather too kind. I would say 'Good morning' in the drawing-room to some cultivated young woman or an immaculate young man, and the next day's paper would have two or three columns of things I never even imagined!" She wished that New York journalists would have the high sense of honor and personal responsibility that English journalists manifested. Rebecca hurried to agree with her.

Mrs. Astor knew about Rebecca's years in Europe, and she mused over her own past travels abroad and over the shift in perspective she had always enjoyed upon her return home. "I believe in a republic," Mrs. Astor continued, "and I believe in a republic in which money has a great deal to say, as in ours. Money represents with us energy and character; it is acquired by brains and untiring effort; it is kept intact only by the same means. . . . Best of all, there is the American idea, demonstrated about us every day, that each man can bring happiness and comfort to himself and to those he loves if he will only set about it, and that education, books, pictures, travel, are all within his reach."

Caroline Astor, called "Lina" by her friends, had been born in 1830 into a family rich in shipping money and, more important, prestige. Schermerhorns in America dated from the founding of New Amsterdam, and when Lina was an infant, her father's wealth was estimated to be around half a million dollars, today's equivalent of around $13 million. Her mother had been a Van Cortlandt. As a girl, Lina was tutored in French and other arts thought necessary for a young lady of wealth and breeding. During her early years, Lower Manhattan had already begun to teem with commerce, and the old Knickerbocker families had begun to hunt for more exclusive enclaves in which to establish themselves. The Schermerhorns settled around the corner from Lafayette Place.

When she was twenty-three, Lina married William Backhouse Astor II, the second son of William Backhouse Astor Sr. William Senior had divided the family fortune between two of his sons, though much of the control over the family business was given to William Junior's brother John Jacob III, who'd been named after their powerful grandfather.

Lina's husband, William Backhouse Astor II, was a pleasure-loving and genial man, known as much for his racehorses and his yachtsmanship as for his wealth, but he never got along with his brother John, who was seven years older. William thought John had a snobbish and superior attitude toward him, which he did, and John thought William wasted his time on frivolities, which was also true. Not having much say over the family business made it especially easy for William to indulge his considerable appetite for fine and fast things.

We don't know exactly what brought Lina and William together.[10] A match by their mothers? Lina's plans for the Astor wealth? In any event, the union of Lina's pedigree and intelligence with William's fortune would forge nothing less than a social juggernaut in what became Gilded Age New York. Their private relationship, however, quickly deteriorated into an arrangement of convenience. By the 1870s, at the pinnacle of Lina's social power and influence, William's role in the lives of his wife and five children was largely symbolic. His extramarital affairs were common knowledge, and Mrs. Astor was more often seen with her favorite "walker"—a man, often gay (explicitly or implicitly) and therefore "safe," who escorts married women to social events—Ward McAllister, than she was with her husband.

"Mrs. Astor," Rebecca asked, treading with some care. "In the Middle West, and even on the other side of the water, we hear charges of special viciousness, even degeneracy, in New York society. Not among the old guard, of course, but among the younger set. Can you comment?"

"I can speak with authority about our young people," Mrs. Astor said, with the sort of assurance common to older people speaking about youth. "I have always kept in close touch with them. They are of a new age and often have ideas different from my own old, conservative ones. And they are full of health and abundant spirits, embodiments of the new age of athletic development and out-of-door sport. It is perhaps true," she allowed, "that they frequently go into excess in amusement, but they are not degenerate and they are not vicious." Young men work hard to manage their fortunes, Mrs. Astor suggested. Didn't they deserve some healthy sports as a well-earned diversion?

Mrs. Astor knew something about young men and their diversions. Her husband, William, had been devoted to racehorses, even fielding a thoroughbred named Vagrant, who triumphed in the 1876 Kentucky Derby.[11] When William's first yacht, at the time the largest privately owned one in existence, was no longer equal to his needs, he had replaced it with an even larger, more sumptuous one, christened the *Nourmahal*, which could be translated as "Light of the Harem."[12] Caroline Astor had seemingly invented the art of refusing to know things that she did not wish to know. This steadfast refusal had insulated her from pity or public embarrassment. Once, upon being asked about one of William's long absences on his yacht, known by everyone in New York to be stocked with prostitutes, Mrs. Astor had said, "Oh, he is having a delightful cruise. The sea air is so good for him. It is a great pity I am such a bad sailor, for I should so much enjoy accompanying him. As it is, I have never even set foot on the yacht; dreadful confession for a wife, is it not?"[13]

She was, of course, lying. Years later, a granddaughter wrote that Mrs. Astor was not a bad sailor at all. In fact, she would willingly chaperone young relatives on windy sailing dates in Newport, "and grandmother was the only chaperone intrepid enough to go. She was never seasick."[14] But Mrs. Astor's refusal to acknowledge behavior she found upsetting extended beyond her management of her wayward husband.

"Our young women," she continued to Rebecca, warming to her topic, "are easily trained in domestic matters and taught to appreciate their responsibility toward the poor. There are no such barriers between the very rich and the very poor as some newspapers would have the world believe. All of my friends do a great deal for the poor, their daughters are brought up from infancy to look upon their charity work as an important part of their lives."

"Yes," she allowed when Rebecca gently pressed her on this idealized picture of society's rising young women, "I have heard that our young women smoke and drink and do other terrible things. I know a great many of them and know them very well. I have known them since they were born, and I am quite sure there is not one in my circle who is a cigarette fiend or who drinks to excess."

Thirteen years after this interview, in 1921, the chief literary chronicler of Mrs. Astor's Gilded Age world, Edith Wharton, would capture this kind of deliberate unawareness in her Pulitzer Prize–winning novel *The Age of Innocence*. "The world of her youth had fallen into pieces and rebuilt itself without her ever being conscious of the change," Wharton writes, describing her character May Welland—and it's hard not to imagine she had Caroline Astor in mind. "This hard bright blindness had kept her immediate horizon apparently unaltered. Her incapacity to recognise change made her children conceal their views from her as Archer [her husband] concealed his; there had been, from the first, a joint pretense of sameness, a kind of innocent family hypocrisy, in which father and children had unconsciously collaborated. And she had died thinking the world a good place, full of loving and harmonious households like her own."[15] That Mrs. Astor's household had not been particularly loving, or even harmonious, was another inconvenient fact she would never admit, certainly not to a reporter and possibly not even to herself.

But perhaps this hard, bright unawareness was born not out of mere denial. Mrs. Astor was businesslike, even unsentimental, about what she saw as her responsibility to the dignity of the family name. "One must have high ideals and do the best one can to realize them," she told Rebecca, a shade of steel in her gray eyes behind the veil. "My ideals in society have always been very definite. I have not realized them, but who does realize his ideals in this world?"

Mrs. Astor had been Rebecca's age when the Civil War ripped the United States apart. And when the South's defeat finally came, she had understood that in the uneasy years of reconstructing the union, someone would have to decide what made American society American. Someone had to set the standard. Someone had to decide what constituted American taste. Someone had to stand ready to demonstrate that the United States need not be overshadowed by the old societies of Europe. New York, after all, was the city of the future, and the United States was the country that held New York.

In this project, Mrs. Astor had had an ally, the transplanted southerner Samuel Ward McAllister. They were about the same age, McAllister having been born in 1827 in Savannah, Georgia. He had married Sarah Gibbons, also from Georgia, and then spent several years in Europe polishing himself. He was determined to know everything that a person of fashion needed to know. He studied court manners, architecture, clothes, food, drink, and resort spots.

When he returned to New York with his newfound social expertise, Ward McAllister established a career as "the most complete dandy in America."[16] In this project, he attached himself to the woman he called his "Mystic Rose," Lina Astor. Distantly related to Mrs. Astor by marriage—his cousin had married William Backhouse Astor Jr.'s sister Emily—McAllister was easily able to enter her circle. Under his tutelage, Mrs. Astor began her swift transformation from old New York to new American elite. McAllister was the one to first to suggest she choose livery for her servants, and he steered her toward collecting French art, hiring a French chef, and serving her dining companions exclusively on French and German china.

Ward McAllister also devised a system of gradation in society that split people into "Nobs" and "Swells." The Nobs had old money and fancy antecedents—like Mrs. Astor and her Schermerhorns and Van Cortlandts and Lorillards. The Swells, for their part, were the *nouveaux riches* then rolling into New York City, their pockets bulging from industrialization, and making a point of social-climbing—like the Vanderbilts and the Fricks. Mrs. Astor and Ward McAllister's great insight lay in how to knit the two together, the old guard and the new money.

They decided that anyone wanting acceptance into society had to be three generations removed from whoever had gotten their hands dirty making the money. Conveniently, Mrs. Astor was the wife of a grandson of John Jacob Astor, in addition to being one of the Schermerhorns, a Dutch family that first settled in New Amsterdam in 1636. Also, to run in the fast crowd that Mrs. Astor and Ward McAllister were fashioning, one had to have at least a million dollars in cash (about thirty million dollars today). As McAllister famously told the *New York Tribune* on March 25, 1888, "A fortune of a million is only respectable poverty."

After the Civil War, a sense of American cultural inferiority persisted, even as the newly reunited United States emerged as an international player in industry and economic power. The country's youth made it seem lacking in tradition, lacking in heritage. Mrs. Astor viewed the enrichment of society as a nationalist enterprise. As one historian of the Gilded Age has noted, "elegant dinners and splendid balls provided one expression of this desire, enacted for the elect but often viewed as adornments for the masses, who could share in their aesthetic triumph through accounts in the press and thus be themselves inspired to more cultivated heights."[17] Together, Mrs. Astor and Ward McAllister decided to establish a social institution that would feel steeped in tradition despite being sparkling new. They called it the Patriarch Ball.

Twenty-five society gentlemen—mostly old Knickerbockers like the Schermerhorns and Van Rensselaers, but also the two Astor brothers—joined forces to form the Society of Patriarchs. As McAllister put it, "We resolved to band together the respectable element of the city and by this union make such strength that no individual could withstand us."[18] The Patriarchs gave balls through Dodsworth's Dancing Academy and, later, at Delmonico's restaurant, and each founder was granted a set number of invitations to distribute. These were highly coveted items for those new arrivals longing to one day be seen as old families. The secret to the Patriarch Balls lay, as McAllister later wrote, in "making them select; in making them the most brilliant balls of each winter; in making it extremely difficult to obtain an invitation, and to make such invitations of great value; to make them the stepping stone to the best New York society."[19] The Patriarchs struck the perfect balance between propriety and ostentation. To create a pathway to this elite, McAllister founded the Family Circle Dancing Classes for young people about to make their social debut. This circle came to be known as the Junior Patriarchs.

Around this time, McAllister coined a term that would long outlive him: the *Four Hundred*. Rebecca had heard the rumors that the term originated from the maximal occupancy of Mrs. Astor's original ballroom on Thirty-Fourth Street. But the answer was perhaps even more snobbish than that. "There are only about 400 people in fashionable New York society," McAllister opined. "If you go outside the number you strike people who either are not at ease in a ballroom, or else make other people not at ease."[20] To be "at ease" suggested not merely wealth but also knowledge of etiquette, of the social codes, of the fashions of the moment, of the complicated quadrille dance steps. Ease was essential but harder than it sounded. Continued the historian of the Gilded Age, "This mingling of the old families with the new, of established fortunes with those of the *nouveaux riches,* and of traditional ideals with European influences set the four hundred apart, marking it as an intrinsically artificial American society, although one that quickly eclipsed the last remaining vestiges of the proper Knickerbockers."[21]

"I am not vain enough to think New York will not be able to get along very well without me," Mrs. Astor continued to Rebecca, reflecting on what she had accomplished. She had codified her social ideals—and not merely the social ideals of New York, but those of a newly reborn nation. "Many women will rise up to take my place," she said, perhaps with the knowledge that such a task would be impossible. "But I hope my influence will be felt in one thing, and that is in discountenancing the undignified methods employed by certain New York women to attract a following. They have given entertainments that belonged under a circus tent rather than in a gentlewoman's home. Their sole object is notoriety, a thing that no lady ever seeks, but, rather, shrinks from." Imagine what Mrs. Astor would think of today's social currency of followers and likes and "Housewives" hungering for attention on reality TV.

Certainly, in the previous decade, society's amusements had morphed from the fantastic into the grotesque. In 1883, Alva Vanderbilt had mounted the first major challenge to Mrs. Astor's social primacy when she threw a masquerade ball to end all masquerade balls.

Mrs. Astor had resisted the Vanderbilt incursion as long as she was able, but she couldn't withstand her daughter Carrie's wheedling entreaties to be allowed to attend Mrs. Vanderbilt's party. Alva let it be known that she couldn't possibly invite Carrie Astor because the young woman's mother had so far refused to call on her. Mrs. Astor had been outmaneuvered. She had no choice but to get into her carriage, stop outside Alva Vanderbilt's Petit Chateau, at 660 Fifth Avenue, and have her footman leave a calling card.

Carrie attended the ball, and her performance in the quadrille was a triumph. In the end, Mrs. Astor had attended as well. She chose for her costume that of a Venetian princess, draping herself in dark blue velvet embroidered with gold thread, pearls, and lace. She wore almost all her diamonds: a tiara of stars glinting in her black hair, drop earrings, bow and lover's knot brooches on her chest, heaps of diamond necklaces, a diamond and pearl stomacher, and bracelets over the wrists of her long white gloves. Ward McAllister accompanied her, dressed in a purple velvet and crimson silk costume as Count de La Môle, lover of Marguerite de Valois.

Alva, too, chose the costume of a Venetian princess. Taking a page from Mrs. Astor's playbook, she received her guests in her François I salon standing before a full-length portrait of herself by Raimundo de Madrazo y Garreta. She was sumptuously dressed in yellow and white brocade with an overskirt and bodice of blue satin with gold thread and beading. Transparent gold sleeves fell from her shoulders. On her head, she wore a velvet diadem featuring a jeweled peacock. Most notable, though, were the strands of pearls stretching to her waist. They had once belonged to Catherine the Great. As Mrs. Astor well knew, perfectly matched pearls were even more expensive than diamonds.

She also knew when she had been not beaten, exactly, but perhaps evenly met. Mrs. Astor was spotted in confidential discourse with Alva during the party, though she never told anyone what was said. The following year, it seemed only right that Alva and the Vanderbilts be included in her annual opera ball. The Vanderbilts may have been viewed as crass, but no one could ignore their money. Not even Mrs. Astor.

The success of Alva's ball demonstrated that the highest peaks of New York society were accessible to those with enough money and boldness. But not all assays of the Vanderbilt kind had been destined for success. Just look at poor Bradley and Cornelia Martin. Ten years before Rebecca's interview with Mrs. Astor, the Martins had married off their daughter and spent several years in Europe. When they returned to New York, they thought the time was ripe to make a dazzling break into society just as Alva had done thirteen years before. But it was now 1896, and New York—indeed, the whole country—was in a widespread depression. No matter: they could accomplish two things at once. They would hold a costume ball so magnificent that the Four Hundred couldn't fail to appreciate it, and if they did it on short notice, their guests would have no time to order their finery from Paris. They would be forced to obtain all their clothes from tradespeople in the city, creating work for the starving underclasses and a much-needed boost to trade![22]

The Martins announced that the ball would be held on February 10, 1897, at the new and very fashionable Waldorf-Astoria hotel. Over twelve hundred invitations would be issued, and the theme demanded period costumes from the sixteenth, seventeenth, and eighteenth centuries.[23] Just as Alva Vanderbilt had cunningly done, the Martins leaked all the extravagant details to the press. Rumors swirled that their costume ball would be the most expensive party ever given in America, that they were transforming the Waldorf into the Hall of Mirrors at Versailles—each rumor more ostentatious and appalling than the last. But this time, the prospect of an opulent ball taking place when so many people were out of work or barely getting by stirred up nothing but public rancor. Local ministers seized upon it as a symbol of moral rot and roundly condemned the Martins from the pulpit. Soon, the couple was receiving hate mail.[24] The threats made against them were so terrifying that Theodore Roosevelt, at the time the assistant police commissioner of New York City, deployed 385 members of the Metropolitan Police around the Waldorf-Astoria on the night of the ball to protect the arriving guests.[25]

Crowds gathered to watch the partygoers pull up in their carriages, just as they had outside Alva Vanderbilt's famous party in 1883, and at ten o'clock in the evening, a team of footmen in eighteenth-century-style livery unrolled a red carpet from the hotel entrance all the way to the curb. By ten thirty, the carriages and sleighs started to arrive. The ballroom had been transformed into a tropical paradise overflowing with out-of-season orchids and roses. Cornelia Martin appeared costumed as Mary Queen of Scots, covered in jewelry worth a hundred thousand dollars at the time, with husband Bradley on her arm as Louis XV. But in sharp contrast to the fawning rhapsodies that the press had showered on Alva Vanderbilt, the papers were harsh about Cornelia, who was inclined to stoutness. And though her jewels were indeed fine, they couldn't hold a candle to the diamonds worn by Mrs. Astor, who showed up in the elegant dark-blue velvet dress she had worn for her most famous portrait and decked out in jewels worth twice Cornelia's.[26] Alva was there, too, though by then she had become Mrs. Belmont, scandalizing society by insisting on her right to divorce her philandering husband. Her new husband, Oliver Belmont, wore a suit of real gold-inlaid armor and could hardly move in it.[27]

The Martin ball opened with the requisite quadrilles, after which came a twenty-eight-course formal supper—suckling pig, caviar-stuffed oysters, duck stuffed with truffles, and so on—which almost nobody ate, with four thousand bottles of 1884 Moet et Chandon champagne, which had been imported expressly for the occasion.[28] The Waldorf-Astoria, reportedly annoyed that an outside vendor was providing the champagne, charged the Martins a six-thousand-dollar corkage fee.

By the time the party was over, the Martins had spent $369,000 (about $12.4 million in 2021 money). Initially, the newspapers were as rhapsodic about their ball as they had been about Alva Vanderbilt's. But just as quickly, the press turned on the Martins. One commentator wrote that it was a "festering sore on the syphilitic body social—another unclean maggot industriously wriggling in the malodorous carcass of a canine."[29] The criticism got so intense that the couple gave up their ambitions of New York entirely and fled to Great Britain. Mrs. Astor didn't know what had become of them; they had effectively ceased to exist.

Perhaps no entertainment better demonstrated the dissipation of late Gilded Age New York society than the dinner given to celebrate completion of the New York Riding Club's French Renaissance–inspired complex in a forested section of Washington Heights in March 1903, the same year Rebecca arrived in New York. The press got wind of the planned extravagant seven-course dinner and camped out at entrances to the stables to try to get a scoop on the details.[30] To dodge the publicity, famous restaurateur Louis Sherry suggested that the dinner be moved to his restaurant, Sherry's.

On the evening of the soon-to-be infamous dinner, the ballroom at Sherry's was transformed into a pastoral idyll, with green turf brought in to cover the parquet floor. Live birds flitted between potted palms and trees, while a night sky, complete with glittering stars and a brilliant moon, had been painted onto the enormous ceiling. And there, at the center of the ballroom, by a real split-rail fence and hitching post, stood a circle of real-life horses. They had been specially shod to protect the floor as they were smuggled up inside the freight elevator. Every guest was invited to settle into a saddle, to which had been affixed a tray for the dinner service and a saddlebag filled with ice and a bottle of champagne. Some of the guests wore white tie, others dressed in the club's colors, and the waitstaff were all kitted out in deep-red riding habits and white breeches. The horses were treated to oats while the guests slurped champagne from long straws, ate the first course of caviar and turtle soup, and took in a vaudeville show.[31] While the dinner was a smashing success among the society set, who exclaimed over its novelty, the newspapers raked the hosts and guests over the coals. A society photographer had been brought in to memorialize the occasion, and soon enough, an image of the plush, well-fed gentlemen on their steeds in an ornate ballroom that most New Yorkers would never see hit the papers. More concrete proof of the moral degeneracy of society's elite could scarcely have been found.

In truth, Mrs. Astor confessed to Rebecca, she yearned for a vision of society like the old French salons, with intellectual hostesses attended by poets, artists, and financiers, where everyone was expected to be witty, well read, urbane, and charming. (Though Mrs. Winthrop Chanler, wife of one of Mrs. Astor's nephews, once noted that Mrs. Astor and her set "would have fled in a body from a poet, a painter, a musician or a clever Frenchman.")[32] If only more politicians were like Mr. Theodore Roosevelt. Then, having them at society events wouldn't pose so much of a problem, Mrs. Astor said and sighed. But too many American politicians bragged about having once worn blue jeans.

"Many people," Mrs. Astor sniffed, "seem to think I could have done a great deal in making New York society as democratic as it is in London and open to any one of intellectual attainments, as it is over there. But one can do only one's best under the conditions."

Mrs. Astor gave her last formal reception in 1905. *Town Topics*, the often sharp-tongued chronicler of society life in America, described her outfit at that event as follows: Mrs. Astor "wore a massive tiara that seemed a burden upon her head, and she was further weighed down by an enormous dog collar of pearls with diamond pendant attachments. She also wore a celebrated Marie Antoinette stomacher of diamonds and a large diamond corsage ornament. Diamonds and pearls were pinned here and there about the bodice. She was a dozen Tiffany cases personified."[33] Her sidekick in those years, a catty young thing from Baltimore named Harry Lehr, with whom she'd replaced Ward McAllister, was overheard describing Mrs. Astor as "a walking chandelier."[34]

"We have to be more exclusive in New York because in America there is no authority in society, and Americans in general are not inclined to admit its possibility," Mrs. Astor told Rebecca with finality. "Each woman is for herself and trying to outdo the others in lavish display and mad extravagance, with little thought of any ultimate good or any ideal."

Whenever Mrs. Astor mentioned her "ideal," her gray eyes lit up beneath her veil. Rebecca knew that Mrs. Astor could be pitiless in her expectations of adherence to an ideal of which she herself was the arbiter. Look at poor Ward McAllister. Once Mrs. Astor's closest confidant, he had destroyed their relationship when he published a tell-all book in 1890 and then, two years later, resorted to publishing the names of the Four Hundred in the newspapers. Caroline Astor could ignore many things, but she could not ignore failure to be circumspect. When McAllister died in 1895, Mrs. Astor failed to attend his funeral.

Rebecca and Mrs. Astor rose from their perch in the reception room for a tour of the impressive house, beginning with the picture gallery, also known as the ballroom. But the doors closeting the great room away were too heavy for the old lady to open on her own, and a footman appeared to help her. The rest of the time, Rebecca and Mrs. Astor rattled through the palace alone.

"This is where I invariably come when I am lonely," Mrs. Astor said softly. She used a large magnifying glass to inspect the paintings on the walls, all of them French, most of them otherwise lacking in distinction. "Yes. I have many lonely hours, you know. I am no longer young. My son next door is a great comfort to me and my grandchildren come often to see me; but of late years I have spent many hours here with my pictures. I have learned to love them dearly."

When they passed the open doors of the drawing room, Rebecca noticed the famous portrait of Mrs. Astor by French painter Carolus-Duran: in it, she was dressed in dark colors as she was today, one glove removed in preparation to receive all of New York society at her literal feet. Mrs. Astor used to receive her guests standing under this image of herself, a redoubling of her power and might that none of her guests could possibly escape.

The two women made their slow way to the dining room so that Rebecca could admire the Beauvais tapestry that Mr. and Mrs. Astor had brought home from Spain. From the dining room, they shuffled slowly into the drawing room, a French confection of Louis XIV furniture with a signed photo of the Duke and Duchess of Orléans conspicuously displayed in a silver frame. The Duke and Duchess had lately attracted attention for their pretense to the defunct throne of France. Rebecca noted aloud the prominence of the picture. Did its place of honor signify Mrs. Astor's support for them?

Mrs. Astor dismissed the idea as preposterous. "They are personal friends," she said, "and were the first friends I entertained in this house." She went on to add that though she supported them in a personal way, she was quick to disavow monarchy. "I am an American," she said from within her French drawing room. "And a very sincere one, and opposed to the overthrow of any republic. The duke is a charming man and he has a vigorous mind, but what do I know, what can I know, of his fitness to rule over France? I have not the slightest opinion on that subject, and no opportunity of forming any."

The minutes ticked by, sunlight slanting lower through the windows as the luncheon hour came and went. Perhaps Mrs. Astor was glad of such congenial company. As they chatted and visited, pausing at times to admire this painting or that item of decorative art, Rebecca could almost forget that she was talking with *the* Mrs. Astor. As Rebecca began to construct the magazine profile in her mind, she determined to conclude it by telling her readers that what she had wanted most from her time with Mrs. Astor was to sit at her feet and learn.

Rebecca was delighted with the reception her article received when it was published. What a coup! She was still basking in the glow when she saw the headline of the *New York Times* the morning of October 30, 1908, only three weeks after the issue of the *Delineator* containing her piece came out. "Mrs. William Astor Is Critically Ill," the *Times* blared over the fold. Rebecca hurriedly read that Mrs. Astor had been attended around the clock for three days by Dr. Austin Flint Jr. She was suffering from a return of a heart ailment that had first reared its head in the summer of 1907, causing her son to announce that she would not be opening Beechwood, their cottage in Newport, for the season. The previous summer, in Paris, Mrs. Astor had been flitting about, shopping for dresses and repeatedly telling anyone willing to listen that she was going to make the approaching Newport season the most spectacular one yet. But when her ship landed in Boston, her health collapsed. "At Boston," the paper reported, "her breakdown had been complete."[35]

Certainly, Rebecca had found Mrs. Astor's youthful vigor muted, but she couldn't have imagined that she was meeting the great lady in the last weeks of her life. Apparently, the *Times* shared her surprise—the article even mentioned Rebecca's *Delineator* interview. It was surreal to see her own words quoted in the *Times* ahead of the paper's solemn pronouncement that "all the members of [Mrs. Astor's] family have been summoned."[36]

The next day's *Times* front page brought the news that Rebecca had both dreaded and expected seeing: "Mrs. Astor Dies at Her City Home." Apparently, Caroline Astor had breathed her last the night before, at around seven thirty, after the evening papers had gone to press. Her daughter Carrie, now Mrs. Marshall Orme Wilson, had been by her side, along with a small crowd of doctors and nurses. Her son was nearby but happened to be out of the room when the last moment came. After her passing, hundreds of telegrams instantly shot around the world, notifying her friends and the newspapers that the reigning queen of New York society was gone.

"Mrs. Astor was not possessed of great wealth as the world rates riches now," the *Times* noted. It listed her various annuities and interests, also mentioning that she had an inheritance from her father, though he "was not wealthy." She would leave all her diamonds to her son John Jacob Astor IV and a five-strand necklace of pearls—yet, when the appraisers got ahold of the latter, they discovered that ninety of the pearls were imitations.[37] Edith Wharton wrote that Mrs. Astor, at the end of her life, was "a poor old lady gently dying of softening of the brain," locked in an eternity of entertainments of "the same faces, perpetually the same faces, gathered stolidly about the same gold plate."[38]

"There are many who believe that with Mrs. Astor has passed away the last leader of New York society," the *Times* remarked. "No one, they say, will ever be able to occupy the place she filled, for the conditions in New York's upper set, which justified the term *leader*, with all it implied, and rendered the position almost as well established as though it had been provided for by the Constitution, have changed materially since this gifted and tactful woman ascended to it."

Rebecca turned the page and was met with the same portrait she and her subject had beheld weeks before in Mrs. Astor's drawing room: Caroline Astor at the peak of her powers, her mouth set in a line that spoke of her inflexibility, her ideals, and the seriousness with which she took largely unserious things.

"Tradition," the *Times* concluded, "wealth, and social accomplishments combined to enable her to hold her position as the head of New York society, when that society was passing through a perplexing era of transition which came with the rapid growth of fortunes in new hands and the newly rich clamoring at the gates."

As for Rebecca, she would go on to enjoy a long career in journalism and marry in England in 1910. By 1920, she would be a widow living in a small apartment that she owned on West 115th Street with a seventy-one-year-old woman for her companion.[39] But where was she living in 1908, when she set out to interview Mrs. Astor and where, presumably, she also read of her death in the voluminous columns of print that unrolled in the aftermath of the great lady's passing? We don't know. Rebecca doesn't appear in the city directories, and the Allerton and Barbizon, residential hotels aimed at single professional women like her, a journalist from Indiana, were still fifteen or twenty years into the future. But in a tidy and respectable room somewhere on a crisp late-autumn day in New York City, Rebecca folded back the front page of the newspaper and read her own words quoted as the world mourned the passing of the last great arbiter of New York's Gilded Age.

5

WALDORF-ASTORIA

1928

I remember escorting Viscount Astor through the
corridors of the hotel. . . . It seemed to me that not once
did he look up—not once did he gaze at the frescoes, the
murals, and all that his own wealth first inspired.

—*Oscar of the Waldorf*

"If you move I'll blow your damned head off."

Joe Smith froze, his gun in his hand. The threat had come from the vague form of a man on his hands and knees, inching toward him on the two-foot-wide ledge five stories up on the rear exterior wall of the Waldorf-Astoria hotel. That night, the sky was overcast, and the courtyard at the rear of the building was darker and gloomier than usual. It was just before dawn, when the city is still draped in shadows and even the most die-hard partiers begin to collapse with relief into their feathered pillows, their spangled finery in a heap on the hotel room floor.

Joe had been waiting for this moment. He had been waiting on this ledge every night for six weeks. From darkness until dawn, he waited with his eyes on a ladder carefully placed to look like it had been left there by accident, and which conveniently ended only about a foot or so from a fire escape. The fire escape led to this ledge, which traced around the back side of the hotel, past the windows of unsuspecting sleepers. Six weeks was a long time to wait, but if there was one thing Joe Smith knew for sure, it was that they always came back.

Joseph Edward Smith, officially the assistant manager of the Waldorf-Astoria hotel and captain in the U.S. Army Reserve Corps, was currently the chief house detective, and he was waiting for a thief. There had been a series of burglaries in rooms at the Waldorf in quick succession, and in each instance, the thief had escaped totally unobserved. The management was beside themselves. The Waldorf-Astoria was the most fashionable hotel in New York City. If word got out that a thief was stealing from guests with impunity, its reputation would be ruined. And Smith was beginning to take this personally. The Waldorf, a later account described, "was his church and any violation of its sanctity was a desecration."[1] He had a good idea of who the culprit might be, too, and if he was right, the thief was a dangerous enough character that Smith didn't feel good about letting one of his guys take care of it. He would catch this man himself.

All the burgled rooms had been entered and exited through a window. This burglar was no ordinary opportunist—the guy knew what he was doing. And no amount of sharp-eyed surveillance in the lobby or corridors would stop him. The guy had guts; Smith had to give him that. To shinny up a fire escape and sneak around on a ledge five stories up was no joke. A plunge to the courtyard below would surely have killed him.

Smith suspected the culprit was José Hermidez, a guy he'd collared the previous year and given the nickname "the Mexican." When Smith caught him the first time, Hermidez had claimed he had turned to a life of crime only recently, and so, he'd been given a slap on the wrist—one year at the reformatory in Elmira, up in the Finger Lakes. But Smith had been a hotel detective for more than thirty years. He'd collared hundreds of people. And in his opinion, the state reformatory was really just a school for the broader education of crooks. When he asked around, he learned that, sure enough, Hermidez had been released from Elmira just before the recent spate of break-ins at the Waldorf began. Of course, he had sworn to the parole board that he was ready to go straight.

Nobody ever goes straight, that's how Smith saw it—not really. And if a burglary is successful, you can bet they'll come back. So, Smith had decided to set a trap. He took stock of all the fire escapes, trying to determine Hermidez's path up the outside of the building. In the Astor Court, toward the rear, he discovered a ladder propped up against a pillar, left by some workmen who had been fixing the façade. That side of the hotel fronted a narrow street rather than the busy Fifth Avenue or the blazing lights of Thirty-Fourth. Less foot traffic, much dimmer, easy to miss. The top of the ladder was a short distance from the bottom of a fire escape, which was an avenue to several ledges wrapping around the outside wall. That must have been the thief's way in, Smith reasoned, and told the façade workers' foreman to leave the ladder where it was. He armed himself, knowing that Hermidez would probably be carrying. And then he waited. It had taken longer than he anticipated, and Smith had idled away the weeks concealed just behind a curtain at an open window, until he saw the telltale shadow of a cat burglar appearing on the ledge, right where he expected. And now, the two men were crouching face-to-face, and the Mexican was threatening to blow Smith's head off.

When the burglar spoke, Smith caught a glimpse of something metallic glinting in the shadows at his waist. Without stopping to think, he raised his gun and fired—bang!—shooting to hurt rather than kill. The burglar cried out in pain and cursed as he tried to inch backward along the ledge, desperate to escape. In an instant, Smith was on the ledge, crawling after him. Hermidez's knees slipped, and for a sickening moment, it looked as though he were about to fall. Smith grabbed the collar of the thief's coat and dragged him away from the edge, but Hermidez scrabbled at Smith's legs, wrapping his arms around them and trying to throw Smith over. For a few moments, which felt like an eternity, the two men struggled on "the knife edge battlefield" on the rear wall of the most glamorous hotel in the world.[2] Finally, Smith broke free one of his pinioned legs, stuck a foot through an open window, and hauled himself and the thief over the sill. The two men tumbled to the floor inside in a tangle of arms and legs. Panting, Smith flicked on a lamp.

"I thought it was you," he told the thief. "And that's the way I wanted to get you."

The house detective's bullet had torn through the would-be thief's shoulder, and a warm stream of blood dripped from the fingers of the intruder's right hand. Turned out, he didn't have a gun after all—what the detective had spotted was the gleam of a flashlight—but Smith had caught him, red-handed.

Nearly forty years before, such a confrontation, seemingly ripped from hard-boiled detective fiction and yet completely true, would have been unimaginable on that particular city block. Before there was a Waldorf-Astoria hotel on that site, there had been two elegant brownstone mansions standing cheek by jowl, belonging to two quickly diverging branches of the Astor family tree. The houses were built for William Backhouse Astor Sr.'s mutually suspicious sons John Jacob Astor III and William Backhouse Astor II, playboy husband of Mrs. Caroline Astor.

But in 1890, John Jacob III died, followed just two years later by his brother. The brownstones became the domains of their sons William Waldorf "Will" Astor and his cousin John Jacob "Jack" Astor IV, though Jack's mother, Caroline, still ruled as *the* Mrs. Astor, the home she shared with her son being the very beating heart of Gilded Age New York society. The property was worth around $35 million, about a thousand times what William Backhouse Astor Sr., the "Landlord of New York," had paid to acquire the land on which the houses stood. At the time, he was considered to have overpaid.[3]

By the beginning of the 1890s, the Astor Estate, consisting of the combined holdings of the cousins (and next-door neighbors and rivals) hovered somewhere in the neighborhood of two hundred million dollars.[4] They already had a hotel in their vast real estate portfolio, the Astor House, established by the first John Jacob Astor in 1836 at Broadway and Vesey Street, in what is now known as Tribeca. Though not as profitable, in absolute terms, as the slum properties that sent a river of cash flowing into the family's coffers, the Astor House had consistently made money and had become a cultural touchstone in nineteenth-century America. The elegant neoclassical building, illuminated with gaslight, was for a time the most famous hotel in the world and one of the first to fashion itself as a self-contained community, able to serve all its guests' needs. But by the 1880s, the hotel was a relic, overshadowed by other, more modern ones being built farther uptown.

When his father died, Will Astor decided he was done with NYC. His mother was also gone, and he was turning his eyes eastward, across the Atlantic. But he had a few loose ends to tie up first. He had begun the process of developing the Hotel New Netherland, on Fifth Avenue and Fifty-Ninth Street, and decided to develop another new hotel on the site of his father's house, which he had just inherited. The location was an emotionally complex one, motivated, as one historian

writes, "by feelings of oedipal succession, long-standing clan antago-
nism and rivalry, and undisguised vindictiveness."[5] He would knock
down his father's home, where Will himself had been born in 1848,
and build a machine for making money in its place. And he would do
this while his detested aunt Caroline—who believed herself to be (and
was) the queen of New York society, though Will felt his wife ought
to hold the title of "Mrs. Astor"—still lived next door, in her elegant
redbrick and brownstone town house with the most famous ballroom
in the history of social exclusion. He would name the new hotel the
Waldorf—ostensibly, after the unassuming small town where the
family's patriarch had been born, but really after himself.

Now, noise has always been a fact of life for all New Yorkers. Even
today, in the app the city maintains for its citizens to report municipal
problems and disturbances, the very first item on the list—ahead of rat
infestations, food poisoning, or buildings without heat—is noise. Not
even the moneyed denizens of the plush Upper East Side are safe from
the predawn jackhammers, the passing chesty boom of the subwoofer,
or the echo of parade music vibrating off distant plateglass windows on
a Saturday afternoon. Maybe the people living in the super-skyscrapers
on Billionaires' Row, on Central Park South, are insulated from the
noise of everyday living by double-paned glass, but it is certain even
they occasionally awaken in the night from the passing hum of the
elevator or a garbage truck making its early morning rounds.

Mrs. Astor would, of course, have had to contend with noise. She
had lived through the Astor Place Riot in 1849, and the Draft Riots in
1863, when it seemed as though the city would be burned to the ground
around her. And she would have been accustomed to the everyday
bustle of life along Fifth Avenue: the rattle of passing carriages, the
nicker of horses, the shouting of touts and buskers. But all that was

nothing, in her mind, to what her irritating nephew unleashed next door to her in 1891.

Once the city's finest home for entertaining, it had become unbearable for daily living. As Will Astor's house next door was razed and then the plot excavated with steam shovels and pickaxes, Mrs. Astor's block of Fifth Avenue became an ungodly sector of noise, with never-ending clouds of dust, hordes of workers coming and going, traffic crawling past, stones being broken, horses whinnying and clomping by, lumber being sawn, and stone being cut. As the Waldorf rose into the sky, story by story, higher with each passing day, Mrs. Astor's town house disappeared into lengthening shadows. Soon, her south-facing windows, once so thick with sunlight that she needed double layers of curtains to keep the paintings from fading, looked out upon a blank brick wall with no distinguishing features except for an open-sided air shaft.[6]

This was an even worse affront than when Will had encouraged his wife to change her calling card to read simply "Mrs. Astor," a direct challenge to his aunt's authority. Even the *New York Times* remarked that the building of the Waldorf was a symbol of "something in the nature of a family feud between the two branches of the Astors."[7] But what were Mrs. Astor and her son to do?

The Waldorf was a success from the moment it opened its doors. Eleven stories high, it was a skyscraper before there was such a thing. The Flatiron Building, still about a decade into the future, would be the same height as the Waldorf when completed some ten blocks to the south. The hotel was, in short, the supreme kiss-off from Will Astor just before he hauled up stakes and packed his bags and his art collections and his cash and tooted off to Great Britain, for all intents and purposes, never to return. "It was," historian Justin Kaplan writes of the Waldorf, "an expatriate's declaration of personal magnificence, blue-blood pride, and superiority in imagination, style, and intellect to the members of his class and the nation at large."[8] Every room had a hand-painted ceiling. The hotel had also imported a European innovation that is now familiar to anyone with enough Marriott points—the concierge, whose job it is to create a sense of exclusivity and atmosphere. Will had even set aside one of the private dining rooms to be remade as an exact replica of the one that had been in his parents' house before it was demolished, right down to identical furnishings and seating for fourteen people, with actual Astor family china.[9] Though Will had designed every last detail of the hotel, he set foot in it only one time in his life. When it opened with a gala party in 1893, William Waldorf Astor did not attend.

The success of the Waldorf, however, signaled the beginning of a change in public life. The Astor House hotel, though it had a few ladies' dining rooms among its other splendors, did not allow unaccompanied women inside. This was because, in the nineteenth century, respectable society women were not seen on their own in public, and the Astor House wanted to remain a respectable institution. The demimonde and café society were a different story, and by the end of the century, even some society women enjoyed the thrill of a dinner at Delmonico's. But the Waldorf was about to transform how things were done. It would invite the public to dine at the Astors' table.

Will Astor leased the enterprise to a man named George C. Boldt, who had been the proprietor of the successful Bellevue-Stratford Hotel in Philadelphia. Boldt was a type that would soon become familiar in exclusive hotels—think of the aloof, formal, yet world-weary manager Barney Thompson, played by Hector Elizondo, in *Pretty Woman* (1990), who is at once discreet, exacting to his staff, harshly dismissive of people he deems not worthy, and yet obsequious and fawning with his richest and most important guests. Boldt knew which of his prominent guests liked which flowers, which variety of cigar, which vintage of wine. For the Palm Garden Restaurant, he hired only waiters who could speak French or German. He insisted that all male staff be clean-shaven, including the hackney carriage drivers who picked up fares at the curb, a decree that so incensed the cabmen that they nearly went on strike.

But even more important than the ineffable sense of European panache he brought to the appointments of the rooms and restaurants, Boldt wanted to make the Waldorf an acceptable place for society women to gather. He knew how much money socially ambitious women were spending on their private entertainments, and he believed that if he put the Waldorf at the center of their plans, the success of the hotel would be unprecedented. He also had the singular insight that would launch a million society events, from that year forward to the present day. In March 1893, in celebration of the hotel's opening, Boldt mounted a concert for the benefit of St. Mary's Free Hospital for Children.

Town Topics reported on the coming festivity in February 1893, saying, "The opening of the Astor Hotel, 'The Waldorf,' has finally been fixed for the 14th of March. It is proposed to make the matter one of profit as well as pleasure. . . . The proceeds will be divided between St. Mary's Free Hospital for Children and another equally worthy charity." And so, the society charity ball was born.

Boldt made sure to invite social figures from New York City, Boston, Baltimore, and Philadelphia, and he let it be known that the event would be strictly limited to fifteen hundred guests. On the appointed day, Fifth Avenue was crowded with carriages delivering partygoers to the new Waldorf Hotel, clogging traffic all the way up to Fifty-Ninth Street. Of course, it was convenient that any out-of-towners coming into Manhattan to attend the benefit could stay at the hotel.

The opening night landed on a Tuesday of "marrow-chilling wetness," which Boldt attempted to stave off by covering both the Thirty-Third Street entrance and the entire sidewalk in awnings. The day was touched with tragedy and disorder that the partygoers didn't see: there was a fatal accident among the staff, and the kitchen workers staged a walkout. But as far as the public knew, the evening was a complete success.[10]

Those attending were invited to explore the sumptuous halls and well-appointed suites, to admire the décor that somehow simultaneously managed to reference the Second French Empire, the Medicis, and Versailles. There was a concert, followed by a supper: "Oysters in bechamel sauce, cutlets of braised sweetbreads, terrapin, various pates, and other rich delicacies washed down with champagne and claret punch."[11] *Town Topics* sniffed, "I must emphatically condemn Mr. Boldt's terrapin. I tried it out of curiosity, and found it as insipid as a beef stew at a farmhouse." But apart from that quibble, the voice of society gossip pronounced the opening of the Waldorf a "joyous and handsome" occasion. "The crowd was heterogenous and promiscuous, but the general effect was one of good color and graceful character. Personally, I shall not soon forget the girl in yellow that stood in the pale music room, near to the gold piano decorated with pink roses."[12]

A new way of socializing had come into being, one that was inviting to and, indeed, under the control of respectable women. The Waldorf opening party combined a glamorous public setting with an opportunity to wear high fashion from Paris and important jewels from Tiffany and Cartier and Van Cleef, to enjoy delicious food and unlimited champagne and music and dancing, all while doing good works and all while being respectable in public. The following day, the party made the front page of the *New York Times*, which included the names of all the guests. And at the center of it stood the Waldorf. The social life of the wealthy classes (and the classes wishing to emulate them), once the purview of private ballrooms and dining rooms, was now going to be lived out in the open—the same way the working classes had done for generations.

Meanwhile, next door, Jack and Caroline Astor were fuming. They had survived all the noise and tumult of the construction, and now they had to contend with hordes of strangers pulling up in carriages in front of the house. But Mrs. Astor and her son knew they had to concede, and they began to plan their retreat. Jack spent two million dollars for Richard Morris Hunt to build an elegant French Renaissance Revival château on Fifth Avenue at Sixty-Fifth Street, a double house—for him on one side and his mother on the other, containing the largest private ballroom in the city. Before it was ready, however, in 1894, they suffered a particular kind of ignominy that was only made worse by Jack's response to it.

On a chilly Saturday night, November 17, 1894, a man named John Garvin was wandering up Fifth Avenue. He was about thirty years old and had immigrated to New York from Ireland some seven years before. He'd found work as a porter, and then he'd made a go of it as a grocer. When that job collapsed, he clerked for a tea merchant, but when he was discharged—the tea merchant thought there was something a little off about him—he had gotten work, such as it was, in heroin-shooting galleries.[13] The financial crisis of 1893–94 had rocked the economic stability of men like Garvin, creating a crisis of underemployed and unhoused "tramps," just as the Great Depression would send men to ride the rails in search of work a few decades later.

Garvin shuffled past the bright gaslights of the new Waldorf Hotel, which was full of hubbub and warmth and good food. As he lingered, staring into the windows at a world of splendor and safety he could never even dream of, he noticed that a lower door on the neighboring brownstone was ajar. He crept inside, roaming the service halls and climbing the back stairs to the top floor, looking for someplace warm and out of the way to sleep. He found himself in the rooms of Jack and Caroline Astor's laundress, Jane Doherty, who was elsewhere in the house, still working. Warm at last, tucked away in the attic of a fine house, Garvin curled up in the laundress's bed and went to sleep.

He was discovered at one o'clock in the morning when an exhausted Doherty tried the door of her bedroom and found it locked from the inside. A party of searchers was summoned, including a policeman, a watchman, the butler, a footman, a coachman, a few other people, and Johanna Best, the housemaid. Finally, they broke open the door and found Garvin in the bed. He was promptly arrested.

On Monday, he was hauled before the Jefferson Market Court for arraignment and charged with disorderly conduct. At that time, the Astors—always mindful of how they would be represented in the press, or perhaps unaware when the arraignment was happening—did not appear to make a complaint. The judge fined the tramp five dollars.

"I didn't want to take nothin'," Garvin said, according to the *New York Times*.

"How do I know that?" the judge asked him.

"Say, you're dead slow," Garvin said. "If I'd wanted anything, don't you s'pose I'd 'a' swiped it?"[14]

The tramp was penniless, and could not afford to pay his fine, so he was remanded to prison. But when Jack Astor heard what punishment had been handed to the man the newspapers were already calling "the Astor Tramp," he was incensed. "It does not seem right to me," Jack told the *New York Times*, "that a man can enter the house of any citizen and only be fined five dollars. My mother is frightfully alarmed over the matter and something must be done to punish this man so he will not repeat his offense. If he goes free there may be hundreds of others doing the same thing, and I cannot have that."[15]

The judge suggested that Jack Astor, who'd been out of town when the incident occurred, have a talk with the tramp, and a meeting was arranged.

"Oh! Think o' them beds," Garvin said to the court officer who led him before the rich gentleman. They both regarded each other, the one critical and bitter, the other affecting nonchalance.

"How did you get in?" Jack Astor asked him.

"Walked in," said Garvin, with what the paper described as "a sleepy, serio-comic air."

"Were you asleep?"

"Cert."

"How came you to lock the door?" Astor pressed.

Garvin looked up at the courtroom ceiling, thinking. "That's so; was it locked?"

"Why didn't you wake when they broke the door?" Astor demanded.

"Eh? Did I break the door?" the tramp marveled.

Confronted with a desperately poor and probably mentally unwell man, Jack Astor, instead of feeling pity, felt resentment. He told the judge that, in his opinion, Garvin had broken into the house intending to burglarize it and had then hid himself, feigning sleep to avoid being caught. Astor informed the court that he wanted to see the tramp prosecuted.[16]

By Thursday, the case—as most things in the Astor orbit did—had ballooned. A crowd had gathered at the courthouse hoping to spot Jack Astor, but he sent his family's butler, Thomas Hade, instead. On

Hade's testimony, a second warrant was issued for Garvin. The charge, upon Jack Astor's insistence, had been elevated to burglary. An affidavit claimed the tramp had forced a door on the first floor of the Astor manse at 350 Fifth Avenue and had gone to the fourth floor intending to steal five thousand dollars' worth of property.

The *Times* reported that "At the mention of $5,000 Garvin seemed to fall into a reverie, as though contemplating the luxury which it represented, and especially the downy couch in the Astor mansion."[17] He had probably never even imagined that amount of money, which is equivalent today to about $173,000. For context, a clerk with steady employment in the period could expect to make in the neighborhood of a few hundred dollars a year. Garvin was destitute. "With a faraway look" the *Times* reported, "he pleaded not guilty."

Once the charge had been elevated to burglary, the bail was set at one thousand dollars. Garvin allowed that he didn't mind going to prison so much, so long as he "got something inside of him." His lawyer sent out for an order of steak with potatoes and eggs. The detective who had arrested Garvin suggested adding an extra order of bread, as the man was fond of it. Clearly, the public sentiment was already firmly on the side of "the Astor Tramp"—so much so that several lawyers tried to persuade Garvin to file suit against the Astors for false arrest, but the defendant kept quiet.

On the Wednesday before this lively scene, a reporter called at the Astor mansion, knocking at the same door that Garvin had ostensibly forced to gain entrance. "After considerable conversation through a speaking tube, unbolting of bars, and ringing of electric bells," the reporter was invited inside to speak to Thomas Hade.

The butler, who had been with Mrs. Astor throughout the forgoing two decades of her reign in New York, was described in the paper as "a sleek, well-groomed, smooth-faced individual of the English type."

He told the reporter that none of the servants had been discharged as a result of the incursion. "Garvin was around here before," Hade said. "The first time he came to the house he asked for Mrs. Vanderbilt, saying he wanted to see her on important business." A maid named Anna broke in to confirm this account, saying that they told Garvin he had the wrong house. She added that he had come by only when the gate was left open and that on several occasions he had asked for something to eat.

"What did Garvin say when the policeman awakened him?" the *Times* asked.

"He didn't say anything," Hade answered. "He leaned back as though he was going to sleep again, but the officer shook him, and told him to get on his clothes. He didn't wish to leave the bed, indeed." Back to the streets of New York City in November? Of course he didn't want to get out of bed.

A sympathetic newspaperman named George W. Turner paid Garvin's initial fine and published an editorial about the case: "This is persecution. It is a bitter and cruel attempt to punish a man, not that he has been guilty of trespass, but that he has been guilty of trespass on the Astor premises. . . . The machinery of the law that is now hounding Garvin at the instance of John Jacob Astor would not have entertained the complaint of a tenement-house resident similarly aggrieved."[18]

Garvin's lawyer offered to cover the $1,000 bail, but Garvin declined. He didn't want to be "under obligations" to so many people, and anyway, he was "tired of walking around, and thought he could rest as well in jail as out."

After gazing at the ceiling while the Astor staff recounted his crime, Garvin was summoned to the stand. He was finally well fed due to his incarceration and seemed amused by all the attention and onlookers, but his shoes were full of holes, and his hair was long and matted. The paper noted that "his hands and those portions of his face left visible by his heavy red beard looked entirely innocent of soap and water."[19]

Garvin once again insisted that he had merely walked through an open door looking for a place to sleep. He'd been asleep, he testified, for four or five hours at 96 Bowery—probably a flophouse—but after being roused, he had made his way up Fourth Avenue, today's Park Avenue, and wound up at the Astor residence. He said he proceeded to the top of the house because he didn't find any beds until he reached the laundress's room.

The case went to the jury, and it took just thirty minutes for them to convict him.[20] When he stood and heard their verdict, "he did not show half as much emotion as on the occasion when he was first informed that an unknown friend would provide him with a substantial breakfast."[21] He faced a fine of five hundred dollars and imprisonment for up to a year, all for sneaking in and falling asleep in Caroline Astor's house.

Jack Astor had won the battle, but the damage to his reputation made him lose the war. He and his mother were revealed as cold, heartless, and indifferent. On top of that, Jack couldn't ignore that the Waldorf was a complete success. For a time, his mother had been considering tearing her treasured home down and building a stable, once they'd moved, so that anyone arriving at her nephew's hotel would have to walk through the omnipresent stench of manure. But when Jack learned that his detested cousin's monstrosity of a hotel was expected to gross more than four million dollars in its first year of business, he formed a new idea for their mansion at Thirty-Fourth Street and Fifth Avenue.[22]

Shortly thereafter, the house was razed, Mrs. Astor's famously exclusive ballroom and all. A fragile peace was brokered through the wall in the Astor family office that divided Jack's staff and interests from Will's staff and interests. Jack hired the architect who had de-signed the Waldorf, Henry Hardenbergh, to build another hotel, and enlisted George Boldt to manage it as well. Hardenbergh had already designed the famous Dakota apartment building, on the Upper West Side (outside of which John Lennon was killed in 1980), and would go on to design the Plaza Hotel (of *Eloise* fame) in 1907 and the Copley Plaza in Boston in 1910.[23]

With a budget of three million dollars, Jack Astor tasked Harden-bergh with filling in the remaining city block along Fifth Avenue, and along the increasingly commercial artery of Thirty-Fourth Street, with a hotel built in the same style as the Waldorf and connected to it, only several stories taller. "Jack's hotel dwarfed, enveloped, and subsumed his cousin's, in outward appearance at least, a victory in their long-standing battle," historian Justin Kaplan noted.[24] Jack planned to name it the Schermerhorn, after his mother, but Will refused to agree to this. Instead, they named it Astoria, for the country their grandfather John Jacob Astor had tried to found on the West Coast in the early years of the nineteenth century. The new Astoria opened on November 1, 1897, and Boldt mounted another benefit to celebrate; the festivities lasted from noon to midnight and churned up inches of froth in the press.

Town Topics looked upon the opening of the Astoria with a jaun-diced eye. "As tickets were sold for this opening, the proceeds from the sale of which realized upward of $5,000 for charity, it could not be expected that the attendance remain socially choice," sniffed the gossip paper of record, "but no one who was present thought to see such a curious combination of people. The makeup of the crowd, and indeed of some of the faces, was the feature of the event, and not the new and gorgeous rooms, the decorations, the music, or the flowers, which were everywhere in profusion. Such a conglomeration of society men and women of position, of actors and actresses, bookmakers, politicians, artists, journalists, country visitors, demimondaines and men-about-town was probably never assembled before in New York."

The shifting nature of society as it moved into the public sphere did not go unnoticed by the gossip paper, which was attentive to the misread social cues of many of the attendees. "And the costumes! Women with hats in evening dress, women without hats in tailor-made gowns, women in ball gowns, their necks and arms bestudded with jewels, and women in fancy-dress costume. I saw one woman in a directoire gown with a white felt picture-hat, and another in a ball gown with powdered hair. It was a strange, wild and weird scene, and one that may never be repeated in New York"[25]—except that it would be repeated. In fact, that description could pertain to everything from the Met Gala to any given evening at Zero Bond today.

The two hotels were connected by corridors, the most famous of which was called Peacock Alley. They could be sealed off if the truce between Will and Jack broke down, but while it held, the hotels would be linked by a hyphen and known thereafter as the Waldorf-Astoria, which, when it opened for business, would be the largest and most luxurious hotel in the world. It was rumored that the daughter of Ward McAllister had suggested combining the names, supposedly saying among her friends, "Meet me at the hyphen."[26]

"Like New York itself," historian Lloyd Morris wrote, "the Waldorf-Astoria crystallized the improbable and fabulous. It was more than a mere hotel. It was a vast, glittering, iridescent fantasy that had been conjured up to infect millions of plain Americans with a new idea—the aspiration to lead an expensive, gregarious life as publicly as possible."[27] The existence of the Waldorf-Astoria and the social life it fostered was one reason that New York, by the turn of the twentieth century, could legitimately be classed among the world's capital cities along the lines of London, Paris, or Rome.

The maître d' of the Waldorf, and now of the Waldorf-Astoria, was Oscar Tschirky, who had become universally known among the select as "Oscar of the Waldorf." You already know all about Oscar of the Waldorf, even if you don't realize it. The Waldorf salad that your grandmother used to make, with apples, walnuts, celery, and mayonnaise? Oscar invented it.[28] How about the chafing dish that keeps the scrambled eggs warm at the breakfast buffet at your hotel in Boise? Oscar again. What about those mid-century elegant dinner mainstays, lobster Newburg and chicken à la king? Oscar's recipes. And what about the velvet rope you've waited behind outside a nightclub where your outfit, sexiness, and overall coolness were judged by a door guy and usually found wanting? You might think the system was invented in the 1970s at Studio 54,[29] but you'd be wrong, because that was Oscar's idea, too.

But perhaps the biggest insight of luxury city hotels like the Waldorf-Astoria and of the men, like George Boldt and Oscar of the Waldorf, who ran them was that they offered a way to buy status. No longer did you have to wait for a coveted invitation to a ball in Mrs. Astor's home. If you had the money, the leisure, and the appropriate clothes, you could make a reservation and sweep into a hotel dining room, putting yourself at the center of glittering luxury, where your every whim was catered to. At the new luxury hotels, you were treated as though you mattered. The Waldorf-Astoria ushered in an era of the democratization of status—or maybe it provided the ultimate proof that the true arbiter of status in American society was money.

Only one symbol of the Waldorf-Astoria's importance was missing. George Boldt would not be satisfied until Mrs. Astor herself was seen dining at the hotel. He once said that he would rather serve an unprofitable glass of water to Mrs. Astor than an expensive dinner to anyone else—because once Mrs. Astor dined at the Waldorf-Astoria, the transformation of American social mores would be complete.

That moment came in 1897, shortly after the Astoria was added and Peacock Alley became the glittering artery through which all American fashion would pass for the next thirty years. Remember the Martins' otherwise ill-fated ball? It was held at the Waldorf-Astoria. Harry Lehr worked to convince a reluctant Mrs. Astor to attend— and attend she did, together with her son Jack, who appeared as Mrs. Martin's ball partner, making him "king" of the ball. The public outrage over that ball, as we have discussed, was so vicious that the Martins eventually fled to Europe to live in obscurity, but the larger transformation was complete.

But grand hotels rarely stay grand for very long, and several events unfolded in succession to seal the fate of the original Waldorf-Astoria. First, when George Boldt died in 1916, his son took over, but things weren't quite the same. And then came Prohibition. By 1924, rumors were already circulating that the hotel's days were numbered. Fashionable New York had continued its march northward, away from Murray Hill, and the stock market crash of 1929 was the final straw. Plans were announced that the grand hotel that had invented public life as we know it would fall to the wrecking ball to make way for the Empire State Building. The hotel's final day of operation, May 3, 1929, was designated an Employees' Day, with every dollar taken in going into a fund for the workers who were about to be unemployed. The two-ton wrecking ball swung on May 4, 1929, caving in the walls of the hotel that had changed American culture forever.[30]

By 1931, a new forty-seven-story Waldorf-Astoria arose on Park Avenue between Forty-Ninth and Fiftieth Streets, on land originally leased from the New York Central Railroad, closer to the heart of fashion and appointed in cutting-edge Art Deco style.[31] Until 1963, it remained the tallest hotel in the world. It changed hands a number of times, passing through the control of Conrad Hilton and then undergoing a substantial renovation in the 1970s and '80s, and losing the hyphen for good in 2009. It was sold in 2014 for over a billion dollars to the mysterious Anbang Insurance Group, which shortly announced the hotel's closure for renovation into condos. Anbang went bankrupt in 2020. The reopening of the Waldorf Astoria, at the time of this writing, continues to be a rumor that never quite seems to come true.

6

Hever Castle

1916

*The death of William Waldorf Astor, though not an event
of great and lasting significance either in the world of
action or the world of thought, will be generally deplored.*

—New York Tribune

On an unseasonably warm day in late September 1880, William Waldorf "Will" Astor was fed up.[1] He was thirty-two years old, annoyed at the press, annoyed at his aunt Caroline, and especially annoyed at New York, the site of all his family's triumphs, origin of all their wealth and prestige and prominence and, yet, disdainful of all his ambitions. Maybe he was even annoyed at his father, John Jacob Astor III, for insisting that Will relinquish his artistic dreams and come back from Europe to take his rightful place in the small, cloistered prison on Prince Street that was the Astor Estate office, just as Will's grandfather, William Backhouse Astor Sr., had been forced to do by his own father, John Jacob Astor. But that afternoon, Will began to mull over what he would come to call his "English plan." Like Harry and Meghan, only in reverse, he decided to give it all up. "On the 20th day of September, 1880," he wrote later, "the thought occurred to me that we should fare better in another land."[2]

Will was born in March 1848, only a short year and two months before the Astor Place Riot that erupted on his grandfather's doorstep. He grew up in the elegant brownstone on Thirty-Third Street and Fifth Avenue that his father had erected next door to his brother William Backhouse Astor Jr.'s home.

Will grew up steeped in his father John Jacob Astor III's sour opinions of his brother and his brother's wife, Caroline Astor. To Will's father's way of thinking, William Backhouse Astor Jr. (though he dropped the "Backhouse" at his wife's insistence) was louche. A dissolute, unserious man given to womanizing, horse racing, and yachting, shirking his responsibility to the family name and the family business. Someone who had left a promising education at Columbia College and become "shiftless, a drifter, a wastrel." One contemporary famously described Will's uncle William as "a one-man temperance society, dedicated to destroying all spiritous liquor even if he had to drink it all himself."[3]

John Jacob III had different principles, and he had raised his son in a strict religious and isolating household. "I was myself brought up severely," Will recalled years later, "and kept upon a pitiful allowance. I lived in an atmosphere of sinister religion filled with hobgoblins. . . . I was a mischievous little animal and everybody kept telling me that I was so bad."[4] Sunday in Will's childhood home was treated as a Sabbath day, with no games or fun allowed. Like many boys of his rather rarified social class, Will was raised by a succession of governesses and tutors, before advancing to Columbia Grammar School. He spent his school days alone reading histories and uplifting biographies, without the company of playmates or friends. This somewhat stern upbringing left Will with two rather disparate sides to his character: On the one hand, he was a loner, and prone to depression.[5] On the other, he was disciplined, deeply controlled, and freighted with the destiny that his father had mapped out for him. "In later life," one historian noted, "Willy's shyness and sensitivity often took the protective forms of truculence, impulsiveness, and a thickening crust of self-reserve."[6] But before he stepped into the role that the Astor Estate was holding for him in the counting room at 85 Prince Street, he had a period of finishing in Europe, first at the University of Göttingen, which his grandfather had also attended, and then in Italy. Perhaps the origin of his escape plan can be found in those heady, youthful days of reading and dreaming. The man who would control the land of New York City first dreamed of being, of all things, a writer of historical novels.

Will and his cousin John Jacob Astor IV, sixteen years his junior and known to all as "Jack," occupied a curious, and perhaps impossible, stratum of life. Edith Wharton summed up the expectations of men in their class in her 1913 novel of manners, *The Custom of the Country*: "For four or five generations it had been the rule of both houses that a young fellow should go to Columbia or Harvard, read law, and then lapse into more or less cultivated inaction. The only essential was that he should live 'like a gentleman'—that is, with a tranquil disdain for mere money-getting, a passive openness to the finer sensations, one or two fixed principles as to the quality of wine, and an archaic probity that he had not yet learned to distinguish between private and 'business' honor." No matter how they felt about it, the Astor wealth made Will and Jack figures of public fascination, doubly so because they were the city's second biggest slumlords, after Trinity Church.

The Astors were born into scrutiny, by both the public and the press. And their money assured them idleness while also stultifying them. If men like Will tried to do anything, beyond engaging in staid professions like banking and the law, they would be roundly mocked. Unlike in Europe, which was accustomed to the purviews of aristocracy, America had neither space nor time for the man of leisure—the word *leisure* defined by Thorstein Veblen as "the nonproductive consumption of time."[7] Will's descendant Michael Astor wrote that "As a young man from the distance of New York [Will] had envied the English their cultural heritage and the apparent ease and serenity of their lives. In England there was a leisured class of people whose lives were an extension of their tastes and inclinations: it might be sport, or art or literature or politics—still very much an unprofessional pastime—or a combination of any or all of these."[8] American culture had no language with which to understand or value idleness. What would happen, though, if Will tried to accomplish something of his own?

By the time he was in his twenties, Will was conforming as expected. At twenty-six, in 1874, he appeared in a contemporary's diary as "nice young Willy Astor," tall, muscular, with "polished manners, an intense and unflinching gaze, and a worldly assurance that belied his essential shyness and melancholy."[9] He could speak French, German, and Italian, had attended Columbia Law, and was working at the Astor Estate counting room. He'd been admitted to the New York State Bar. He'd even had his first love affair. In Italy at the tender age of twenty-one, he had fallen desperately in love with a local girl. "She was a figure of statuesque beauty," he wrote in his later life. "It was a strange and delicious emotion, an intense dreaming and anguish. I became humanized and lifted out of my youthful savagery. . . . But . . . we were not allowed to marry."[10] Maybe that's part of why he was so fed up that September day in 1880. He never forgot the unnamed Italian woman he had loved. In his later years, he would fictionalize her in *Pall Mall Magazine*—it helps, when writing fiction, if you also publish the magazine to which you are submitting—writing that "Across her face floated a swift tinge of tragic passion—as unfathomable as the depth that lurks between the rose leaves." He stayed in touch with the woman until she died in 1909.

In short, by his mid-twenties Will had grown into what one historian characterized as "a solitary, rather melancholy figure who concealed romantic yearning behind a brusque and stern facade."[11] About this time, he traveled to Boston on business, and William Dean Howells, that city's answer to Edith Wharton, took Will to meet Henry Wadsworth Longfellow at his house on Brattle Street in Cambridge.

"Frankly," the poet wondered to the Astor in his living room, "when you foreclose a mortgage, do you not feel some compunction for a fellow creature?"

"No," said Will. "We could never feel the emotion you suggest, because we are not taking the Mortgagor's money from him but our own."[12] He was an Astor, through and through.

Will had always known he would take his place in the Astor Estate. "In boyhood," he wrote, "I was taught that I and the Estate would some day be one and that my life would be judged by my success or failure in its control."[13] After studying business and law at school, he worked in the role of every junior staff member in his half of the estate's offices—the Astor equivalent of starting in the mailroom. Like other Astors who dreamed of other worlds, Will found his taste for art and history subsumed into his duty to the discipline of the countinghouse.

Still, he hungered for more. In the summer of 1877, the smooth, cultured, educated, and wealthy young man delivered a shock to his family. "I startled and amused my relatives," he wrote later, "by declaring my wish to stand for election to the New York State Legislature, a body endowed with infinite power for mischief."[14] In his letter accepting the Republican nomination, he enumerated his commitment to party principles, his belief in the "maintenance of law and order," and in "equal rights for all, and honest money."[15] Will had a pretty good start in his political career, moving smoothly from the office of assemblyman to the state senate.

In 1878, with his star on the rise, the time came for him to settle down. He married Mary "Mamie" Dahlgren Paul, a Main Line belle from Philadelphia, when he was thirty, in a true love match. She was pretty and vivacious and fun, and she broke through Will's controlled exterior to tap into the romantic hiding underneath. In quick succession, the couple had five children, only three of whom lived to adulthood: Waldorf, Pauline, and John. Meanwhile, Will and Mamie held grand entertainments in their house at 4 East Thirty-Third Street, the house where he had grown up. Will even urged Mamie to compete with his aunt Caroline for the title of "Mrs. Astor." That was his first mistake.

His second mistake was political. In 1881, after having served as a New York State assemblyman and a New York State senator, he decided to run for the U.S. House of Representatives for the Seventh District, a Tammany Hall–controlled area that contained many squalid Astor-owned tenements. He would, in later years, reflect on his political life as "a fine roll in the mire—unfamiliar streets, outlandish slums, villainous drinking saloons, Negroes trying to be white, speeches inane, humorous, half mad."[16] But how could Will have expected to succeed? Did he really think he was going to be able to glad-hand toughs in bars and factories? The same kind of toughs who had tried to tear down the Astor Opera House with their bare hands?

When campaigning, he'd hand out cigars and lay money on bars, treating everyone to rounds of drinks. In German immigrant sections of the neighborhood, he could trot out his German and talk about his family's peasant roots in the old country. But he wouldn't canvass the Astor tenements, and when he had to "press the flesh," shaking hands with potential voters, he always kept his gloves on.[17] The moment he was finished sharing fake smiles and back slaps with the New Yorkers whose votes he so desperately wanted, he'd be whisked away in the closed carriage, drawn by matching bay mares, that had been waiting for him at the door.

Will was defeated by only 165 votes.[18] The *New York Times*, which had supported him in his earlier forays into the political arena, turned on him, accusing him of being beholden to the Republican Party machine. "The moral," the paper opined, "is that the possessor of an honored name, of great wealth, of sound ability, and of unexceptionable private character may throw all these advantages away when at a critical moment in his political career he forgets what is due to his constituents as well as to his own independence and self-respect."[19]

Soon enough, other city papers joined in the pile-on, jeering at the rich boy's willingness to sell out without even having the ability to win. Will Astor's political defeat and subsequent public drubbing made him bitter, and that bitterness against the American press lasted until the end of his life. "Tobacco-spitting journalism," he described it, done by "trained vulgarians." His innate classism was pretty close to the surface, it turned out, and he was enraged that he could be publicly humiliated by people so uncouth. He could not bring himself to beg for votes from people he disdained, and he tried to justify the loss any way he could, save for looking at his own unfitness. "We were too prosperous," he wrote in his later years. "We liked the amenities of foreign travel; we had been known to employ alien servants, French chefs and English butlers. We were un-American."[20] Before too long, Will's pervasive sense of alienation, this realization of his un-Americanness, would result in his turning his back on New York and the United States entirely—with a reverse immigration back to Europe. The sting from his public shame still fresh, Will's "English plan" began to take shape.

Fortunately, Will and Mamie would soon be offered a taste of another life. In August 1882, President Chester A. Arthur tapped Will as envoy extraordinary and minister plenipotentiary to Italy. "Go and enjoy yourself, my dear boy," the president said. "Have a good time!" Secretary of State Frederick Frelinghuysen agreed: "Young man, don't write me many dispatches."[21]

Will took their exhortations to heart, and soon enough, he found himself in Rome, with no real duties to speak of but with all the freedom to revel in his own cultivation and to experience leisure without the wagging disapproval of American customs to constrain him. He and Mamie rented the Palazzo Pallavicini-Rospigliosi, where they gave elegant parties and were fêted at the court of King Umberto and Queen Margherita. Their social success was immediate and glittering, with the queen exclaiming over Mamie's beauty and refinement. Of course, it's hard not to wonder if part of the splendor of Italy, for Will, was connected to the other beautiful woman who had opened his heart in his youth. He felt alive again, alive with romance and possibility, and he could indulge in sculpture, drawing, and reading about Italian art and history as much as he wanted. He even finally wrote a novel, entitled *Valentino: An Historical Romance of the Sixteenth Century in Italy*, which one historian calls "the first of three gloomy, highly charged historical novels."[22] Scribner published it in 1885. Will followed it four years later with another sprawling historical drama, set in Milan. But neither book sold very many copies.

While in Italy, Will finally had the opportunity to become a serious collector of art and antiquities. His tastes spanned everything from Old Master paintings to antique furniture, from Shakespeare folios to arms and armor, and he even acquired a hat once worn by Napoléon.[23] (Perhaps Will was the model for Connor Roy, on *Succession*, the wealthy first son of a New York dynasty who turns his dilettantism, first, to collecting, bidding on a block of goods at auction rumored to include Napoléon's penis, and then, to running for president on a platform against the "great dangers: usury and onanism.") Will dreamed of using his collection to imbue his sprawling assortment of private palaces with the beauty and refinement of antiquity. His most astonishing acquisition while he was stationed in Italy was a gigantic balustrade lifted from the Villa Borghese Gardens, complete with statuary and fountain—but he kept it in storage, waiting for the perfect placement opportunity to present itself.

In 1885, when the presidency changed party hands, Will and Mamie were obliged to resign their post and return to the United States. It was a sullen homecoming.

First, Will's mother died in 1887, followed shortly by his father, John Jacob III, in 1890, of heart disease. Two years later, Will's uncle William-no-longer-Backhouse Astor Jr. died of an aneurysm in his hotel suite in Paris, leaving Will's cousin Jack to step into his father's shoes. The two cousins inherited the homes next door to each other right around the same time. When his father died, William Waldorf Astor's inheritance, though hard to quantify exactly, was estimated at somewhere between $150 and $300 million,[24] which the *New York Times* suggested made him the "wealthiest man in America, if not the world."[25]

As the elder of the two cousins, Will presumed himself now to be the head of the house of Astor. (His aunt Caroline, *the* Mrs. Astor, dismissed Will as "a prickly sort of person," nowhere near as fun and charming as her own son, his cousin Jack, who, in her estimation, would be better suited to be in charge of family affairs, despite his being the younger of the two cousins.)[26] Will and Mamie had been overseas during the great Vanderbilt-Astor showdown of 1883, which had seen the Vanderbilts finally admitted to New York society, but only on Mrs. Astor's say-so. Caroline, around that time, had changed her calling card to read simply "Mrs. Astor," instead of "Mrs. William Astor." Of course, Mamie was now also technically "Mrs. William Astor."

For a time, both social New York and the long-suffering postmaster of Newport had to contend with two women both technically called "Mrs. William Astor," both insisting on being addressed simply as "Mrs. Astor," who lived literally next door to each other. Social wags called this the "Battle of the Cards," for the calling cards each woman wielded as her weapon. Will and Mamie lost the battle, naturally. Everyone lost to Caroline Astor. But this social defeat only added to Will's sense of pique.

By 1890, his mind was made up. He tore down the house where he grew up, began building the Waldorf Hotel, and made ready to sail for England. As you know, Jack and Caroline Astor would cave, erecting the Astoria on the adjoining plot and after negotiating a fragile truce, the two hotels would become one, joined by capacious corridors that rewrote American public life. But Will wouldn't be there to see it. "America is not a fit place for a gentleman to live," he sulked. "America is good enough for any man who has to make a livelihood, though why traveled people of independent means should remain there more than a week is not reality to be comprehended."[27] He "washed his hands of America and American methods," as historian Justin Kaplan put it, an interesting approach given that it was American methods, or American capitalism, that had made the Astor fortune in the first place. But Will decided that he would "no longer be connected in any way to that country."[28]

He wasn't shy about broadcasting his bitterness when his move to England was officially announced, and the response was what might be expected from nativist and patriotic newspapers in New York City: he was denounced as a traitor at the level of Benedict Arnold. The press was merciless, saying that the Astor coat of arms should be "a skunk, rampant, on a brindle ox-hide."[29]

Will repaid the media with a perverse practical joke. We don't know for sure if he planted the story or not, but on July 12, 1892, two years after he and Mamie had decamped for England, the *New York Times* blared the headline "Death of W. W. Astor. He Suddenly Expired Yesterday in London." Will felt vindicated—the paper was as vindictive and sloppy in its reporting as he'd always asserted, but on top of that, its editors had revealed themselves as hypocrites, willing to trumpet his virtues now that they thought he was dead. The premature *Times* obituary waxed rhapsodic on Will's career in public service and politics, even going so far as to praise his common touch with the American people—though the *Times* perhaps had some doubts. "For some mysterious reason," it reported, "there seemed to be a disposition on the part of the Astor family to suppress in London the news of Mr. Astor's death."

The *Times* was also a bit sly in its account of Will's youthful character: "Never a brilliant young man, either in his college life or at the bar, Mr. Astor was one of the plodders who managed to accomplish his ends after a deal of hard work." It added that he had met Mamie at one of the Patriarch Balls at Delmonico's, and praised her rich olive complexion and her "most attractive manners."

The *New York Tribune* was as loose in its fact-checking as the *Times*, but was less hypocritical, announcing that Will's death was "not an event of great and lasting significance either in the world of action or the world of thought."[30]

The following day, the *Times* reported rather sulkily that "Mr. Astor Not Dead. Reported as Rapidly Recovering—Investigating a False Dispatch." Turns out, Will had only had a severe cold. But his wife was deeply annoyed, having received telegrams of condolence from all over the world.[31]

As they turned their attention to settling into their new life abroad,

Will and Mamie ensconced themselves and their children in a stately home in the London neighborhood of St. James's. However, the jewel in the Astors' English crown, as it were, was Cliveden House, a grand estate nestled amid 376 acres of gardens, lawns, and woods only twenty-nine miles from London. Will first rented Cliveden in 1893 for five months, and when the rental term came to an end, he bought it outright from the Duke of Westminster for $1.25 million (about $41.7 million today). The Duke, like many Gilded Age aristocrats, was rich in titles and prestige without actually being rich in funds. The sale of Cliveden reportedly dismayed Queen Victoria, who said, "It is grievous to think of it falling into those hands."[32] But the sale went through, though there was some argument between Will and the Duke over who should get to keep the estate's visitor book, with its signatures and names dating back to the seventeenth century. Will, of course, wanted the guestbook for his collection of antiquities and autographs, while the Duke was presumably trying to hold on to a last shred of his patrimony and his pride.[33]

Once Cliveden was his, Will set out to transform the estate into his own private fief. The main house, originally built in 1666 by the Duke of Buckingham, had been allowed to molder as the cash needed for its upkeep dwindled. Will was determined to rescue it from "the neglect and abandonment into which that dreadful old creature, the Duke of Westminster, had allowed it to sink."[34] But Will was also an Astor, and wary of press and publicity, so he immediately closed Cliveden off to visitors. For more than a hundred years, the estate had been open to tours and boaters who liked to picnic on the banks of the river that wound through the property—English tradition dictated that estates like Cliveden were in some ways part of the public's heritage.[35] But Will, like all the Astors before him, didn't think he owed the public one goddamned thing. Cliveden would be private, for his family alone.

When Will was in residence, he had his personal flag, with an invented coat of arms, raised each morning at nine to signal his presence. But signal to whom? The formerly open iron grille gate had been replaced with a solid wall topped with shards of broken glass, so no one outside the grounds could see or access the house without great effort. Will's neighbors had nicknamed him "Walled-Off Astor."[36] Will was so controlling of the life inside Cliveden that he even determined the windows of time when his visitors were supposed to write letters or go into town, and he insisted that all the clocks run one hour behind, as he rejected "English summer," or daylight saving time, as ridiculous.

Then his world shifted. His wife, Mamie, died in 1894, when she was only thirty-eight. Will brought her body back to New York to be buried in the family vault at Trinity Cemetery, but neither his cousin Jack nor his aunt Caroline attended. Mamie had represented another tie to New York loosened and ultimately undone.

Back in England, Will found himself alone, unmoored from the way he thought his life was going to be. He was a rich widower, in good health, with plenty of staff to cover the tedious work of raising his children. He wanted to enjoy himself as much as he could—which wasn't easy, as he was self-serious to the point of being ridiculous. He created a man cave, essentially, for his business and extracurricular engagements with women, building an office and apartment in London at 2 Temple Place—a neo-Gothic building that is now an art gallery—on Victoria Embankment, "a house, in a sense, to house other houses," as social observer Cleveland Amory put it.[37] He lavished $1.5 million on the creation of a study where he could stash his various collections—artwork, autographs, antique musical instruments. The room was seventy feet long, with a thirty-foot ceiling, two giant chandeliers, and floors layered in Persian rugs and tiger skins.[38] There was a huge portrait of himself and the same writing table he had used during his charmed time in Rome with his wife a decade before. It was in Rome that a fortune-teller had warned him that his life was in danger (not a big leap, given the instability of the times and Will's prominent fortune). He had become increasingly paranoid, worried for himself and his children. He slept with a pistol by his bed and installed a security system that locked all the windows and doors with the touch of a button, like something a Bond villain would have in his lair.[39]

Perhaps as an outgrowth of his never-ending war with the American press, Will turned his attention to British newspapers. Doubly useful for a man of literary ambitions, he purchased the *Pall Mall Gazette* and founded *Pall Mall Magazine*, in which, in addition to that of Rudyard Kipling and Thomas Hardy, he published his own work. Unfortunately, many of his assays into the realm of the literati would have benefited from the steadying influence of a good editor. For instance, when Will penned an article debating the true identity of William Shakespeare, finding it impossible that a butcher's son from Stratford could have written such beautiful plays, it was roundly mocked; the *New York Times* made fun of it in a dispatch from its London correspondent, novelist Harold Frederic, who remarked of Astor that "the second syllable of his name is clearly superfluous."[40]

Will embodied a curious contradiction: he was insecure in his status, yet possessed an "unshakable sense of being in the first rank of the blue-blood elect."[41] His wealth and an education superior to that of many of the aristocrats around him were proof of this, in his mind. In truth, he seems to have been a smart guy, but perhaps he never felt assured of this, as any achievements he might have been able to seize for himself would inevitably have been dismissed as due to nepotism or privilege.

"William in particular had a capacity for silence and isolation along with a thickening crust of reserve and a habit of making brusque and ill-considered responses to what he saw as challenges to his dignity," Justin Kaplan writes. But his daughter Pauline later recalled, "My father was not at all hard hearted, in fact he was very sensitive. I often felt he needed help and sympathy, and yet it seemed impossible to reach him through his defenses of reserve and a certain aloofness. . . . His true self seldom appeared and his motives were often misjudged."[42]

Even though Will was now an expat, with no intention of living Stateside ever again, his business office siphoned money from the very marrow of New York. His half of the Astor Estate was collecting up to six million dollars a year in rents—around two hundred million in today's money.[43] American dollars streamed into his coffers from office buildings and apartment houses on the Upper West Side, from vast blocks of dilapidated tenements, and from his half of the old Astor House. Money churned out of the Waldorf half of the Waldorf-Astoria and out of the seventeen-story New Netherland, which had so many rooms that it had its own telephone exchange office. H. G. Wells once remarked that William Waldorf Astor extracted rents from his New York City properties "as effectively as a ferret draws blood from a rabbit."[44] All this cash, all this value, leached away across the Atlantic, never to be seen again.

Will officially renounced his American citizenship in 1899. The public verdict was swift: W. W. Astor was an ingrate who had sapped his family's fortunes from New York City and absconded with them to England. He was a coward who had failed, both in achieving higher public office (even failing at buying it) and challenging his aunt's primacy in society. He now lavished his American spoils on multiple British institutions—universities, hospitals, charities—all in the hope of buying the legitimacy abroad he had so craved at home.

The public rage was due, in part, to the belief among reformers that the astronomical value of Astor properties did not reside in the properties themselves, but in the labor of the immigrants who had come to New York and transformed the city by the sweat of their brow into the international capital it was. Without those immigrants, those workers—and without the accident of John Jacob Astor's having gotten his hands on the deeds to that property first—the Astors would have had nothing. And yet, they had not repaid the favor to the people of New York.

On Broadway, near what would shortly become Times Square, rioters burned a life-size effigy they named "William the Traitor."[45] Police broke up the melee, but not before a smoldering hole was created in the asphalt. The *New York Times* covered the protest on its front page, opposite an item about Will's cousin Jack getting a company together to fight in the Spanish-American War. Will read all these stories and used them to feed his already simmering rage. For their part, the English aristocracy viewed him as the worst kind of arriviste, buying his access into society, gobbling up and bowdlerizing architectural and historical treasures, and even purchasing his own good press. Eventually, though, not even the staid English aristocracy could resist the Astor millions.

Will returned to New York quietly for a quick visit in 1904, to check on the opening of a new Hotel Astor, located near where his effigy had been burned. He was fifty-six and hadn't been back to the city of his birth in five years,[46] but the reporters who hunted him down on the *Majestic* while she waited to exit quarantine found his accent was still that of a Manhattanite.

Will's new project, the Hotel Astor, would come to fill the entire block of Broadway between Forty-Fourth and Forty-Fifth, on Longacre Square, which that April was renamed Times Square, the "Crossroads of the World." When finished, the new hotel soared twenty-two stories high, the tallest building in Midtown. It would be less snobbish than the Waldorf-Astoria, more aligned with the commerce and changing cultural styles of the new American century. The Hotel Astor didn't intend to serve as a display case for society and those who nursed social aspirations. Instead, it was built for tourists and businessmen, the increasingly mobile and moneyed middle class.

The twentieth century was here. The Hotel Astor had air-conditioning, fire and smoke detectors in each room, electric-powered fire doors, its own ice-making facilities, and its own incinerator. All the floors were served by elevators, and the building on the Great White Way blazed with 14,000 electric lights.[47] Despite his imperial pretensions, Will was happy to be seen dining in public at the Hotel Astor, and happy to emblazon his name on it. For the first time, the name "Astor" would be associated with something explicitly middle class. Will's partner in the Astor even designed the china service to be decorated with China asters—blossoms rather than Astor family coat of arms. The "Astor" idea was spinning away from Will's family's hands. While his trip was a success, and the hotel even more so—it was expanded in 1910, with the adjoining Astor Theatre and a roof garden added—Will faced a hard enough time from the press on that 1904 visit that he swore never to set foot in New York City again.

Safely back in Britain, he focused on burnishing his aristocratic bona fides in pursuit of a peerage. He succumbed to an ailment that was taking hold widely in white upper- and middle-class America around the turn of the twentieth century, arguably in response to the waves of immigration from Europe that were changing the literal face of the United States. He fell in love with genealogy. Desperate to locate in his family tree some distant sprig of nobility, Will paid exorbitant sums to try to demonstrate a connection between himself and a Crusader named Count Pedro d'Astorga of Castile, which was patent nonsense. He yearned to redeem John Jacob from being remembered as the immigrant German butcher's son he was, even blaming American democracy itself for what he saw as his great-grandfather's tarnished posthumous reputation.

"Originally 'the poor man's country,'" Will wrote, "the United States had been undermined and betrayed in national purpose by envy, resentment, and a misguided hatred of wealth, distinction, and achievement."[48] He felt that John Jacob's singular genius in business had been lost in caricature, in a fetish for his humble beginnings, or out of a populist resentment of his incredible success. Ultimately, Will hit on an essential contradiction at the center of the American fantasy of itself: "It is not democratic to climb so high."[49]

Despite his grumbling, Americans in the 1890s and early 1900s were as preoccupied with the doings of the wealthy and successful as they are today. We look to examples like Cornelius Vanderbilt and John Jacob Astor as proof positive that resounding wealth and success are theoretically within anyone's reach, provided that person has enough gumption. But we also want to punish them for their success. The two patriarchs both remind us of what is possible and underscore everything that we haven't been able to achieve ourselves. Maybe a noble bloodline would justify the Astor success in the popular mind? But it was not to be. No matter how hard Will tried, the first John Jacob was, and always would be, the rapacious son of a butcher.

Eventually, Will gave up on his genealogical quest, telling himself that nothing he did would offset the ingrained American resentment toward inherited wealth. "I do not believe," he wrote to a friend in 1905, "that anything would avail to change the ordinary acceptation in America of my great-grandfather's life and character. He will go down as a 'Dutch sausage peddler,' and my fate promises to be the same if the American press can make it so."[50]

By 1905, Will had lived in England for fifteen years, six of them as a subject of the Crown.[51] That year, his future daughter-in-law Nancy Langhorne, soon to be Lady Astor, visited Cliveden. "I went over the building a couple of years ago," she recalled later to her biographer, "and my recollection is of a theatrical sumptuousness. It was excessively grand with stone carvings, ebony pillars, carpets that allowed no sound of a footfall and heavy doors through which no sound could penetrate. By touching an invisible spring on his desk Mr. Astor could shut and fasten every door in the building, not only the hall door, but of every room, so that whoever was inside at the moment was shut in a box and unable to get out till the spring was released."[52] The butler at Cliveden confirmed Lady Astor's impression, saying, "The room doors had no handles inside. If you shut a door, it locked and you could not get out. But guests were told of this and shown a secret panel and how to slide it back. Inside the panel was a button, by pressing which you could open the door. . . . The first Viscount seems to have been afraid for his life. Two revolvers always lay by his bedside."[53]

If nobility could not be found in the archives of history, there was one other place to look: real estate. In 1906, Will had picked up Hever Castle, a grand manor house in Kent, where Anne Boleyn had grown up. For four years, he rained ten million dollars down on Hever to make it align with how he imagined it had been four hundred years in the past.[54] He dug a moat. He built a brand-new drawbridge and portcullis. He restored the battlements. He added a deer park, fountains, a boating lake, a power plant, and waterworks. Hever Castle was Will's own private Medieval Times village, surrounded by a twelve-foot-high wall. Everything in it that was supposed to be old was actually new—new bridges over the new pond, a new forest, a fresh yew hedge maze. He even commissioned a fairy-tale thatched-roof Tudor village, on the other side of the moat and drawbridge, to house the servants and staff. He filled the manor to overflowing with his collection of art, arms and armor, and artifacts, and then he added Anne Boleyn's actual prayer book and bed, and told anyone who would listen that her headless ghost stalked the halls. He sequestered himself in a fantasy of the era of absolute monarchy—albeit one with the modern conveniences of electricity and indoor plumbing. He lived there alone, surrounded by medieval antiquities he had purchased while biding his time, waiting for the day he would enter the peerage. He even opened the drawbridge for the British Society for Psychical Research to come look for Anne Boleyn. She wasn't there.

As the twentieth century progressed, Will grew even more regressive. He turned sixty-four in 1912, the year his cousin Jack died on the *Titanic*, but if he was affected by the loss, it didn't show. He became more British than the British, aligning himself against egalitarianism, social reform, and home rule for Ireland. His views were put forward in the *Pall Mall Gazette*, the left-of-center newspaper he'd bought in 1892, which grew to be reactionary under his ownership. It advocated the closing of public spaces to women to stop suffrage activists from demonstrating and took a stand against international arms reductions as well as death duties and taxes. According to Will, *Pall Mall* was a paper "written by gentlemen, for gentlemen."[55] He still vacillated between two origin myths—that of the plucky, honest German peasant with the grit and genius to take full advantage of the capitalist system to make his staggering fortune and the imaginary connection to the Spanish Crusading knight. Usually, he preferred the latter.

He deployed his wealth strategically, even when it could be overwhelming. When his son Waldorf married Nancy Langhorne in 1906, Will bestowed on his new daughter-in-law a fifty-five-carat diamond and gave the groom Cliveden—all of it, complete with the vast collection of antiquities and artwork inside. A generous gesture, yes, but also one that meant there would be no room for Waldorf, or Nancy, or their tastes, perspectives, wishes, or dreams. Ultimately, Will was laid up with gout and didn't attend their wedding.

Nancy posed an interesting challenge to Will. She was a Southern belle, born in Virginia in 1879, and would go on to become, in 1919, the first woman seated in the House of Commons.[56] Though he died before her election, the prospect of it must have stuck in Will's craw. She was a member of the Conservative Party, though she was in favor of reform and of votes for women. Will loved fine wine; she was a temperance booster. He'd suffered under a religious upbringing; she was an outspoken Christian Scientist. And then she had the temerity to redo Cliveden to suit her tastes.

"The keynote of the place when I took over was splendid gloom," Nancy Astor wrote later. "Tapestries and ancient leather furniture filled most of the rooms. The place looked better when I had put in books and chintz curtains and covers, and flowers."[57] Chintz! Feminine, approachable chintz. Gone were the Roman sarcophagi, the suits of armor, and the funerary urns that Will had scattered throughout the gardens at Cliveden. Instead, Nancy turned it into a house where people actually wanted to be.

But then, maybe Nancy had more in common with Will than people suspected. Certainly, she would have understood his conundrum of being at once unable to work and unable to be idle. One of her favorite stories concerned her father, Chiswell Dabney Langhorne, a plantation enslaver who had been ruined in the Civil War. When he finally made some money again, at the end of his life, he bought Mirador, an 1820 Georgian house near Charlottesville, where Nancy and Waldorf were married. Chiswell was eager to retire to a life as a country gentleman, enjoying nothing more arduous than hunting, shooting, and fishing, because, as Nancy, now "Lady Astor," said to her biographer in 1960, "Only Yanks and n——ers work."[58] And yes, she actually said that.

By the time Will gave away Cliveden, he regarded Hever Castle as his summer place, and he had decided to spend future winters in Italy, which had never lost its romantic allure for him. He bought land in Sorrento, within view of Pompeii and Mount Vesuvius. "So far as beauty is concerned," he wrote to a friend, "it is as near Paradise as anything I expect to see."[59] He named the place Sirena—as Italy, after all, had been a siren's call echoing throughout his life—and there retreated even further into his fantasies of the past. "Child of the century of steel, steam, electricity, and America's leap to world power," notes Justin Kaplan, "he tried to create at Sorrento an alternative world bathed in the light of the Roman Empire at high noon."[60] He began filling the estate with classical antiquities. He even put ancient Greek and Roman vases that had been excavated from the grounds into the villa's wine cellar and stocked the kitchen with antique earthenware dishes, iron pans, a grain mill, and even a bronze mortar. The chairs around the dining table were cushioned only in bear and wolf skins.

Will had women come to Hever Castle in the years of his widowhood and to his private office-cum-pied-à-terre in London. That he managed to do this without attracting attention and without any of the women selling her story—in an age after blind-item gossip columns but before the invention of nondisclosure agreements—is nothing short of remarkable. Rumors occasionally bubbled up of his involvements with society women, but nothing came of them. Then, in 1913, at the age of sixty-five, William Waldorf Astor fell in love. And he fell hard.

Maybe it was the sumptuous Italian surroundings that did it, but he became most desperately smitten with Lady Victoria Sackville, who at fifty-one was beautiful, with exquisite skin and long flaxen hair.

She possessed a worldly elegance and sophistication cultivated by her upbringing in a French convent after her mother, a Spanish dancer, bore her out of wedlock. Her father had been minister to the United States from Great Britain, and so, like Will, she existed in this strange mid-Atlantic world, neither British nor American, but somehow too much of both. Lady Victoria was used to being adored. She was married to Lionel Sackville-West, who was also her cousin, though by this time they were leading largely separate personal and sexual lives. (Victoria's daughter, called Vita, would go on to become a novelist, poet, journalist, and Virginia Woolf's lover; her fluid relationship with her own gender and sexuality would serve as inspiration for Woolf's novel *Orlando*.) One of Victoria's lovers before Will had been Pierpont Morgan.[61]

Uncharacteristically for an Astor, most of whom were religious in the destruction of all their correspondence, Will wrote Victoria passionate love letters that survive today. "A woman in the flower of her prime—like yourself—needs a romantic attachment," he pressed. "Without it the heart grows cold. It is as necessary as daily bread, and not even Knole [her husband's estate] and four acres at Hampstead can take its place. It is the consciousness that someone is thinking of you, desires you, longs for the touch of your beautiful body that keeps the heart young."[62] They had known each other socially for years, with Will not having the courage to approach her romantically. Then, one charmed afternoon, she came to see him at Hever Castle. He would later recall it as "l'après-midi d'un faune," referring to the romantic symphonic poem composed by Claude Debussy in 1894. "That momentous Saturday," he wrote to her, "was the psychological hour for which you and I have unconsciously waited."[63] When their hands met, something wonderful awakened. He pledged discretion, promising that if she returned in the afternoon to his office on Embankment, she should arrive "veiled and unannounced," to be admitted only by him. His butler, he assured her, was trustworthy.

Victoria led him on a little, declining an afternoon assignation and suggesting, instead, that they meet in Switzerland with friends, to enjoy a "picnic without refreshments" (presumably an early twentieth-century equivalent to "Netflix and chill").[64] Sadly, for Will, by the winter of 1913/14, Victoria had already moved on, rekindling her relationship with a Swedish baron she'd run into while traveling to Sorrento to visit Will at Sirena. She arrived in a chauffeured Rolls-Royce at Will's treasured ancient Italian haven only to break up with him. He was crestfallen. They agreed, as so many exes do, to remain friends, but his subsequent letters to her were all signed with the formal "W. W. Astor," while his love letters had been signed "Will."

When their affair ended, something in Will died—some small glimmer of hope, or freedom, or youth. Soon, he started shaking off things in his life that had constrained but also defined him. He sold off his publishing enterprises. He signed his Manhattan real estate holdings, worth about seventy million dollars, over to his sons Waldorf and John Jacob V, including the site of the demolished Astor House, the Waldorf half of the Waldorf-Astoria, the Hotel Astor, the Astor Theatre, the Hotel New Netherland, and several apartment buildings and office blocks, some of which were named Astor and some not.

He still had one unmet goal in his life: elevation to the peerage. On this, he refused to give up. He even reportedly once arrived at a party wearing a robe made of ermine and velvet, designated only for peers, though he hadn't been given any reason to hope he'd be named one. In his obsession with titles, Will was no different from the other Americans who, after rising in social rank because of their wealth in a country that had deliberately cast off hereditary titles, tripped over themselves trying to get close to aristocracy. Will set about his project of legitimizing his own aristocratic pretensions in the most American way possible: by donating money. He showered his largesse on Conservative Party politicians both before the Great War and after, he rained money on British universities, he blasted a hose of cash at British hospitals and the Red Cross and at public funds for wounded servicemen. One estimate puts his wartime largesse at upward of $5 million—or $151 million today.

He needed to spend that much because while trying to break into Edwardian British society, he had violated a lot of spoken and unspoken codes—painting his carriage brown, for instance, a color reserved for the royal family.

Cleveland Amory tells this story: "When a distinguished British naval captain, Sir Berkeley Milne, came to a concert at his house, having been brought by the lady, who had been invited by Astor, with whom he happened to be dining, Astor met him at the door and summarily told him to leave. The next day he published in his paper: 'We are desired to make known that the presence of Captain Sir Berkeley Milne of the Naval and Military Club, Piccadilly, at Mrs. Astor's concert last Thursday evening, was uninvited.'"[65] This caused a rift between Will and the Prince of Wales, who had accepted Will to his Carlton Club, of which Milne was also a member. The Carlton Club asked Will to apologize to Milne, which he grudgingly did. But in general, the British aristocracy held its nose and overlooked Will's behavior, which they considered boorish, including his disparaging remarks about Edward's mistress ("royal strumpet," per Will), South Africans, and Jewish people.[66]

Then, finally, it happened: Will's name appeared on King George V's New Year's Day Honours list on the first day of 1916. He was named a baron, and appeared in the House of Lords dressed in the robes he had so craved . . . for upward of twenty minutes. He returned the following year, when he was elevated to viscount. After feverish correspondence with the College of Arms and the editors of Debrett's *Peerage*, he chose the motto "Ad Astra" (To the Stars), with an emblem of a falcon surmounted by an eagle and three stars, flanked by an Indigenous American on one side and a fur trapper on the other, each a representative of a population that the first John Jacob Astor had manipulated and swindled in the making of his fortune.

Society gossip magazine *Town Topics* celebrated the occasion with a bit of doggerel:

> The honor's but a doubtful one; it comes too late in life
> For one who's stood so many snubs and bucked such social strife;
> It stinks too much of sordid gold, of cunning thought of self,
> As though Britannia yearns to finger more of Astor's pelf.

No matter how high and mighty he rose, no matter how fine his homes and his fabrics, William Waldorf Astor couldn't shake off the stench of bloody fur.

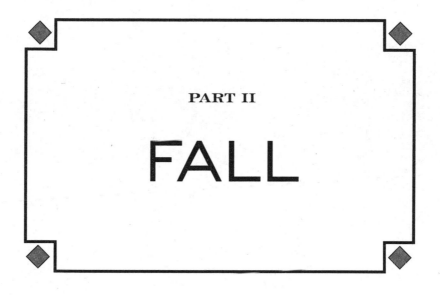

PART II

FALL

7

ROKEBY

1875

> *Of course Rokeby, like a lonely orphan, would inevitably call me back, but for the moment I was free.*
>
> —*Alexandra Aldrich*

When William Backhouse Astor Sr. died the day before Thanksgiving in 1875, the public was eager to discover how his estate, estimated to be worth in the neighborhood of one hundred million dollars, would be distributed. Unsurprisingly, the bulk of the cash and real estate holdings were divided between his sons John Jacob III and William Backhouse Jr., thereby establishing the division in the Astor family office that would come to be symbolized by Peacock Alley connecting the Waldorf and Astoria hotels a generation later. But William Backhouse Sr.'s disgraced and ignored third son, Henry, was not to share in his father's fortune.

Henry rarely appears in Astor family trees. He was large, given to sudden rages; he hated society and business, but loved buying drinks. He lived in a gardener's cottage at his father's Catskills retreat, Rokeby, and was married to Malvina Dinehart, a ruddy farmer's daughter and Henry's social inferior in the eyes of the Astors. Malvina had done something no woman marrying into the family had ever done: she refused to give up her dower rights, which, under the law, allowed her a percentage of her husband's estate if he died before her. For this unpardonable sin, Henry was disowned.[1] Instead, the third beneficiary of William Backhouse Astor Sr.'s will was Maddie Chanler, his granddaughter by his daughter Emily. Maddie was left property worth around five million dollars, including a brownstone on Madison Avenue, Rokeby and all its contents, and several other allotments of cash and real estate.

Maddie was born Margaret Astor Ward. Her mother, Emily Astor, had been the sparkling, musical, favorite daughter of William Backhouse Astor Sr. In 1838, Emily married Samuel Ward Jr., who was as witty and sociable and rich a partner as any Astor might wish for his most celebrated daughter. At a time when marriages were as much an alliance of common economic interests as of passions, Emily and Sam actually loved each other desperately.

The pair settled into blissful domesticity, planning to spend their summers at Rokeby. Their second summer there included their new infant daughter, whom they had named for Emily's maternal grandmother, Margaret Armstrong. The house rang with the laughter of Sam's visiting sisters, Julia, Louisa, and Annie. Julia would grow up to be the writer Julia Ward Howe, who penned "The Battle Hymn of the Republic." Her memories of the summer she spent at Rokeby draw a sharp distinction between the somewhat stiff formality of the Astors and the puppy-like chaos of the Wards. Through that summer of wildflowers and clucking chickens and rounds of singing at the piano, no one could have known that Rokeby, and not Manhattan, was going to be baby Maddie's real home.

Emily died in childbirth shortly after that summer, and when she died, some glimmer of warmth was permanently extinguished in the Astor family. The Astors took Maddie Ward up to Rokeby to live. Sam, too flighty and fun-loving to play the part of the grieving widower for very long, fell in love again, marrying a scandal-tainted woman by the name of Medora Grymes. The Astors were furious at what they took as his desecration of Emily's memory and refused to have any further connection with him. Threats were made around Maddie's inheritance, and ostensibly to protect her interests, Sam relinquished parental rights over his daughter. Within a very short span of time, she effectively lost both parents —her mother to death and her father to legal chicanery.

Though surrounded by cousins and uncles who were devoted to her welfare, Maddie passed a rather dour childhood, like so many other Astors before her, largely devoid of playmates her own age. She saw her father once in a while, always with her own mother's nurse along as a sharp-eyed chaperone. She was trained in the etiquette rules decreed by her aunt, *the* Mrs. Astor, mastering the reserve, formality, and understanding of social gradations that the Astors thought necessary for a family of self-anointed royalty. When Maddie grew to a marriageable age, the family supervision of her grew almost martial. Her grandparents Margaret and William Backhouse Astor Sr. carefully vetted any possible suitor, worried over the depredations of fortune hunters.[2]

Happily, John Winthrop Chanler ticked all the necessary boxes for an alliance. He had studied at Columbia and was already a lawyer in New York, with unimpeachable family connections. The two were introduced by John's sister, who also helped massage an approval from the Astor grandparents. The young couple's engagement was announced to universal delight in 1861, and they were wed the following year in Maddie's grandfather's living room in his home on Lafayette Place.

A surviving photograph of Maddie from around this time shows a placidly smiling young woman with kind-looking, downward-sloping eyes. She was twenty-three when she married John Chanler, who was thirty-five and embarking on a political career that would see him serve six terms in Congress.

Their union was a happy one, and Maddie started bearing children, almost one a year for more than a decade. Archie was the first to arrive, in October 1862; Winthrop, or "Wintie," appeared in October 1863; and a daughter, Emily, named for her late grandmother, was born the following year. Elizabeth, or "Bess," arrived in 1866, and then Willie in 1867, born while the family was in Newport for the summer. Son Marion was born in 1868, then Lewis in 1869, Margaret in 1870, Robert in 1872, Alida in 1873, and Edgerton, the baby, in 1874.

The household was a wild and rambunctious place. The Chanlers weren't at Rokeby full time; in 1870, they moved into an elegant brownstone on Madison Avenue in Murray Hill, built on Astor land, a gift from Maddie's grandfather that he would later deed to them in his will. Baby Margaret, who was born at that house, would remember it as typical of the Gilded Age—paneled in dark woods and somewhat depressing, with room upon cavernous room.[3] Maddie was raising her children to be members of the elite society into which she herself had been born. The four oldest—Archie, Wintie, Emily, and Bess—were even presented at the Children's Ball given by Andrew Johnson at the White House on December 29, 1868.[4]

But all wasn't easy in the Chanler home. In 1872, the same year that Maddie and John Chanler welcomed baby Robert (who would be called Bob), they lost Emily to scarlet fever. Maddie took the loss of her daughter hard. She had thrown herself into motherhood, never seeming fazed by the demands of a quickly growing brood. One story that persists about her finds Maddie at a gathering of ladies, where she pulls out her knitting and brightly remarks that she's begun her yearly quota of seventy-two pairs of winter stockings for the children.[5]

When Maddie's maternal grandfather, William Backhouse Astor Sr., died three years after her daughter Emily, she was heartbroken, but pleased to be named mistress of Rokeby. The stately old house had been her refuge, and its history was well known to her. The land on which Rokeby stood had been granted to her maternal great-grandmother's ancestors, the Livingston family, by James II, king of England, in 1688.[6] The oldest part of the house began construction in 1811, though the War of 1812 caused a hiccup in its progress, as the manor's owner at the time, John Armstrong Jr., was called away to serve. By 1815, Armstrong was back in the Catskills, licking his wounds and finishing construction of the big house. In those days, the estate was called La Bergerie, French for "sheepfold," because the Armstrongs were raising a herd of merino sheep that had been gifted to them by Napoléon Bonaparte.[7] The original house was two stories, in classically Federal style, with a hipped roof and an elegant cupola. Inside, a central entry hall opened onto three rooms on either side, connected by a genteel curving staircase.

William Backhouse Astor Sr. had purchased the property from John Armstrong Jr. for fifty thousand dollars in 1836, allowing his father-in-law to continue living there, ruling the roost from the patriarch's seat at the head of the long dining table. William's generous gesture may have come as a surprise, as one historian has called his overall bearing "dour and morose," but his wife, Margaret Armstrong Astor, was a country girl at heart, and William didn't enjoy entertaining, either. The couple preferred to spend their time in Rhinebeck, where William expanded the house from a gracious twenty rooms to a staggering forty-eight by adding the third floor, a whole north wing, and a Gothic Revival library inside an octagonal tower.

Margaret Astor had a romantic streak and loved the dramatic

landscape of the Catskills. She wasn't alone. This is when the Hudson River School of American landscape painting also found romantic inspiration in the craggy rocks, the liminal colors of water, and the blasted tree trunks of a region that, within one generation, had gone from being wilderness frontier to a resort area for people living in the increasingly crowded city at the mouth of the river. Around the time her father began construction on their country home, one of Margaret's favorite authors, Sir Walter Scott, was putting the finishing touches on a grand epic poem that he called *Rokeby*, which would so inspire Margaret that she would rename the big house in its honor.

Margaret's granddaughter Maddie adored Rokeby, but her stewardship of it lasted only a matter of days. The very afternoon she took part in her grandfather William Backhouse Astor Sr.'s funeral cortege up Broadway in damp and miserable weather, Maddie came down with pneumonia. Two weeks later, on December 13, 1875, she died. She was only thirty-seven years old and pregnant with her twelfth child.[8]

She left her fortune to her husband and their ten surviving children—but Rokeby to the children alone. Her oldest son, Archie, was thirteen and took his mother's death hard. The little ones didn't feel it quite as keenly, he didn't think. On the day she died, they had been hustled out of the house—ostensibly, to go Christmas shopping. When they returned, they were told that their mother was dead.

Little Margaret was five years old. She remembered not feeling sorrow, instead saying, "She has gone to join dear Emily in heaven!"[9] Archie and twelve-year-old Wintie, however, mourned their mother. They knew that her extreme Astor reserve and propriety in public had masked a loving person who could romp and play in the nursery with abandon. Bess, for her part, felt the mantle of responsibility descend upon her shoulders, the sense that she would have to be her siblings' mother now. She was nine.[10]

When Maddie died, something broke in her husband. John Chanler needed help with the children, and so, his unmarried cousin Mary Marshall was summoned from South Carolina to take charge. Miss Marshall was of a rigid and Calvinist bearing, inflexible, but she loved her little cousins and was able to summon depths of patience that surprised everyone when managing the increasingly chaotic brood.

John's estimate of the children's needs, for which he had to apply to the court as executor of his wife's estate, ran to around forty thousand dollars a year (about a million dollars today), which included the upkeep of Rokeby; salaries for a governess for the little girls and to pay Mr. E. B. Bostwick, a friend of Archie's who had been engaged as a tutor for the younger boys; plus boarding schools for the other kids; a nurse for the baby; someone to keep the house; and the expenses of everyday life, like food, firewood, lights, and medical care. The enormous house required a full domestic staff of a cook, a laundress, several maids under the supervision of the housekeeper, and a butler. The outside staff included a coachman to drive them, grooms to look after the horses, a gardener and his staff, and a farmer and his own set of assistants.[11] Rokeby was a miniature town, a self-contained organism powered by Astor patrimony.

John felt that his two oldest boys needed a gentlemanly education in England and planned to enroll Archie at Rugby and Wintie at Eton. Their sister Elizabeth Winthrop Chanler, universally called "Queen Bess" in the Chanler household, for her regal air, was to be enrolled at Miss Sewell's finishing school for young ladies on the Isle of Wight. And so, in the early summer of 1877, Archie, Wintie, Bess, and their father all set sail across the Atlantic.

Archie flunked the entrance exams at Rugby, but his father managed to secure a place for him at another school, Hillbrow.[12] Wintie proved too old for entry to Eton, but John greased the wheels and finally got him in over whatever objections Eton might have had. Bess, too, was safely installed in her finishing school. While in England, John got regular missives from the younger boys' tutor. Mr. Bostwick's job was mainly to see that the boys learned some Latin declensions in between playing with their rabbits, goats, and chickens, but John was satisfied enough with that for the time being. He enrolled his next younger son, William Astor Chanler, called "Willie," at St. John's Military Academy in Ossining, where the older boys had gone, and then returned to Rokeby at the end of the summer.

Archie tried his best, but his new teachers reported that he was not a promising student. Wintie wasn't much of a scholar, either—he preferred horseback riding—but somehow he never came off quite as disappointing to his father as Archie. When Archie wrote home to John on September 29, 1877, he included another mediocre report card, but embellished stories of his athletic prowess to make up for it.[13] The letter made its slow way to Rokeby, finally arriving in late October, but his father never had a chance to read it. Weeks before, he had caught a cold while playing, of all things, croquet. It worsened into pneumonia, and he died suddenly on October 21, 1877. He was just fifty-one.

Archie didn't know this yet, as cables were still shooting the news across the Atlantic Ocean, but he and Wintie and Bess and Willie and all the little ones who were romping across the rolling landscape around Rokeby were now orphans. In a letter to his siblings back at Rokeby, Archie described how he had learned the news of their father's death. It was up to him to tell the little ones that everything was going to be all right. But was it? They were in a sense alone in the world now, though surrounded by a bustling retinue, all of whose livelihoods were dependent on the income from the inheritance of the "Astor orphans."

"My dear Brothers and Sisters," Archie wrote:

I am very well and am trying to bear up under this great
affliction, which God has seen fit to send us, as well as I can.
Dear Cousin Bob . . . first told me that he had some very [bad]
news to tell me, and I asked him what, and he said that dear
Papa was dead. Of course I was nearly knocked off my feet by
the blow. But Cousin Bob comforted me and told me that I must
be the strongest as I was the oldest, and bear up against it. . . .
Cousin Bob and I went for a walk and talked it over, and he was
awfully kind to me and comforted me a great deal. . . . Wintie is
bearing up very well, and so is Bessie. . . . We are all in perfect
health, and are in as good spirits as we can afford. Give my
love to Mr. Bostwick and dear Bunk [Willie] and let him read
this letter as it is for him as well as for you and I only send it to
Rokeby as you are nearly all there. Write to me soon. How are
you all. Keep cheerful as possible.

From your loving ARCHIE.[14]

John had arranged his will to attempt to keep the children together and specifically protected from any attempt by Sam Ward,
their maternal grandfather, to seize control of their inheritance. He
did so by putting Astors in charge: John Jacob III and his son, Will,
together with a handful of other socially prominent and connected
people, were tasked with the guardianship of the orphans and their
wealth.

Rokeby was left to the orphans equally, though Archie, as the
oldest boy, got a few other things, including another farm nearby.[15]
He also received the contents of the house, the farm equipment, and
an extra inheritance designed to keep the estate running. Though the
guardians were of impeccable reputation, they were all ill-equipped to
manage ten children suddenly living alone in a grand country estate.

None of them was prepared to take all ten children to live with them, but the children couldn't bear to be separated. All their guardians were old; some were childless. Patrician heads bent together, worrying over what was to be done with the Astor orphans.

Mary Marshall was the one who ultimately made the decision, by volunteering to stay on as their de facto adoptive mother. The children could remain at Rokeby with her watching over them, and the guardians could look on from the safe remove of Fifth Avenue.

Like the epic romantic poem that inspired its change of name, by 1877 every room at Rokeby was already thick with associations, images, and memories for the Astor orphans. They lived in the shadow of General Armstrong at the head of the dining table and of William Backhouse Astor Sr. settling down to read by the fire in the library he had built. Not to mention the memories of their recently departed parents.

Rokeby was full of ghosts, and so the ground was laid for the creation of a strange, unique world in which the Chanler children lived surrounded by the shadows of their forebears. They galloped through halls that had been the haunts of Armstrongs and Astors, everyone talking all at once, occasionally banging on the piano to the presumed frustration of the instructor who came up from Vassar to teach them the instrument. The orphans were masters at alienating tutors and governesses, so they would be freed from their lessons, and they whiled away the hours playing with the animals—dogs, cats, chickens, rabbits, birds, goats, ponies, and sometimes even a raccoon or a snake.[16] Only three rules were enforced within the quickly evolving self-determination of the children. Rule number one: No hitting. Rule number two: No showing off. And rule number three: "A bore must shut up."[17]

The children sorted themselves to some extent. Archie, Wintie, and Bess formed a set, the oldest ones off at boarding school. Lewis and little Margaret were only a year apart in age, so they formed another set, though Lewis liked to taunt his sister by telling her there were bears under her bed who lived in the daytime in an armoire, which a terrified Margaret would dash by at top speed. The two littlest were Alida and Edgerton, and they were a tight pair, both liking to go out in springtime to look for snakes peeping their noses out of their holes. Only Bob, homely to look at and oppositional in temperament, lacked a confederate among his siblings. He preferred to roughhouse with the farm children and was so in tune with animals that while still a child, he reportedly broke a steer because he wanted to harness it to pull his sled. He refused to do any lessons or to come to dinner on time, hunted rabbits instead of going to church, and declined to explain how he passed his time on the days he disappeared off by himself.[18]

A sense of mystical unreality clung to the halls of Rokeby. Mary Marshall, for instance, reported at breakfast one morning that a cousin of theirs had appeared standing at the foot of her bed the previous night, and no one batted an eye when they all later learned that the cousin had already died.[19] Miss Marshall had each child analyzed by a noted phrenologist, who took the measure of the bumps and ridges of their skulls to learn their futures. Incredibly, the man found that they were all destined for great things. The children would attend the loud and rousing Irish wakes held by the kitchen staff, and they believed that the two angels bearing swords on the frame of a mirror in the "White Room" would descend to the floor and dance "in a terrible manner" if the fire were allowed to go out.[20]

Archie, Wintie, and Bess continued on at their respective boarding schools, escaping having their heads measured and judged by the quackery of the moment. Shortly after sending his first condolence letter to his younger siblings, Archie reached out to them again.

"I am awfully glad to hear that you are all well and are in good spirits again," he wrote. He was delighted to hear that everyone was going to stay together with Cousin Mary. "How I wish I could be there with you around the fire in the dear old library." He assured them that he and Wintie and Bess were doing fine, that they were healthy and missed everyone, and he sent his love to the lengthening list of adults who were charged with wrangling his siblings.[21]

Archie remained a mediocre student. Wintie did better, in part because by the time he got to Harvard, he had acquired international polish and, in addition, was perfectly happy to pay other undergraduates to write his papers for him.[22] Archie blundered his way into Columbia, and after receiving a master's degree there in 1884, he was admitted to the New York bar. He had come into his inheritance the year before, and in 1885, he set off on his Grand Tour, having already developed something of a wanderer's character, even spending some months with General George Crook as he stalked the Apache leader Geronimo.[23] He passed a pleasant summer in Europe, though he caught fleas on a night train to Paris, and then joined up with Wintie and a friend and journeyed through the Caribbean, where he tasted yams for the first time and wrote that, when cooked, a yam "looks like a potato and tastes like castile soap."[24]

Eventually, the duties and possibilities of life as an Astor heir would not be ignored. Archie ended up back in New York and made the rounds of his many clubs. Then, in 1887, while visiting Wintie and his new wife in Washington, Archie spent Christmas outside Charlottesville with the Rives family, whose daughter Amélie he had met at Newport the previous summer. Archie by this time had grown into himself. He was handsome; stood over five feet, ten inches tall; and had refined his physique with amateur boxing, so he moved lightly, like a panther. He affected a French beard and mustache, and his manner was sweet and serious, but perhaps a bit guarded and sad, too.[25]

Amélie was beautiful, but like Archie, she had a wandering, curious spirit. She was already a published poet, and that Christmas, she flirtingly confessed to Archie that she was at work on a novella and that he was the model for its hero.

The novella, called *The Quick or the Dead?*, was excerpted in *Lippincott's Monthly Magazine* the following year. The salacious romance, in which the protagonist is torn between her sexual obsession with her dead husband and her growing attraction to his nearly identical, living cousin, caused an immediate storm of publicity, and when it was published in full as a book, it was a commercial success, selling 300,000 copies, which would have made even Sir Walter Scott gnash his teeth with envy. Wintie remarked in his diary that the book was "A most sensual bit of rot . . . Distinctly horrid." But he admits that Archie, who was indeed the transparent inspiration for the romance's protagonist, had been "very well drawn."[26]

Archie fell hard and fast for Amélie, whose gray-eyed beauty was intoxicating and whose mind turned in ways both fascinating and bizarre to the society in which she lived. Once, Amélie had terrified a childhood friend by saying, "Do you think if I drank a whole cupful of warm, bubbly blood, I would see a real fairy?"[27] But Archie, eldest of this unusual brood of self-determined and self-directed orphans, was irresistibly drawn to her artistic brilliance.

The Chanlers were stunned when a tiny item appeared at the bottom of the front page of the *New York Times* on Sunday, June 3, 1888, picking up a mention from the *Baltimore American*. "Miss Amelie Rives to Marry," the announcement read.[28] A fuller account appeared the following Tuesday, with an "intimate lady friend of Miss Rives" providing the scoop that Amélie and Archie had met at Newport and that, though he owned Rokeby, he lived in Paris. They planned to marry in the autumn, after which he and the "authoress" would make their home in Paris, where she could continue her literary work and "occupy herself at the easel."[29]

But the papers didn't have the full story. Everyone at Rokeby was in a dither, partly because Amélie, while enjoying her considerable literary publicity, had been romantically linked to a number of other young men. To make matters worse, less than two weeks later, on June 14, without anyone in the Four Hundred being notified and especially none of the guardians, Archie and Amélie were married at her family home in Virginia.

Wintie was apoplectic. The only sibling in attendance at Archie's wedding was seventeen-year-old Margaret, who had been taken into her brother's confidence. The bride and groom hadn't even sent a telegram to Rokeby.[30]

In Canto V of his epic poem, Sir Walter Scott sets Rokeby on fire. Archie's wedding had a similar effect.

The eve, that slow on upland fades,
Has darker closed on Rokeby's glades,
Where, sunk within their banks profound,
Her guardian streams to meeting wound.
The stately oaks, whose sombre frown
Of noontide made a twilight brown,
Impervious now to fainter light,
Of twilight make an early night.[31]

Five days later, Wintie was finally calm enough to send his sister Margaret a letter. "If ever two people deserved a good spanking, those two are Brog [Archie] and you. Of course, you were but as putty in his hands, and backed him up in his absurd mysteries—but still your own common sense, if no other feeling, should have told you that he was quite wrong, in what he did. . . . All of us at Rokeby heard it from an outsider & the daily papers."[32] He followed this missive with another letter, even more enraged, saying, "In the most important epoch of his life he has made a fool of himself and hurt his wife in the eyes of the public."[33]

Before the nuptials, the orphans' aunt *the* Mrs. Astor had heard a rumor that Archie was to be married, but all the siblings at Rokeby had dismissed this as gossip. Now they all looked ridiculous to the most powerful social broker in New York. Mr. Bostwick, for his part, had just returned from a trip to Baltimore, having spent the whole time dodging questions about why none of the siblings except Margaret was at the wedding. Even the nearby farmers were alive with curious chatter about the scandal of Archie's marriage. Wintie's wife, Daisy, worried that if Archie and his new bride didn't come back to Rokeby, and soon, they would be unable to control public speculation over a family rift.

When Wintie finally wrote to Archie, he couldn't hide his pique. "Dear Brog," he wrote. "Just a line from an outsider to disturb the bliss of Armida's garden. Ask for and read the two letters I have written to Margaret in the name of the Rokebyites and use your own judgment about repeating the contents. Love to Armida,"[34] he wrote, referring to the Saracen sorceress in a poem by Italian Renaissance poet Torquato Tasso. "We don't want any cuttings from the *Herald* or any other of your friends the journalists. P.S.: The weather here is very warm, 93 in the shade today. I wonder if you wouldn't find it cool in spite of the thermometer."[35]

Archie's response was swift and cutting: "Dear Wintie," he said. "I have just received your note of June 21st, and I shall want an apology from you in writing before anything further can pass between us."[36]

But something else was afoot in Archie's seeming mad flight of passion with Amélie Rives. While the fire of their marriage was still smoldering, Amélie wrote to Margaret, her sole defender among the boisterous and imperious Chanlers at Rokeby. "Margaret, tell me as though you were my own sister as well as Archie's," she implored, her letters as florid as her fiction, "have you ever thought in the bottom of your soul, that Archie's mind was not quite right? He laughs at me in such a dreadful way at times, until I am crying & trembling with terror. And the more I cry & beg him to stop or to tell me what is the matter, the more he laughs."[37]

Amélie seemed to push aside her doubts, and by the time the newlyweds descended upon Rokeby after a sparkling season at Newport, with Amélie enjoying the fullness of her literary accomplishment, the orphans had begun to warm to her. Wintie's wife, Daisy, found her charming and as widely read as she; Willie and Lewis found her beauty enthralling; and even recalcitrant Bob thought her gorgeous and pious and worthy in all respects.

By winter, however, something had begun to go seriously wrong with Archie. Only five months into their marriage, Amélie wrote to Margaret to confess that Archie would be going to Paris without her. They separated for two years, with Amélie returning to her parents' house to write a novel. The couple reconciled after the agreed-upon separation, on which neither commented publicly, but Archie's tendency to be solitary, explosive, and erratic began to spiral out of control.

The year 1888 was largely one of dispersal for the orphans. Wintie was already married, Archie made his scandalous secret marriage, and Willie came of age while at Harvard that year and bailed on his studies to go adventuring. And the orphans were now fewer in number: Baby Edgerton had died of a brain tumor in 1882, followed by Marion, of pneumonia while still a student at the preparatory boarding school St. Paul's, in 1883. Of the eleven original Chanler children, eight lived to adulthood. By 1888, only four were still minors: Lewis, Margaret, Bob, and Alida. Bess had come of age the year before and was living independently.

The aging guardians decided that the minor girls should enroll in the same finishing school that Bess had attended, and they bestowed on the girls an extra allowance for gloves and ribbons. Lewis was studying law at Columbia, which left only Bob at home at Rokeby with Daisy and Wintie that winter. In the spring, Wintie would spirit his seventeen-year-old brother off to Europe, ostensibly in furtherance of his education, but more likely to keep Bob away from the farm girls.[38]

Due in large part to his increasingly odd behavior, Archie's tumultuous marriage with Amélie ended in divorce in 1895, but the strange drama of Rokeby wasn't finished with the Chanlers. The following year, Archie was playing at billiards when he noticed the balls had resolved themselves into the shape of the Big Dipper constellation. He racked them up again, broke them, and the same thing happened. He repeated the experiment a third time, with the same results. He took a pencil out of his pocket to note this strange phenomenon, but instead of obeying him, his hand wrote the words "Get a planchette," a reference to a kind of Victorian-era Ouija board.[39] The term *subconscious* had not yet entered popular discourse, and so, Archie was at a loss to describe the words he was able to produce with the planchette. He would come to believe that he had discovered a new sense, which he called his "X-faculty."[40] But the messages he was receiving weren't always logical. Sometimes they gave him faulty stock tips, or urged him to burn himself with coals. But his interest in what was then called automatic writing flourished. He even claimed that his psychic powers had caused his eyes to change color from the light brown of his youth to an unsettling gray.[41]

His siblings were concerned, as was a friend of his, the architect Stanford White, who paid Archie an unexpected visit with a doctor in tow. The two men persuaded Archie to return to Manhattan, worrying that too much time alone was sending him off the deep end. Archie reluctantly agreed and checked into his preferred city hotel, the Kensington. While there, he received a communication via "vocal automatism" that he should go into a "Napoleonic trance," during which he would "reenact the deathbed scene of Napoleon."[42] A few days later, the sculptor Augustus Saint-Gaudens dropped in for a visit, and Archie's "X-faculty" suggested the moment for his Napoleonic trance had come. He asked his friend if he wanted to witness the experiment, and Saint-Gaudens said why not. Archie stretched out on the bed, holding a shaving mirror over his head. For about ten minutes, he stared into the mirror with his mouth open, then began gasping for air. Slowly, he lowered the mirror to the bed, his eyes closed, and the trance began. Petrified, Saint-Gaudens begged Archie to stop, which he did.[43]

The next day, Stanford White returned with the doctor, and Archie offered to repeat the experiment. Supposedly, while in his dissociative trance, he heard White whisper, "It is exactly like Napoleon's death mask! I have a photograph of it at home."[44]

The following day, the doctor returned again, this time with someone he said was an oculist who wanted to examine Archie's color-changing eyes. The three men had a long discussion of parapsychology as the oculist peppered Archie with questions and listened to his long disquisitions on the medical field in general.

But, it turned out, the oculist wasn't an oculist after all. He was Dr. Moses Allen Starr, professor of nervous diseases at the College of Physicians and Surgeons in New York, president of the New York State Neurological Society and of the American Neurological Association.

And he had in his possession a court order that Archie's siblings had obtained to commit him involuntarily on the grounds of insanity. Archie argued with the doctors while brandishing a loaded revolver he had stashed under his pillow. As you might imagine, this didn't help matters.

The next day, two detectives appeared and escorted Archie to Grand Central Terminal and then onto a train to White Plains and the Bloomingdale Insane Asylum, where he would remain locked up for the next two and a half years.

Archie had sold Margaret his shares in Rokeby for a nominal fee when his marriage began to fall apart. She then persuaded her sisters to sell their shares to her, becoming Rokeby's sole proprietor.

On Christmas Day 1900, the Astor orphans gathered around the Rokeby dining room table. Lewis was there with his wife and three children, Bess with her husband and his three sons from his first marriage. Willie regaled them all with tales of adventure and of his new life in politics, and Alida was there with her family—she would go on to live until 1969, the last living remnant of the original Four Hundred. Margaret had lately returned from travels in Asia and stood to give a toast that, from that day forward, became the ceremonial toast given at all special days at Rokeby: "To all who have been here; to all who are here; to all who would like to be here."[45]

Not all the living orphans were there, however. Wintie was off on a shooting party in Sardinia. Bob was living in Paris. And Archie? The month before, on Thanksgiving Eve, he had vanished from the Bloomingdale Insane Asylum. Doctors, orderlies, and security staff searched all over and found no trace of him. The only clue was a note discovered in his room, addressed to Dr. Samuel P. Lyon, the facility's medical superintendent: "My dear Doctor," it read. "You have always said that I am insane. You have always said that I believe I am the reincarnation of Napoleon Bonaparte. As a learned and sincere man, you, therefore, will not be surprised that I take French leave. Yours, with regret that we must part, J. A. CHANLER."[46]

Archie did eventually resurface, in a private clinic in Virginia, where he successfully petitioned a court in 1901 to declare him sane. In the ensuing years, he wrote a number of books about his time in the asylum and his belief in his X-faculty and gave public lectures railing against psychiatric abuses and the siblings who had committed him.[47] But in 1919, he reconciled with them. Archie died in 1935 at the age of seventy-two. Margaret lived to be ninety-three, dying in 1963.

As for Rokeby? Amazingly, it still stands today, and is still well loved and meticulously maintained by six of Margaret's descendants. The Astor money is gone, but Rokeby persists, sustained by rents, hosting weddings and photo shoots, and making hay.[48]

In 2010, the *New York Times* visited Rokeby, looking for ghosts of vanished Astors. "Not many venture into the vast, shadowy front rooms," the *Times* noted, "which are kept as a shrine to previous generations—a practice that irritates some members of the younger generation—and the French wallpaper is pocked with moisture stains and peeling off in sheets. In the shuttered, paneled Gothic library, Teddy Roosevelt's photograph sits on a shelf thick with dust . . . in a parlor, a bust of Julia Ward Howe . . . is propped on a chipped radiator."[49]

"Maybe we are the museum," Richard Aldrich told the *Times*. Richard is the tenth generation of Livingston descendants to make their home at the former sheepfold. The paper described his "bent figure and stained clothes" as "testament to four decades' worth of wrangling with this drafty, unwieldy house."[50]

"The house gives each of us—the impoverished descendants—an identity," Richard's daughter Alexandra Aldrich confessed in a memoir she wrote of growing up at Rokeby. "And we live off the remains of our ancestral grandeur."[51]

8

HALIFAX

APRIL 15, 1912

We will meet in Heaven.

—Carving on a fragment of a Titanic *deck chair retrieved off the coast
of Africa on January 4, 1913, attributed to Colonel John Jacob Astor*

Could Jack have survived if Rose had made room for him on the door?
You know who I mean: Jack Dawson, the earnest American artist-
cum-drifter who falls in love with society bride Rose DuWitt Bukater
in the 1997 James Cameron–written and –directed film, *Titanic.* Jack
saves Rose, first from a life of cosseted excess in a loveless marriage
and, next, from certain death. He accomplishes the former by sharing
Rose's love of avant-garde art and by looking like Leonardo DiCaprio,
and the latter by making sure that Rose climbs atop a floating piece of
wreckage as they wait for rescue in the frigid North Atlantic waters
off Halifax, Nova Scotia. The two clasp hands, and Jack reassures
Rose that she will die an old woman, safe in her bed. Rose promises
never to let him go. He (spoiler alert) dies of hypothermia, clutching
Rose's hand, just as a lifeboat comes within hailing distance, and Rose

is saved, to go on living the life of freedom and passion Jack inspired her to live.

Fine, but couldn't she have moved over just a little? This fan theory has sparked debate ever since the film was released, even being tested on the television program *Mythbusters*.[1] First, internet fan boards will inform you, the item to which Rose clings in the movie is not a door. It's a piece of paneling from *above* the door in the RMS *Titanic*'s first-class lounge.[2] Second, it wasn't a question of space, but of buoyancy. If they'd only used Rose's life jacket to give more buoyancy to the paneling, and propped themselves up on their elbows to keep their bodies out of the water, they both could have survived.

Oh, well.

But what if Jack never existed?[3] What if he is the fevered invention of a young woman's mind as it cracks under the pressures of class and gender expectations in 1912? The idea of Jack as a fantasy has been proposed by some fans of the film, perhaps because he does seem too good to be true. He's honest, noble, good-humored, and confident. He's weirdly knowledgeable about how to survive a maritime disaster. He laughs in the face of snobbery. He's able to make love in the backseat of a car without getting bruised by the gear shift. He's got great teeth and skin, even though it's 1912 and he's broke.

As it happens, there really was a Jack who died on the RMS *Titanic*. Like Jack Dawson, his precise character is hard to pin down, and no matter what he accomplished in his very real life, it has been overshadowed by his spectacular death. The stories told about him have overwritten the reality of his life. Like the other passengers on the *Titanic*, he has been transformed from a living, breathing person into a symbol.

When he died, he was known as Colonel John Jacob Astor IV, but everyone called him Jack. We have met him already—when he was living with his mother, Caroline Astor, and battling with his cousin over the Waldorf-Astoria. He was mocked in the press as "Jack Asstor" for his callous treatment of the poor, but became a colonel during the Spanish-American War and was praised for his volunteer efforts. He was a devoted son, a miserable husband, and a difficult father. He was a hardworking slumlord and an inept yachtsman. At the time RMS *Titanic* set sail from Southampton, he was traveling with his eighteen-year-old second wife, the former Madeleine Force, after enjoying a long honeymoon in Europe away from the prying eyes of the press, who were breathless with the scandal of his divorce and quick remarriage to a woman two years younger than his son Vincent. The newlyweds were on their way home to New York.

As would happen when my great-uncle Alfred Vanderbilt died in the sinking of the *Lusitania* in 1915, when Jack Astor perished as the *Titanic* sank in the predawn hours of April 15, 1912, the world could talk of nothing else. Word of his death blazed above the fold in newspapers around the globe, claiming the headlines before any other victim's name was mentioned. Jack was the head of what was left of the American branch of the Astor family, the wealthiest and most high-profile person among a first-class manifest of many extremely wealthy and high-profile people: Benjamin Guggenheim; "Unsinkable" Molly Brown; Macy's owner Isidor Straus and his wife, Ida; heir and book collector Harry Widener. And plenty of people lost their lives whose names did not make the headlines: immigrant families traveling in steerage, cooks, porters, men whose job it was to shovel coal into the boilers to fire the engines that kept the *Titanic* cruising at a steady twenty-one knots into eternity. But when the tragedy struck, "Jack Astor" was the name on everyone's lips.

Newspapers were breathless in their coverage, recounting eyewitness reports of Astor assisting his young wife into the lifeboat and getting out so that a woman could have his seat. Some reports insisted that he had offered his life jacket to a woman and faced death coolly, pulling his cigarette case out of his pocket and waiting calmly at the ship's rail for the inevitable.[4] Americans experienced the horror of the *Titanic*, first and foremost, through the tales of Jack Astor, whose body was one of ninety-one found floating in the Atlantic by the Canadian cable ship the *Mackay-Bennett* twelve days after the *Titanic* sank. As with the others, it was hauled out of the water, packed in ice, and eventually offloaded in Halifax.[5]

But the ocean liner's loss quickly moved from a tragedy rapidly unfolding over the news wires to something else entirely. How quickly? The first film version of the *Titanic* disaster was made in Germany in August 1912, only two months after a minister aboard the *Montmagny*, the last ship actively searching for *Titanic* bodies, reported that the life jackets on the floating corpses were coming apart and releasing the dead into the depths.[6]

The film, called *In Nacht und Eis* (*In Night and Ice*), was a silent reenactment with a thirty-five-minute run time—an epic length by the standards of the day. In it, Jack Astor appears early and often—an older gentleman in a drooping handlebar mustache and smart hat escorting his elegant young wife around the ship. One of the first title cards announces, "Another well-known billionaire gets on board with his young wife . . . . The young woman will be saved while her husband drowns, because he remains to help others."

As in many films from this early era, scenes change abruptly, often without much context. We see the ship with four smoking funnels. We see a band. Then the film cuts to a shot of the ship far off at sea; in 1912, transitions and point of view, storytelling conventions we now take for granted in cinema, were still being established.

We then read that "Notable passengers tour the boat deck," and get a better look at the actors playing Jack and Madeleine Astor strolling arm in arm, a pleasant-looking young woman, a wide straw hat secured under her chin with a veil, enjoying the soft sea air with a plush and well-fed gentleman by her side. *In Nacht und Eis* features several elements that would later become hallmarks of *Titanic* cinema, including special effects showing the ocean liner at sea (a toy ship, in this case, drifting through a water tank), a scene of Captain Edward Smith handing over command to his first officer, and a shot of sweaty men shoveling coal into boilers as the ship builds up to full speed. Then, after the film shows us a shot of choppy ocean waves through binoculars—despite the actual collision having taken place during a dead calm—a title card announces, "Wireless telegram: 'Watch out! Icebergs in the area.'"

The action then moves inside, to the Café Parisien, which was one of the real dining areas on the actual RMS *Titanic*. Jack and Madeleine Astor appear in evening dress, settling down at a table near the band. A waiter pops champagne for them and their party. When the long-awaited collision finally comes, a model boat bumps against a papier-mâché iceberg, and the actors all tumble together convincingly. Then we cut to the site of the most exciting action: the wireless room! (The focus on wireless communication makes sense given the era in which the film was made: this was cutting-edge technology.)

Near the end, on another title card, we read about something that will become another motif in *Titanic* cinema: "From the lifeboats floating in the water with rescued passengers, one hears the ship's band on board play 'Nearer, My God, to Thee.'" The captain, we are told, is swept overboard and saves a drowning man but refuses rescue for himself. And then the movie is over.

It isn't especially affecting as a film. There are no characters to speak of, only abstractions. Jack Astor is really only a mouth into which champagne can be poured. But German cinema wasn't done with him or the famous disaster. In 1943, Nazi propaganda minister Joseph Goebbels ordered a film called *Titanic* to be made, both to demonstrate the might of the German film industry and as propaganda criticizing American and European capitalism. To that end, Jack Astor now becomes the villain, first appearing when one character whispers to another, "Here comes the one man on board who could give his wife the *Titanic* as a birthday present." This Jack Astor looks sharp, and so does the woman playing Madeleine, a high-cheeked, heavy-lidded seductress of a certain age (in contrast to the real Madeleine's shocking youth) sporting a huge feather headdress. The president of the White Star Line announces that the ship is steaming at twenty-six and a half knots, a world record. The coal shovelers are offered bonuses if they can maintain that speed. Newspapers all over the world receive word of the speed record as unscrupulous board members wire to buy half a million more White Star shares. But the stock price plummets because Jack Astor is short-selling, planning to seize control of *Titanic*'s corporate owner and make a fortune for himself. "Tangible assets create power," this calculating, youthful Jack Astor says, "and power is a means to whatever you want." To Madeleine, he silkily adds, "For me, more power. For you, more jewelry."

The film portrays Jack Astor as the stereotype of an American capitalist, fascinating given the real man's German heritage and the Nazi obsession with ethnicity. A passenger named Lord Douglas comes to Jack Astor for a loan, and Astor pushes Douglas to agree to his business scheme, underlining the Nazi view that the Old World European aristocracy had become pawns of the capitalist class. As the action unfolds, we are treated to several displays of moral rot: Jack Astor beating a man at snooker; Madeleine Astor flirting openly with Lord Douglas.

In this *Titanic*, the racist ideologies of Nazi propaganda are as much in evidence as the political ones. The camera lingers on a woman in steerage who kisses two different men before jiggling and stripping her way through a suggestive dance. Sporting dark curly hair and a prominent nose, she is clearly coded as Roma or Jewish, while a blonde woman with Bavarian braids—simple, honest German peasant stock, we are presumably meant to conclude—glaringly disapproves.

Then the iceberg is spotted, almost impossible to see in the flat, calm water late on a moonless night. It rips through the hold, and seawater pours in, with special effects markedly improved over the 1912 production. Meanwhile, up in first class, the idle rich unknowingly while away the last hours of their lives dancing a waltz. And in steerage, the simple, honest peasant folk notice that the engines have stopped.

The telegraph operator refuses to accept another telegram from Jack Astor, who is concerned with continuing his stock scheme.

"All you know is your money. Nothing else," Madeleine snarls to Jack.

"With good reason. Money is the only value I believe in," he responds coldly. Astor wonders aloud if he can find someone to sell him a place in a lifeboat. He dies holding his wife's jewel case with the Heart of the Sea diamond inside, but with his pitiless heart empty and cold.

As the orchestra starts up with "Nearer, My God, to Thee" the telegraph operator sets his canary free from her cage. Finally, a closing title card soberly informs us that "The deaths of 1,500 remain unatoned for in England's eternal quest for profit!"

Jack Astor made a perfect villain because his wealth and fame would have made his name recognizable to an audience in Nazi-occupied Europe. In their view, his death goes from being a noble tragedy to the inevitable result of his and America's presumed preoccupation with money at the expense of all else.

When Hollywood turned its attention to the maritime disaster a decade later, in 1953, with a Barbara Stanwyck vehicle also called *Titanic*, it, too, had an agenda for which Jack Astor was a useful tool. The film is largely the story of Barbara Stanwyck's character repairing her marriage to an English cad, restoring the stable nuclear family unit. By the 1950s, American cinema was twenty years into the reign of the Hays Production Code, which limited the sexual and ethical content allowable in movies. American culture was also well into the Eisenhower years and the Baby Boom. As Jack Astor, actor William Johnstone speaks his first line on board to Madeleine: "Stay right here. I'll try to get a chair," with a solicitous pat of his wife's hand. This version of Jack and Madeleine at least gets the May-December romance right. Jack sports a white mustache, and Madeleine looks about twenty, demure under an early 1950s vision of a 1912 veiled hat.

"I'm not the first woman in the world who's going to have a baby," Madeleine says, and smiles at her husband.

"As far as I'm concerned, you are," Jack answers.

Our final view of these idealized Astors occurs as Barbara Stanwyck's redeemed husband rescues some Basque passengers from steerage and puts them in a lifeboat with Madeleine Astor. We last see Jack on deck with all the other doomed men, looking wistfully at his pregnant wife.

And then it's 1997, and we're back with Jack and Rose and the blue diamond borrowed from the Nazis, riding the ship of dreams. What is so compelling about this story?[7] Maybe it's the tension between hubris and death. Maybe it's the vast gulf between the haves and the have-nots, locked together in a common fate. When Jack Dawson nervously joins Rose in first class for dinner, we have a guide through late Gilded Age society as Rose explains to him who everyone is. "There's the Countess of Rothes," she whispers. "And, ah. That's John Jacob Astor, the richest man on the ship. His little wifey there, Madeleine, is my age and is in a delicate condition. See how she's trying to hide it? Quite the scandal."

The Jack Astor in Cameron's film is called JJ, presumably because having two Jacks in the movie would have been too confusing. This Jack Astor has well-preserved soap opera good looks, coming across as distinguished rather than elderly, and his elegant young wife looks beautiful and slightly pregnant (the only film in which her pregnancy is visible). Once again, Jack Astor is being called upon to symbolize the decadence of his social class: his age difference with his wife makes their relationship more sordid, less authentic, than the budding one between Jack and Rose. The world of this *Titanic* revolves around romance and whether that romance counts as legitimate.

Fellow passenger Molly Brown (played by Kathy Bates) reassures Jack Dawson, who is nervous about rubbing elbows with first-class passengers, by saying, "Ain't nothing to it. Remember, they love money, so pretend like you own a gold mine, and you're in the club." Then she shouts, "Hey, Astor!"

"Well, hello, Molly," Astor says. "Nice to see you." In real life, Molly Brown had just spent a chunk of the winter season in Egypt, where she had stayed with the Astors.[8]

Rose says, "JJ, Madeleine, I'd like you to meet Jack Dawson."

"Well, Jack," Astor says in a polished American accent. "Are you of the Boston Dawsons?"

"No, the Chippewa Falls Dawsons, actually," our hero says with an impish twinkle.

Astor responds, "Oh, yes," with narrowed eyes, pretending to know what that means. We are meant to enjoy Jack making a fool of Jack, to relish the popping of a bubble of snobbish hot air. Madeleine, affirming Rose's reading of her as mere arm candy, has no lines.

We all know what happens next—at least, if we're among the millions of viewers who've seen James Cameron's epic. At the dining table, Jack goes on about making each day count, and before long, we are treated to the ubiquitous steerage dance party (also seen in *Titanic* 1943), with somebody playing spoons while Jack and Rose dance a jig.

Our last moment with Jack Astor is passed under the glass dome at the top of the first-class staircase. He's wearing his life vest, which means that the newspaper accounts of the real Jack Astor giving it to a woman, or facing death at the rail with heroic stoicism, have been forgotten. Then the ocean explodes through the roof, raining glass shards and thick water on everyone, and Jack Astor disappears from public memory for good.

History is cruel, as is Hollywood. In 1912, Jack Astor was the most famous passenger aboard the doomed ship, the lede in every news account. In 1943, he was the starring villain. By 1997, he was so minor a character that he was given only a few unmemorable lines.

So, who was Jack Astor? Was he a mustachioed swiller of champagne? A solicitous, if elderly, newlywed? A sharp-suited, short-selling villain? A distinguished gentleman, licentious but otherwise boring?

John Jacob IV was the youngest child and only son of William Backhouse Astor Jr. and *the* Mrs. Astor. He was educated at St. Paul's and Harvard, but when he made his official appearance in society in 1887, the gossip rag *Town Topics* called him "one of the richest catches of the day and at the same time voted so much less brilliant than his father that it is very questionable whether, were he put to it, he could ever earn his bread by his brains."[9] Ouch. Be that as it may, he was by all accounts meticulous, a tinkerer who enjoyed engineering projects and learning how things worked. He was regimented enough that he volunteered to serve in the Spanish-American War and, thereafter, preferred to be addressed by his rank, which was colonel. And he did, indeed, sport a drooping handlebar mustache.

When he assumed control of his portion of the Astor Estate after his father's death, he could often be seen behind the barred windows of his two-story redbrick office building on Twenty-Sixth Street, surrounded by his three managers and twenty-two clerks, busying himself with the family's considerable real estate and hotel holdings.[10] He certainly had no need to devote his attention to business, and the other half of the Astor Estate was managed by his cousin Will in absentia and with half as many clerks. However, it's possible that one reason Jack took refuge in his elegantly appointed office was to avoid his first wife, Ava, pronounced "AH-vah."

"Ava was the most beautiful woman I have ever seen," said one grande dame at the time. "It was an era of great beauties, but they all took a back seat to her. When she walked into a room every eye was on her. But she was cold, hard, selfish, and mean to her husband. I don't think she was capable of loving anyone."[11]

Ava Lowle Willing had been a Main Line Philadelphia debutante, the belle of the Newport season in 1890, and declared "bride of the year" when she married Jack Astor in 1891.[12] The match delighted Caroline Astor, but there were rumors that Ava's parents pushed her into it.[13] Baby William Vincent Astor appeared exactly nine months later, almost to the minute—but then no other children arrived for another ten years. Ava was both beautiful and difficult. Writer James Fox reflected that "Nature had designed Ava to be admired by men, and this was her occupation. She was also magnificently selfish and spoiled, sharp-tongued, fearless in her pursuit of pleasure, furiously social and permanently dissatisfied."[14]

The difference in Jack and Ava's characters is described by Gilded Age society fixture Elizabeth "Bessie" Drexel Lehr in her memoir. Ava would fill their house with guests addicted, as she was, to bridge. "Their host," Bessie Lehr wrote, "who detested bridge and was far more at home going at top speed in his new racing car or at the helm of his yacht in a storm than in his own drawing room, shambled from room to room, tall, loosely built and ungraceful, rather like a great overgrown colt, in a vain search for someone to talk to."[15]

Some of Jack Astor's enthusiasms were extreme enough as to be almost comical. An early adopter of automobiles, he once took a test drive of a steam-powered engine along Fifth Avenue with Ava and their son, Vincent, which resulted in the car being engulfed in flames.[16] An avid sailor who had placed his private vessel *Nourmahal* at the service of the U.S. military during wartime, he also once plowed into the Vanderbilt yacht and was sued for $15,000 in damages. He worried inordinately about a pirate attack, even going so far as to mount four guns on the *Nourmahal*'s deck. "But John Jacob guessed wrong," one observer noted drily. "No pirates attacked and the *Nourmahal* met disaster only in the form of some rocks that were clearly behaving in an aggressive way."[17]

"Dinner was not an enjoyable meal for him," Bessie Lehr recalled. "Never a brilliant conversationalist at the best of times, he would be wanting to discuss what Willie Vanderbilt's new car was capable of doing, or whether the chef Oliver Belmont had brought back from France was really better than his own. . . . It was the same thing the next morning. He would come downstairs ready for church in cutaway coat and immaculate topper, only to find rubbers [hands of bridge] in progress already. So he would sit alone in his front pew, come back to lunch off a tray in his study, and return to New York in the afternoon, a lonely man in spite of all his acquaintances."[18]

Jack finally found the courage to end his disastrous mismatch with Ava after his mother, Caroline, died in 1908. He learned that the divorce was final while on a cruise with Vincent on the *Nourmahal* in 1910 and was so excited that he hurried back to New York and threw a party for 150 people at a cost of $25,000.[19] Presumably those people didn't try to make him talk about bridge all night, either. The divorce was scandalous enough by itself, but the public drama became feverish at Jack's announcement that he intended to get remarried, and to someone young enough to be his daughter.

When Jack got involved with Madeleine Talmage Force, she had only recently turned eighteen. Most of his friends thought he couldn't possibly be serious about marrying her. Why go to all the trouble and expense when he could easily take her as his mistress? "Appearances must be respected," Vita Sackville-West wrote of this time and social milieu, "though morals might be neglected."[20] But marry they did, in September 1911, in the ballroom of Beechwood, the Astor family summer palace in Newport. Jack was forty-seven, hardly the elderly man portrayed on-screen. But the age gap was considered so sordid that the couple had difficulty finding a clergyman willing to perform the ceremony.[21]

In an effort to escape some of the public scrutiny, the newlywed Astors fled, first wintering in Egypt and then to England, for the glittering social season, which was marked by the coronation of George V and Queen Mary. But by springtime, Madeleine was pregnant, and she wanted to have the baby in the United States. So, they booked passage home on the maiden voyage of what was being hailed as the finest ship ever to plow the North Atlantic, uncertain what kind of social reception awaited them upon their arrival back in New York. The "boat train" left Waterloo Station punctually at nine thirty in the morning, carrying in its gold-tassel-trimmed mahogany car about a dozen men whose combined net worth exceeded three hundred million dollars, among whom Jack Astor was both the richest and the most whispered about.[22] In addition to his wife and her maid, he was also traveling with an Airedale named Kitty.[23]

According to Walter Lord's definitive 1955 account of the *Titanic* disaster, *A Night to Remember*, after the iceberg ripped through the hold and it was clear the ship was sinking, most of the prominent society passengers on *Titanic* clung together. Lifeboat number 4 had been lowered onto A Deck, but a row of sealed cabin windows and a collapsed piece of rigging stood in the way of filling it with waiting first-class women and children. While crewmembers tried to find an axe to break the windows so that passengers could get out of the cabin and reach the lifeboat, the Astors, Wideners, Thayers, Carters, and Ryersons waited on the Promenade Deck, having been told that women, children, maids, and nurses would be loaded soon. By 1:45 in the morning, Second Officer Charles Lightoller was standing with one foot in Lifeboat 4 and one on a windowsill, with a heap of deck chairs piled up to make a rickety staircase. Society men waited nearby to help pass women and children up the pile of chairs and through the window to reach the lifeboat.[24]

Jack helped a terrified Madeleine, bundled in a canvas-and-cork life preserver and ungainly at five months along in her pregnancy, up the pile of deck chairs and through the cumbersome window frame. He then asked the officer if he might accompany her, as she was "in delicate condition."[25]

Lightoller said no. No men could get into lifeboats until the women and children were loaded first.

Walter Lord wrote, "Astor asked which boat it was, and Lightoller said, 'Number 4.' Colonel [Archibald] Gracie was sure Astor merely wanted to locate his wife later. Lightoller was sure he planned to make a complaint."[26] This was, after all, the same Jack Astor who had insisted on charging a destitute tramp with felony burglary for falling asleep in his servants' quarters twenty years before. He was accustomed to getting what he wanted from people he outranked.

The lifeboat carrying Jack Astor's young, pregnant wife and her maid was cut loose and hit the water fifteen feet below at 1:55 a.m.[27]

By 2:05, Captain Smith was releasing the crew from their duties, telling them it was now every man for himself.[28] On the boat deck, as the Wideners and John Thayer clustered together, Jack Astor stood alone.[29]

Astor's final moments aboard the RMS *Titanic* are subject to conjecture. August Weikman, a barber, told a newspaper, "I asked him if he minded shaking hands with me. He said, 'with pleasure.'" But Weikman also said he left the ship at 1:50, so he wouldn't have been the last man to see Jack Astor.[30] Washington Dodge, a passenger from San Francisco, reported that he saw Jack Astor standing with a society fellow named Archie Butt: "They went down standing on the bridge, side by side. I could not mistake them," he told the newspapers. But Dodge had escaped in Lifeboat 13, which by the time the *Titanic* sank, was already half a mile away, and Dodge wouldn't have been able to see this.[31] Let's not get too sentimental, though, about Jack Astor, Harry Widener, and the rest. Despite the policy of "women and children first," the loss rate was higher for third-class children than it was for first-class men.[32]

When she arrived in New York City after the ordeal, Madeleine Astor collapsed into a waiting retinue of two automobiles, two doctors, a nurse, a secretary, and her stepson, Vincent Astor.[33] Jack Astor's sudden and unexpected death seeded family tension that would never be entirely resolved. His will left $5 million in trust to his daughter, Alice, from his marriage to Ava; $5 million to his new widow, Madeleine; $3 million for her unborn "*Titanic* Baby," who would be John Jacob Astor VI, called "Jakey"; and the rest—a staggering $69 million, in 1912—to his son Vincent. (This disparity precluded any possible relationship between Vincent and Jakey in their adulthood.) When Jack Astor's body was retrieved from the ocean, he was identified by the initials sewn into his clothes. He did not die from drowning, but was killed by blunt force trauma, possibly from a falling funnel. Found on him was a gold pocket watch, stopped by water, which Vincent carried for the rest of his life.

In 1894, when he was thirty years old, and three years into his miserable first marriage, Jack Astor had published a science-fiction novel entitled *A Journey into Other Worlds*. Fond of mechanisms and technologies of travel, ungainly and awkward, rich and somewhat unaware of what wealth could mean, Astor imagined that men of the future would control the weather and be able to make it rain on demand. He dreamed of a time when space travel would be made possible by "apergy," a force that would be the opposite of gravity. Some of his fantasies seem almost prescient: All transportation on earth becomes electric. War has been rendered so awful because of airplane bombing that the world now lives in peace. "The love story is handled with far less skill than the sections dealing with science or business—true in the author's life as well as in his writing," one twentieth-century critic notes.[34] But the main plot revolves around protagonist Colonel Bearwarden being hired by the "Terrestrial Axis Straightening Company" to shift the earth's axis to become perfectly vertical.[35]

Today, the rusted outline of the pier entrance where the RMS *Titanic* was supposed to have landed after her maiden voyage, where

Jack and Madeleine and her maid and Kitty the dog would have come tripping down the gangplank to streamers and cheers and newspaper flashbulbs, can be seen silhouetted against the gray and lumpen Hudson River by anyone who loiters in the right spot on the High Line downtown.

As for Jack Astor—the real Jack Astor—the man who once dared to dream that the right engineering and technology could bring about a world that spun under the delicate sunshine of an eternal spring, all that remains are the celluloid images of him, strolling the decks in elegant clothes, sipping champagne on a ship that will never arrive.

9

BLACKWELL'S ISLAND

1910

*The history of all hitherto existing society
is the history of class struggles.*

—Karl Marx and Friedrich Engels[1]

When newspapers all over the world reported John Jacob Astor's death on the *Titanic*, it was not the first time in the twentieth century that John Jacob Astor had died.

Nearly two years earlier, on August 20, 1910, New York City newspapers trumpeted the death of John Jacob Astor at the age of seventy-four. But it wasn't the multimillionaire John Jacob Astor whom everyone had heard of. This John Jacob Astor was an indigent resident of the City Home for the elderly, an almshouse on Blackwell's Island. Also known as Welfare Island, it was the thin strip of land in the East River between Manhattan and Queens now called Roosevelt Island.

Beginning in the early nineteenth century, Blackwell's hosted a penitentiary, with the first of what would become many hospitals and sanitariums on the island erected to care for the prison inmates. After

1839, Blackwell's was also home to the New York City Lunatic Asylum, made notorious as the subject of Nellie Bly's undercover exposé from 1887, *Ten Days in a Mad-House*.[2] The combination of convenience to Manhattan and isolation from it made the island perfect for housing desperate New Yorkers who had nowhere else to go. Blackwell's soon added a smallpox hospital, a workhouse for minor offenders, and the alms hospital for the indigent. It was here, in the shadow of Manhattan, that the other John Jacob Astor died.

News of the death of this surprisingly named man flooded the wire services, as hungry then as the media are now for eye-catching stories. Information about John Jacob Astor's death reached readers as far away as Arizona and Montana. The Boston *Herald* dressed up the wire service human interest story with details of the "real" Colonel John Jacob "Jack" Astor socializing in Newport that same night. He was preparing to depart on his yacht the *Nourmahal* with his son, Vincent, for Bar Harbor after attending a dance given in honor of the officers of the Atlantic Fleet. As he sipped champagne, he would also have been eagerly awaiting news that his divorce from Ava had become final.

Two weeks later, the *New York Times* reported on the glittering summer season at Bar Harbor, noting that "Col. John Jacob Astor, who with his son, Vincent Astor, has been here for some time, has been both host and guest at a number of affairs. . . . On Monday he entertained at dinner, his guests including the Misses Madeline [*sic*] and Katherine Force, Mrs. W. H. Force, A. E. Gallatin, and Vincent Astor."[3] This mention marks the first time that Jack and Madeleine, who was seventeen years old at the time, were linked in print—one year before their wedding.

The John Jacob Astor who died on Blackwell's Island shared more than a name with the wealthy and famous colonel. He had been born in Walldorf, in Baden, present-day Germany, the same small town where the first John Jacob Astor, Jack's great-grandfather, was born 150 years or so before him. Like that first John Jacob Astor, this one had immigrated while a young man, landing on the shores of New York hungry for work. Rather than selling beaver skins to amass a monstrous fortune, this John Jacob labored his whole life rolling cigars until, at age seventy-two, his eyesight failed. The two John Jacobs may actually have shared more than a name and an origin point—Colonel John Jacob Astor's great-grandfather was supposedly the brother of the indigent John Jacob Astor's grandfather (likely Melchior, the original Astor brother who did not leave Walldorf). If true, this meant that the John Jacob Astor who died penniless, blind, and alone in the Blackwell's Island almshouse was the second cousin once removed of one of the richest men in the world, a man who bore the exact same name.

The first John Jacob Astor to immigrate to the newly minted United States had come with flutes to sell and a rapacious hunger for success and wound up attempting to seed an entire Pacific empire with the encouragement of the president. In many respects, his incredible story is part of a long-standing myth about America—that it is a beacon of equal opportunity for anyone with enough grit and determination to make a go of it for himself.

But the other John Jacob Astor also lived an immigrant's story in the United States of America. The New York Municipal Archives *Almshouse* ledgers record his life as a stark list of facts and dates. Admission age: 74. Marital status: Widowed. Death age: 74. Birth date: About 1836. Birthplace: Germany. Admission date: July 27, 1910. Death date: August 19, 1910. Occupation: Cigar maker. His address is given as 307 East Twenty-Ninth Street, which was a rooming house that served mostly German and Irish immigrants. And perhaps as a joke, he listed Jack—the colonel enjoying a glittering season in Bar Harbor blissfully unaware of almshouse life—as his next of kin.

The indigent Astor was buried three days after his death, in the Lutheran section of All Faiths Cemetery in Middle Village, Queens, at the same time as a handful of other men who had died at the almshouse that week.[4] Not a potter's field burial, but not far from it. Within these unassuming boundaries unfolds a life that is as much a part of the American immigrant story as the kind celebrated by Horatio Alger in his nineteenth-century up-by-the-bootstraps fantasies. It's a harder story, though, and one more commonly shared. Not all bootstraps go up, no matter how hard you pull.

We don't know much about this John Jacob's life in Walldorf before his immigration, but Walldorf today is a small town of around 15,000 people most known for being the original John Jacob Astor's birthplace, for its cultivation of white asparagus, and for the extermination of its Jewish residents after the synagogue was destroyed on Kristallnacht. The U.S. Census of 1910, just before the indigent John Jacob's death, gives his year of immigration as 1862. The teeming New York City into which he arrived as a young laborer of around twenty-six would have been a shockingly different place from the sleepy town of his origin.

By the late 1850s, New York already had a population of around eight hundred thousand people—large for today, but staggering by the standards of the time.[5] Just as Vanderbilts and the more famous Astors were making Murray Hill the most fashionable district of the city, and only a few years before truly palatial Gilded Age homes began to rise up along the commodious expanse of Fifth Avenue, the poor of the city lived crammed together along the waterfronts and in the "Bloody Ould" Sixth Ward. This newly arrived John Jacob Astor found himself in a city with a burgeoning population of Irish immigrants and a bustling free Black population as well. He could not have known that he was stepping into a tinderbox moments from ignition.

John Jacob Astor

Mrs. John Jacob Astor
(Sarah Todd)

A later watercolor of John Jacob
Astor, by an unidentified artist

William Backhouse Astor Sr.

Edwin Forrest

William Charles Macready

ASTOR PLACE OPERA-HOUSE RIOTS.

An engraving of the Astor Place Riot at the Astor Opera House

Caroline Schermerhorn Astor, *the* Mrs. Astor, in an 1890
portrait by Carolus-Duran

The double mansion at 840 and 841 Fifth Avenue, built by Jack Astor for himself and his mother, Caroline Astor

The gallery at Mrs. Astor's mansion at 840 Fifth Avenue

John Jacob "Jack" Astor IV

William Waldorf "Will" Astor

Mrs. Astor's Thirty-Fourth Street mansion, dwarfed by her
nephew's new Waldorf Hotel, circa 1893

A view of the Waldorf-Astoria from around the turn of the century

Hever Castle

Cliveden

Rokeby, showing the library addition added by William Backhouse Astor

The Astor orphans with their cousin
and guardian, Mary Marshall

John Armstrong "Archie" Chanler

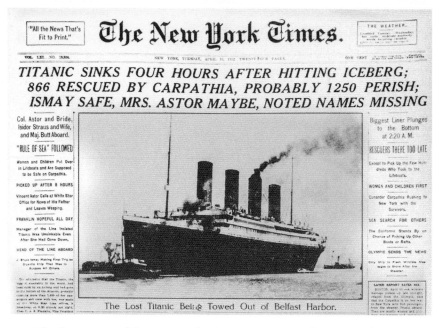

The New York Times.

VOL. LXI...NO. 19,830.　　　NEW YORK, TUESDAY, APRIL 16, 1912.—TWENTY-FOUR PAGES.　　　ONE CENT

TITANIC SINKS FOUR HOURS AFTER HITTING ICEBERG; 866 RESCUED BY CARPATHIA, PROBABLY 1250 PERISH; ISMAY SAFE, MRS. ASTOR MAYBE, NOTED NAMES MISSING

Col. Astor and Bride, Isidor Straus and Wife, and Maj. Butt Aboard.

"RULE OF SEA" FOLLOWED

Women and Children Put Over in Lifeboats and Are Supposed to be Safe on Carpathia.

PICKED UP AFTER 8 HOURS

Vincent Astor Calls at White Star Office for News of His Father and Leaves Weeping.

FRANKLIN HOPEFUL ALL DAY

Manager of the Line Insisted Titanic Was Unsinkable Even After She Had Gone Down.

HEAD OF THE LINE ABOARD

J. Bruce Ismay Making First Trip to Dieantis Ship That Was to Surpass All Others.

Biggest Liner Plunges to the Bottom at 2:20 A. M.

RESCUERS THERE TOO LATE

Except to Pick Up the Few Hundreds Who Took to the Lifeboats.

WOMEN AND CHILDREN FIRST

Cunarder Carpathia Rushing to New York with the Survivors.

SEA SEARCH FOR OTHERS

The California Stands By on Chance of Picking Up Other Boats or Rafts.

OLYMPIC SENDS THE NEWS

Only Ship to Flash Wireless Messages to Shore After the Disaster.

LATER REPORT SAVES 866

The Lost Titanic Being Towed Out of Belfast Harbor.

The front page of the *New York Times* announcing the *Titanic* disaster
(Tuesday, April 16, 1912)

Ava Lowle Willing, the first wife
of Jack Astor

Madeleine Astor,
Jack's second wife

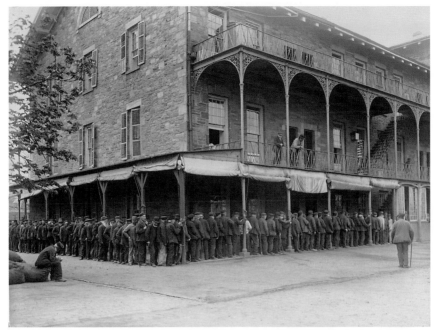

The almshouse on Blackwell Island, where the other John Jacob Astor died

Cigar makers working inside a tenement

A view of the Astor Hotel's neon sign, 1955

Nourmahal, Vincent's ship

Vincent Astor on board a ship, circa 1920

Vincent in later years

Anthony Marshall and Brooke Astor, with
Charlene Marshall in the background

Anthony and Charlene Marshall in court in 2013

Brooke Astor in 2002, at age one hundred

Mary Astor, born Lucile Langhanke

The year after he disembarked, German John Jacob Astor was required to register for the draft for the Civil War. His reported age was twenty-seven. He was unmarried and living at 183 Division Street, and the occupation given on his draft card was "segar maker." Division Street was mere blocks away from the Five Points neighborhood, the notorious slum controlled by warring gangs. The date of Astor's draft card falls within a set of people registered in May and June 1863. The first names of unwilling draftees into the Union cause would be called up by a public lottery the following month, in July.

Things didn't go quite as expected.

But first, it's worth taking a moment to understand what kind of world Astor was living in as a young, unmarried immigrant man in Manhattan in 1863. If he was lucky enough to be employed, a German or Irish laborer might expect to earn a dollar a day.[6] Cigar rolling took place both at home, as piecework, and in crowded sweatshop factories.

Living conditions for the laboring classes of New York were tight to a degree that contemporary New York City—no stranger to close conditions—would find impossible to imagine. The Old Brewery in the Sixth Ward, an infamous slum dramatized in the 2002 Martin Scorsese film *Gangs of New York*, and the similarly ramshackle and crawling Old Match Factory at Forsyth and Stanton Streets, contained around a hundred families each, crammed into tiny subdivided compartments with no ventilation or easy exit in the event of a fire. Old houses and mansions were carved into warrens of rooms. Windowless cellars were retrofitted into living quarters totally belowground.

This period also saw the erection of real tenements, many of them on Astor-owned land. The Astor Estate was one of the biggest landlords of tenement slums in the 1850s and '60s, which were designed from the outset to house as many people as possible, generating maximal profits for their developers. Two buildings would go up on a lot that measured 110 by 25 feet—one building in front, one in back, with a row of latrines in between. Each building might stand seven or eight stories high, with 3-foot-wide hallways connecting the apartments. A tenement typically contained six or eight of these "suites" per floor. The "suites" consisted of two rooms. One measured 8 by 10 feet with a 7-foot ceiling and was typically used as a common room for cooking and washing or as a workroom if the tenant took in piecework like sewing or cigar rolling. The other room, measuring 7 by 8, was used for sleeping. By way of comparison, these dimensions are roughly equivalent to a modern parking space, an elevator, or a prison cell used for solitary confinement. Though the "suites" were originally designed for occupancy by one family, renters often took in lodgers, and the two rooms would regularly be occupied by two, three, and sometimes even four families at a time.[7]

One reason for the intensifying congestion of New York City was that development north of what is now Midtown Manhattan, around Fifty-Ninth Street, was next to impossible until the widespread adoption of the steel-cable equipped steam shovel after 1870. Without technology that was able to grade and cut through the rocky outcroppings of Manhattan's natural landscape, development and street layout on a major scale were out of reach. Until the steam shovel came along to flatten the land, more and more people arrived in the city with nowhere to go but the same few square miles. Waves upon waves of immigrants from Europe poured into the same neighborhoods with no option but to subdivide, crowd in, and subdivide again.

Why not settle into a nearby area and commute, like so many New Yorkers do today? Staten Island wasn't crowded, and Brooklyn lay just across the East River, but, in the 1860s, the technology to build bridges over the East and Hudson Rivers didn't exist, so the only way to cross the water was by ferry—and the Staten Island Ferry was expensive. The Brooklyn Ferry was a bit cheaper, but unreliable. In winter, the steamboats had to dodge ice floes in the harbor and East River that were occasionally deadly. Congestion and transportation were already such a problem that, in 1858, city authorities banned steam engines from traveling along the streets south of Forty-Second, as they were too dangerous. (Can you imagine dodging a steam locomotive in Times Square?) But this meant that any trains moving overland into downtown Manhattan had to be unhitched from locomotives, attached to horses, and pulled the rest of the way.[8] Omnibuses, called "stages," plowed the city, dragged by horses. Built for twenty-five people, they routinely carried seventy or more and were notoriously slow.[9]

After Commodore Vanderbilt took over the New York and Harlem Railroad in the 1850s, the accident rate went down and the train equipment was upgraded. Railroads to Fordham, in the Bronx, and Yonkers, in Westchester, were faster than the streetcars and stages that moved within the city proper.[10] By the 1850s, New York was already dreaming of rapid transit, but the choice lay between digging tunnels through solid rock, a prospect that was risky, expensive, and filthy, or erecting elevated train tracks and running trains, known as "Els," above the streets, which would turn the avenues beneath them into dank tunnels under showers of smoke and ash. The Els didn't start going up until the 1870s.

In the meantime, more and more immigrants poured into the city, crowding into the slums that were their only option within walking distance of their jobs. The German John Jacob Astor would have lived in a crowded Division Street tenement, one stacked deep with other unmarried young immigrant men, not because he wanted to, but because he had to be close to the factories where he might be able to get work rolling cigars.

The miserable tenements where Astor and young men like him lived weren't cheap, either. Apartments on Hester Street, just around the corner from Division, cost between $5 and $6.50 a month in 1856, six years before Astor arrived.[11] A report investigating tenement living at that time said that "the place literally swarmed with human life, but life of so abject and squalid a character as to scarcely merit the name."[12] Housing was in such demand, however, that landlords were able to reap huge profits. Per square foot, it cost more to rent a hovel in the Five Points than a mansion in Murray Hill.[13] Money invested in tenement housing paid an annual return of 25 to 100 percent. By contrast, middle-class housing paid 10 to 25 percent, and residences for the wealthy yielded only 5 to 10 percent.[14]

Those living in tenements were careful to pay their rent before any other expense—before they bought food or fuel or redeemed their Sunday clothes from pawnbrokers. Beyond the ever-present risk of eviction, unpaid rent allowed landlords to seize tenants' belongings and sell them to make up the shortfall. If they didn't pay their rent, they lost everything—including their place to sleep. And if evicted, a tenant might find himself blacklisted among the dominant landlords of the city, unable to rent anywhere.[15]

Housing options for the poor who could not afford tenements were grim indeed. Desperation might lead a laborer like Astor to cellar lodging houses in the Five Points or down by the waterfront, where shared beds were let for five or ten cents a night. As a last resort, an immigrant worker might settle into the shanties in the rocky middle part of Manhattan, squatting in what is now Central Park.[16]

The squalor of Lower Manhattan in this period was unparalleled. Despite being an island, surrounded by fresh ocean air and steady breezes, Manhattan had the highest death rate in the developed world.[17] The year 1863 saw the death of 1 out of every 35 people in New York

City. In contrast, the death rate in London—the putrid London of Charles Dickens that gave rise to the adjective *Dickensian*, and only twenty years before Jack the Ripper—was 1 in 45. Some doctors of the period hypothesized that as many as two thirds of the deaths in New York City could have been prevented by better sanitation.[18]

The crucial point was that 1 in 35 was the *average*. It depended on where in Manhattan one lived. In Murray Hill, the wealthy neighborhood of mansions and brownstones on top of a rise within gasping distance of the East River, the death rate was a much more reasonable 1 in 60. Some tenements in the Fourth and Sixth Wards had death rates as high as 1 in 19.[19] To put this into perspective, the death rate in the United States in the middle of the Covid-19 pandemic (2021) was 1 in 119.[20]

The relentless overcrowding and lack of ventilation weren't the only factors contributing to the dismal sanitation conditions of Lower Manhattan. Much of the city in the early 1860s lacked sewers, and the streets became clotted with excrement and garbage in a thick layer of mud. Many of the few sewers that did exist flowed uphill, causing backups and flooding. Any sewage that made it through the nascent drainage systems emptied raw into the Hudson and East Rivers. The volume of human and animal waste pouring daily into those rivers was so massive that the tide couldn't carry it all away.[21]

Not even the slowly ballooning wealth of the pre–Gilded Age era could insulate New Yorkers from the city's squalor, in part because neighborhoods of the rich and the poor sat cheek by jowl, as they do today. As one historian put it, "mansions and fever nests, townhouses and slaughterhouses stood side by side."[22] The pampered denizens of Murray Hill were bedeviled by goats roaming loose from the Dutch Hill squatters' camp a few blocks away. Residents of tony Gramercy Park—even today an exclusive enclave accessed only by a key—had to guard against catching typhoid from the tenements on Third Avenue.

In short, the New York City where John Jacob Astor, cigar roller, lived in July 1863 was a crowded, congested, cough-filled, filthy, stinking cesspit of gaping inequality. And on top of that, it was summer. Summer in New York City is hot and humid, and with offal and sewage tainting the rivers, not even a quick swim could offer passing relief.

Into this concentrated maelstrom of sickness and squalor we have to add a distant civil war that was pulverizing the bodies of young men in numbers never before imagined. New Yorkers generally believed that the Union was going to lose. The Union Army of the Potomac under Major General Ambrose Burnside had suffered wholesale slaughter at the Battle of Fredericksburg, in Virginia, in December 1862. Meanwhile, Ulysses S. Grant had repeatedly failed in his many maneuvers against Vicksburg, Mississippi, a Confederate stronghold to the west. The CSS *Alabama* was successfully raiding Union shipping operations up and down the East Coast, including off the coast of New York.

Then, on January 1, 1863, the Emancipation Proclamation was passed, freeing enslaved people living in Confederate states. (Enslaved people living in border states, like Maryland, were not freed.) Among low-wage workers and immigrants in New York City, the Proclamation stoked several fears at once. First, that it would only harden Confederate resolve, making reunion impossible, and the war would drag on. Second, and more practically, New Yorkers—like our German John Jacob Astor—would also have worried about an influx of free Black workers into an already saturated labor market. People living on the edge of poverty in New York City in 1863 were contending with runaway inflation. Retail prices had risen 43 percent since

1860, while wages were up only 12 percent.[23] There was labor unrest, war fatigue, anxiety, and frustration among the laboring classes of Lower Manhattan. And then, in March, it got worse.

In March 1863, President Abraham Lincoln put forward the Enrollment and Conscription Act, instituting a draft of young men to serve the (failing) Union cause.[24] The draft came first for single men ages twenty to forty-five—of which the German John Jacob Astor was one—and for married men ages twenty to thirty-five, turning only then, once the first two classes of draftees were used up, to married men ages thirty-five to forty-five. Of course, exceptions could be made. Men with a disability or who provided the sole source of support for aged parents or orphaned children could obtain dispensation against being sent to the meat-grinder battlefields a few states away. They could also buy their way out if they were rich—three hundred dollars to save your life. But who in the German John Jacob's neighborhood could ever put his hands on that much money?[25] Recall that, at this moment, someone like him would have been making about one dollar a day.

Opposition to the draft was immediate and fierce in the Five Points and all along Division Street. Astor and the men with whom he had immigrated and now bunked and worked would not have seen the draft as an opportunity to serve their new country and certainly not as a moral imperative to help liberate fellow men and women living in bondage. Instead, they would have viewed it as a trampling of the rights of their state and their rights as individuals. They would have resented being forced to fight a war they thought they were bound to lose, by a government in which they had no real say, one that did nothing for them, except create more competition for the meager, low-paying jobs they were already fighting to retain. This bitterness was publicly stoked by New York State governor Horatio Seymour, a secession-sympathizing Democrat, and further inflamed by rabble-rousing antiwar newspapers.

All the same, John Jacob Astor wiped the tobacco stains from his hands and went to register in May or June 1863, alongside other newly arrived young men from Germany and Ireland. And on a hot and hazy Saturday, July 11, 1863, at the Ninth District enrollment office at 677 Third Avenue at Forty-Sixth Street, the first names of drafted men were drawn and read aloud.[26]

There was grumbling but not much else. People trudged home, back to their crowded tenements and shared bunks and airless basements. The next day was Sunday, a day of rest for many New Yorkers in 1863. A day to sit around, be a little idle, smoke and talk. And talk they did. Mostly about the draft.

Then, on Monday, July 13, 1863, all hell broke loose.[27]

Young men, mostly unmarried Irish and German immigrants, gathered in a mob in Central Park and then headed for the draft office, intent on destruction. The vicious New York City Draft Riots had begun.

"The riot which commenced on the first day of the Draft was ostensibly in opposition to it," one contemporary account reported, "but early took the character of an outbreak for the purposes of pillage, and also of outrage upon the colored population. For the first three days, business in the city was almost entirely suspended, the railroads and omnibuses ceased running, the stores on Broadway, the avenues, and throughout the greater portion of the city were closed, and prowling gangs of ruffians rendered it unsafe to walk the streets."[28] The Metropolitan Police were no match for the rioters, and the New York State Militia was on its way back from fighting at Gettysburg. From Monday the thirteenth through Tuesday the fourteenth, when the militia finally arrived and joined with the police to fire on the rioters, the mob murdered eighteen people, of whom eleven were Black. By Wednesday, rioters had torched fifty buildings, including the Colored Orphan Asylum, two police stations, three provost marshal's offices, and a "block of dwellings on Broadway."[29] The police and militia finally put down the riots with an unknown number of casualties, estimated by one source at between four and five hundred people. All told, the mob did $1.2 million in damage, about $27 million in 2021 money.[30]

A tenement at 134 Division Street, within sight of Astor's building, was looted by rioters, who torched all the furniture inside before the mob was dispersed by police.[31] Census records don't offer a plausible explanation for why that particular building would have drawn the ire of the mob in which the German Astor may have played a part. The victims could have been Union sympathizers, but more likely, they were free Black workers in a neighborhood with precious few people like them, being targeted by a racist mob.

The Draft Riots were the most vicious race riots in New York City history. A group of men dragged one Black man, who already had a serious head wound, out of a streetcar and chased him to the steps of the Astor House hotel, where he took refuge behind an Officer Wells. Wells held the mob off with a revolver while the wounded man hid behind the hotel columns, and later reported that the crowd was bellowing racial slurs.[32] At the time, the Astor House was the most famous hotel in the country. Abraham Lincoln had stayed there on his way to his inauguration. Months after the Draft Riots, in 1864, Confederate sympathizers would attempt to burn it down.

The German John Jacob Astor does not appear on the list of people who were scooped up and charged by police. No records indicate that he was hurt in the rioting, but it's very possible he could have been among the mob. New York City was a teeming metropolis with a Democratic majority and a vast immigrant underclass, and its populace was being called upon to participate, against their will, in a Republican project of nation formation.[33] Astor would have lived in a community of Copperhead Democrats, violent opposers of the Civil War who supported the right of the Confederacy to secede or who were tired of the bloodshed or who wanted the Confederacy to win—or all the above.

Further, in Astor's world, riots were almost predictable, especially in spring and summer. Rioting often marked Election Day, which in the 1860s was a holiday usually fueled by free-flowing alcohol supplied by party bosses; or the Fourth of July; or labor disputes throughout the economic upheavals of the 1850s.[34] Another contributing factor: so-called Sabbatarianism. In the mid-nineteenth century, Protestant clergy had stopped all music and dancing on Sundays. New York City at the time had no public parks, no excursion trains, no municipal swimming pools. So, on Sundays in the 1860s—as on the day before the Draft Riots began—young and broke New Yorkers like the German John Jacob Astor had little to do but sit around and drink.[35]

John Jacob Astor managed to escape the Draft Riots unscathed, as far as we know, and also seems to have avoided service in the Union Army. At least, his name does not appear on the rolls of men receiving Union pensions in the 1880s. We next see him on October 1, 1868, when the Superior Court of New York County naturalized him as an American citizen. At the time, he was living at 9 Bayard Street, which was also in the Five Points, across Pell from Division Street. His citizenship was witnessed by a German émigré named Johannes Bernard, who lived on Christie, right around the corner.

By the time of the census of 1870, John Jacob Astor's life seemed to be on an upswing. He was living in Ward 10 and married to a woman named Theresa. He was thirty-four years old, and she was forty-three. Both were German. They had no children. His profession was given as "segar mauft," and she was listed as "keeping house." However, it's likely she was running some kind of garment manufacturing or piece-work out of their home, as most women of her class did. They shared their dwelling with three other families, all of whom were German by either birth or heritage. One woman who lived with them was listed as manufacturing "drawers" (probably ladies' undergarments). Jacob—he didn't seem to be going by "John" as much—and Theresa listed the total value of their household as $1,500. They were still living a hard life, very far away, economically and socially, from the glittering world in which Jacob's distant cousins' lives were unfolding in Murray Hill. But they were doing better than they had been. They were getting by.

By 1880, Jacob and Theresa Astor had moved uptown, to Sixth Street. It would seem that Jacob, at age forty-four, was enjoying some fruits of his labor, having moved away from the Five Points and appearing on that year's census for the first time as the head of his own household. While they never had children, Jacob and Theresa took in boarders for extra income at this residence, a very common practice at the time. They lived with William Eochem, a sixty-three-year-old widower who was a tailor; William's thirty-year-old son, Albert, an unemployed varnisher; and William's thirty-eight-year-old daughter, Lazzie, who was also a tailor. However, this otherwise promising picture of Jacob Astor's life in 1880 holds a faint foreshadowing of harder days to come. There's a hatch mark next to his profession, suggesting he was unemployed.

The next decade of Jacob's life is lost to history. The 1890 census was largely destroyed by a fire. A few fragments remain, but Jacob doesn't show up in them. Whatever happened in his life over that decade and the next is unclear, but by the 1900 census, there has been a drastic change. John Jacob Astor is no longer in New York. Records of a "John Astor," a white male, show up in Lynn, Massachusetts, a small industrial waterfront city on the North Shore of Boston. This Astor's neighbors in the boardinghouse where he's recorded as living are mostly men, but there are some women, too, laborers like him. "Boardinghouse" may have been an overly generous description of where this "John Astor" was living—perhaps it was more like a shelter.

What was Astor doing in Lynn? Maybe he went north looking for work in the shoe factories and struck out there, too. The occupations of his fellow boarders included bartender, shoemaker, shoe cutter, shoe stitcher, and servant, but for Astor, there's a lot of blank space. If it's him, Theresa is long gone. So is his apartment. So is his status as head of his own household.

By 1901, when he was sixty-five years old, John Jacob Astor was admitted for the first time to the almshouse on Blackwell's Island. He entered on March 9 and was discharged two days later. His occupation is still listed as "cigar maker." This begins a long, painful decade of decline. He entered the almshouse again in 1903, this time for three and a half months. Then again in 1904, when he stayed a month. Nearly a year later, he was back, but he could no longer pretend he was able to support himself. He remained there for an entire year, through November 14, 1906, and now his occupation was given as "orderly." He had begun to lose his eyesight and became dependent on the hospital to give him a place to live and odd jobs to do.

Our last picture of this other John Jacob Astor comes from the 1910 census. From this record, we learn that he could read and write. He gave his immigration year as 1862—the year he showed up in America, a young man from a small German town, with his wits and his hands and his strong back, and entered an unforgiving city that would offer him hard work and long days and very little else. One wonders if he thought much about the days when the city around him burned, when men like him, young and angry and hungry and tired, torched the buildings and people they blamed for their condition, only to see rich men like his distant cousins just build it back up again and, somehow, make even more money doing so.

As an old man of seventy-four, eyes dimmed from a lifetime of working bent over a table rolling tobacco, John Jacob Astor was living out his days as a lodger in a men's rooming house at East Twenty-Sixth Street, with other men largely of German extraction. He must have felt like an outlier, as the other lodgers all ranged in age from their twenties to their fifties. He would have been the elder statesman of the rooming house, which was being run by a twenty-six-year-old man and his sister. Jacob's occupation was given as "servant," and his marital status, "widowed." Maybe it was true. In any case, his wife was gone. Did he think about Theresa, when the census taker asked him this question? Did he remember meeting her in a beer hall? Did they dance and get sweaty and fall laughing into each other's arms?

A few months later, the same rooming house proprietors would be giving their interviews to the newspapers, who were turning John Jacob Astor's life into entertaining copy. That is, a few months later, he would be dead.

John Jacob Astor was admitted to the almshouse for the last time on July 27, 1910, and died on August 19 at the City Home for the aged. The New York Episcopal Diocese burial records show that he was buried two days later, along with Jan Van Buskirk, age seventy-four; Harry Curtain, age eighty; and William S. Joerke, age seventy-seven. The four men were laid to rest by the same minister—his name is difficult to decipher in the records, probably because it was written so speedily. On that particular day, he seemed to have been in charge of all group burials for the City Home. This John Jacob Astor wasn't buried in the potter's field at Hart Island, at least, where New York still lays to rest its anonymous and indigent citizens. So, it seems likely the people who were interviewed about him in the newspapers had scraped the money together for his burial.

John Jacob Astor didn't make his fortune. He didn't seed a dynasty or agonize over who should inherit his money. He never got a call from the president. Most of us don't. Did he do things he was ashamed of? Did he have small pleasures and triumphs? Did he kiss women in dark alleys, eat hot corn from street sellers, drink too much, get into fights, breathe deep of the ocean air, hold the hand of his dying wife?

Would we even know he once existed if it weren't for his name?

10

MRS. ASTOR'S BAR

1910 TO 1966

Here is the city's world of pleasure at your very door.

—*From a 1922 advertisement for the Astor Hotel*

Bob Eissner had been a bellman at the Astor Hotel for fifteen years, but this was his last day. The storied hotel was finally closing. On June 30, 1966, Eissner idled near the front desk trading memories with some of the other employees and a reporter for the *New York Times*.

"This man came in with 29 pieces of luggage," he said, remembering the biggest tip he ever received. "He was a military man, but he wasn't wearing a uniform. It took three of us to handle all the bags. When we got them up to his room he handed over a roll of bills and told us to split it. It was almost $175. We got more than $57 apiece." (One hundred seventy-five dollars in 1966 is equivalent to about $1,500 in 2021.)

Luis Gonzalez, a bellman there for six years himself, was impressed by the guest's generosity. "Know what we get regular?" he asked the *Times* reporter. "Maybe $18, $20 a day."

"What I liked best," recalled Larry Pearlman from behind the newsstand, "was watching the celebrities going into the Grand Ballroom at eight o'clock at night and then reading about them in the paper at eight o'clock the next morning." He paused. "There was real excitement here in the old days," he said.

The old days were certainly long gone. When it closed, the Astor Hotel was a hollow wasteland of seven hundred empty rooms spread over ten floors and connected by more than a mile of hallways painted pale green, with doors of slate blue and red figured carpeting going shabby with age. The final guests—there were only about twenty of them—had to be checked out by noon the day the paper went to press. The last longtime resident, General Omar N. Bradley, once the chairman of the Joint Chiefs of Staff and chief of staff of the U.S. Army, had already moved out of his two-room suite on the eighth floor, leaving behind nothing but a box of tissues and a scale.

The hotel had been pitched to Will Astor, who held the lease on the land, as the successor to the original Waldorf-Astoria. When it opened in 1904, it stood on the corner of Broadway and Forty-Fourth Street, but it was expanded in 1910 to cover the entire block of Broadway up to Forty-Fifth. The timing was perfect. The *New York Times* had just moved its headquarters to Forty-Second Street, and the construction of sparkling new theaters and billboards lit by electric lights ushered in the era of the newly named Times Square, with that section of Broadway nicknamed the "Great White Way," a seductive playground of pleasure and theatricality. The Astor was an immediate success—so much so that Jack Astor began building the Knickerbocker Hotel nearby to capitalize on the opportunity.

The Astor Hotel's sumptuous event rooms bore the kind of names

meant to signify class and sophistication to a post–Gilded Age customer: "Trianon," "Versailles," "Emerald," and "L'Orangerie" (where
showman Florenz Ziegfeld proposed to Broadway actress Billie Burke,
better known as Glinda, the Good Witch of the North in *The Wizard
of Oz*). On the roof, a restaurant and gardens featuring a bandstand
and observatory enjoyed commanding views of the glittering lights
of the city.

If you entered through the front doors and walked straight through
the lobby, you'd find yourself in the Astor Bar, which the *Times* made
only glancing reference to in its article about the hotel's closing, noting that it had been a haunt for "show people" like George M. Cohan,
"composer of [the] World War I rallying songs 'Over There' and
'You're a Grand Old Flag,' among many other Broadway hits," whose
statue is prominently featured in Times Square.

What the staid editors of the *New York Times* were only hinting
at was made clearer in print that same month by Paul Forbes, writing
in a small independent Philadelphia magazine called *Drum*. Forbes
offered a very different perspective on the hotel's demise. "New
York's tear-stained tributes to the glory that was the Astor Hotel have,
for one reason or another, omitted one item of nostalgia," he noted.
"The fact that for some years—notably during World War II—that
eminent hostelry, however unwilling, housed one of the best-known
gay bars in the world."

It turns out there was a giant coterie, a semi-secret brotherhood
of gay men spanning at least two generations, for whom the Astor Bar
was something of a life raft—though, in its final years, a sometimes
treacherous one. Beginning in the 1910s, the bar, which Paul Forbes
and likely more than a few of its gay patrons lovingly and cattily referred to as "Mrs. Astor's Bar," served as a meeting point for men,

especially servicemen and those who wanted to rub shoulders (or more) with them. "On his way to the wars," Forbes writes, "on his way home from the wars, on leave from the wars. In that crowded, cozy corner he knew he could find plenty of congenial souls who shared his philosophy of eat, drink and be merry, for tomorrow we die."

Though Times Square was considered a glamorous destination when the hotel opened, the surrounding blocks were dotted with cheap rooming and boardinghouses that catered to people who worked in the Theater District as actors and dancers, waiters, and any number of other roles auxiliary to the theatrical life.[1] As historian George Chauncey has noted, "the eccentricity attributed to theater people and 'artistic types' in general provided a cover to many men who adopted widely recognized gay styles in their dress and demeanor."[2]

With so many "show people," as the *Times* called them, living and working around Times Square, it's not surprising the area became a popular cruising spot for gay men, and the Astor Bar was just one venue—there was also the Oak Room, the men's-only bar on the first floor of the Plaza Hotel, by Central Park—but the Astor was more convenient. Before too long, the sidewalk outside the hotel was dubbed, to those in the know, "the meat rack."[3]

One regular, who recalled arriving in New York City in 1917, at the age of eighteen, and going with friends "to the chic bars like the Astor," said the place had the appeal of being both "discreet, and adventuresome."[4] Discretion was important. Gay men and lesbians may have had established footholds in Times Square, Greenwich Village, and Harlem, but homosexuality was still considered a disease or perversion by mainstream American society and was criminalized for most of the twentieth century. In 1903, New York City police conducted the first-known raid on a gay bathhouse, the Ariston Hotel

Baths, arresting twenty-six men, seven of whom were sentenced to between four and twenty years in prison on sodomy charges.[5]

An arrest or even an accusation of being a "fairy" or a "pansy," as gay men were called then, could result in being fired from one's job and enduring public disgrace. As a result, gay men and women created a world within a world, a system visible only to one another, with its own folklore, its own terms and slang, its own gathering places, and its own standards of behavior.[6] It was a world instantly legible to its own members, but thickly coded enough to escape notice by those who didn't belong.

On July 1, 1919—forty-seven years almost to the day before the Astor Hotel closed—the *New York Tribune* reported on the scene at the Astor Bar in the hours before the federal Wartime Prohibition Act went into effect, banning the sale and manufacture of alcohol. "At the Astor Hotel bar the doors were closed at 10 o'clock and kept closed thereafter, except when men inside left and on those occasions an equal number of anxious liquor seekers was admitted," the paper observed. "Similar measures were adopted by the Astor bar on armistice night."

Those men waiting to be admitted to the bar spilled out into the street, eventually creating a scene that had to be broken up. "Half a dozen sailors stood in front of the Hotel Astor for a time during the shank of the evening," the paper reported, "and passed a quart bottle of whiskey from one to another until they became boisterous and were persuaded by a policeman to go elsewhere." The shooing away of sailors when they got rowdy hints at the secret of the Astor Hotel bar's considerable success as a gay enclave: rigorous avoidance of attention.

But Times Square began to change with Prohibition. Many of the bars, restaurants, and cabarets closed down, and as Chauncey notes, when the saloons catering to working-class and immigrant men went out of business, there was a proliferation of New York's sexual underground.[7] Around Times Square, speakeasies popped up, relying on organized criminal groups and payoffs to police for protection, and second-rate hotels in the area increasingly turned a blind eye to prostitution, both female and male, to make up lost profits from liquor sales.

A man named Martin Goodkin recalled his adventures as a gay teenager in New York during the early 1920s, saying that "From the 'gay side' of the Astor Hotel bar to the bushes behind the Forty-Second Street library [in Bryant Park, another institution that at one time bore the name "Astor"], to the public tearoom right outside of Fordham University . . . to the eighth floor restroom in the RCA Building to the restroom across the street in the parking garage . . . and on and on and on, New York seemed to be one big cruising ground."[8]

In 1920 alone, more than 750 men were convicted in Manhattan of "homosexual solicitation."[9] Well-dressed, masculine-presenting young men hustled along Fifth Avenue between Forty-Second and Forty-Ninth Streets, often picking up middle-class gay clients on their way home from the theater. More effeminate men worked along Forty-Second Street as far as Eighth Avenue, soliciting both gay and straight-identifying working-class men from the nearby Hell's Kitchen neighborhood.[10]

By the time the Depression started in the 1930s, the transformation of Times Square from an elegant theater district to a tawdry venue for all manner of vice in entertainment was almost complete. Two major theaters were converted into burlesque houses, featuring borderline pornographic billboards outside and barkers advertising the strippers to be ogled within. The district grew more masculine in character as a result, with movie "grindhouses" showing lowbrow action films on a continuous loop and a proliferation of men's restaurants and bars. This shift in character attracted young sailors and servicemen, who found themselves on the loose in the city looking for adventure. At the same time, some young men turned to hustling out of desperation, soliciting men even if they weren't gay themselves.

The neighborhood around the Astor Hotel, which had once been a glamorous theater district, was increasingly a sexual marketplace with particular appeal for gay men. And with the rollback of Prohibition in 1933, gay life could move from the street into the bars. But in New York, the State Liquor Authority had the power to revoke the license of any bar caught serving liquor to gay clientele, on the grounds that their very presence in the bar qualified it as "disorderly."[11] So, to get around this, some bars began tacitly enforcing a code of discretion. Obvious, or "campy," behavior by men, or "butch" behavior by women, was actively discouraged.

Herein lies the secret of the Astor Hotel bar's success. As Chauncey writes, "The Astor could maintain its public reputation as an eminently respectable Times Square establishment, while its reputation as a gay rendezvous and pickup bar assumed legendary proportions in the gay world."[12]

How did they do it? Well, the bar at the Astor, 150 feet long, was oval, with the right-hand side widely known along gay whisper networks as the place to be; the left, for the heterosexual customers. The divide in clientele was designed to protect both the men—who ran the risk of being arrested, disciplined by the military police, or attacked—and the bar's liquor license. Hotel management ignored the unspoken reason for some clientele gathering on the right ("gay") side of the bar, provided they did not draw attention to themselves. "The management would cut us down a little bit when it felt we were getting a little obvious," recalled Nat Fowler, a regular at the Astor Hotel bar during the 1940s. "If you got a little too buddy, too cruisy . . . too aggressive, they'd say, cut it out, men, why don't you go somewhere else? You had to be much more subtle."[13]

Of course, no such strictures were imposed on the other side of the oval. Straight men could drape their arms over one another's shoulders and be "as chummy as they wanted," because they were seen as "butch."[14] The Astor Bar's gay clientele could drink and cruise and pick up whomever they liked, but they had to do it with such subtlety that the straight men among them—including the ones from out of town who found themselves standing on the wrong side of the oval—wouldn't notice.

Just imagine the scene! Soldiers and Marines drinking alongside "show people" and business travelers. Some, no doubt, were there just to have a cocktail with friends, but others were searching for something more, their eyes subtly scanning the crowd—looking for what, exactly? A slight smile? An almost imperceptible nod of the head?

Was that slap on the back the sailor down the bar just gave his chum a sign? Did his hand linger on the other's shoulder a second too long? What about the Marine next to him? So many cues and codes to catch and read. *That handkerchief in the breast pocket. The way he holds his cigarette. And that laugh.*

It was exhausting at times trying to read it all, but also exciting. That moment when your eyes locked, even for a split second, through the smoke and the noise, and there was that spark of recognition, of seeing yourself in the other man's eyes, and seeing his interest in you. And knowing it was now just a question of how and when, not if.

Paul Forbes reflected on the depth of this subtle coding in his reminiscence for *Drum* magazine in 1966. "An unattached, unsophisticated female wandering into the place might, at first glimpse, have imagined that she had stumbled into heaven," he writes. "All those handsome soldiers and sailors and officers—and no women—if they hit the right side of the oval bar, that is."[15] Forbes goes on to say that no one ever really understood why the right side of the oval was gay and the left "square," though he notes that "there was as prim and distinct a separation as at a Quaker meeting."[16] But like Nat Fowler, Forbes also points out that the management would cut off anyone they took to be, as he put it, "getting out of hand."

Though unsophisticated out-of-towners might have been at sea in the crush of sailors around the oval bar, everybody else knew what was going on there. Consider Forbes's account of Daphne, the bar's cigarette girl. "As leitmotif," he recalls, "the bar in its heyday boasted a sort of one-woman Greek chorus in the person of Daphne, the cigarette girl. Daphne, young in neither age nor experience, missed very little that went on. And what she saw and heard seemed to deepen a basic inborn cynicism. Moving deftly through the crush of handsome young men with her tray of assorted tobacco, Daphne would cry softly, 'Cigars, cigarettes, hairpins, snoods.' On one occasion she was reported to have sidled up to a particularly gorgeous hunk of Marine and—having decided he was on the right side of the bar by choice rather than by accident—whispered, 'God, I wish you would change your mind.'"[17]

Circumspection was the secret to success at the Astor Bar. "The approaches were all extremely indirect," a former service member named Burt Miller remembered. "I didn't know what the folkways of gay bars were, so I had to wait till somebody approached me and then I had to try to figure out what the nuance was." Another service member, Ben Small, agreed. "You really had to behave yourself there," he said. "Play like a little gentleman. But you knew that the guy on your right and the guy on your left were gay, and [you went] though all of this nonsensical straight conversation: 'Hi. Where are you stationed? Where do you come from? Where are you staying while you're in town?' 'Well, I'm at the Y.' 'Oh, so am I. I'm in room 222. Drop by for a drink.' And that was the extent of it. There was certainly nobody running up and putting their arms around each other or, the greatest sin of all, groping in public."[18]

Norm Sansom, who had been tossed out of the Army for being gay, happened to work in a shoe store right across the street from the Astor. He would drop in just about every day. "I used to bring the bartenders free nylon stockings, which was like gold!" He laughed. "And so I could have anything I wanted. I never paid for a drink in my life at the Astor Bar."[19]

In fact, the Astor Bar was so well known as a gay meeting place during World War II that the bartenders would even serve as a clearinghouse for messages between gay service members and their friends. The recollection of Joseph "Bud" Robbins, a young sailor who enlisted in June 1944 after graduating high school, paints a picture of what a welcome haven the bar was. He recalled some of his time in the Navy to historian Steve Estes for an oral history project. "As I looked back on it, it was fun. I went into the Navy after having seen *Anchors Aweigh*. And I really thought I was going to sing and dance my way through the service," he said, chuckling at the memory of his naïve younger self. "As Gene Kelly and Frank Sinatra had done. I had that in the back of my head."

Robbins was stationed in Manhattan for a time. "In New York in those days, the Astor Hotel bar was a notorious place for men to meet," he said. "Somehow, I found that out and wandered in there. It was very easy to be picked up by officers, and taken to nice places. . . . I don't think I was blatant," he reflected. "I was so naive, you know. I didn't think I was cute; I didn't think I was good looking. I had pimples, and I was skinny. I was not the kind of person that I would find attractive. I was sort of surprised when people did come on to me."

But not every interaction was so seamless and suave. Robbins remembered another incident that embarrassed him. "This warrant officer saw me standing on the steps of that hotel, the Astor. He came up and talked to me, and wanted to know if we could go to his room. I thought, 'Well sure, why not?' He was sort of butch looking. Anyhow, I fell asleep, and in the morning he was gone, and there was a twenty dollar bill on the dresser." Robbins laughed again, shocked at himself. "I took it down, holding it like this"—he mimed holding something between two fingers, as if it were dirty—"and there were these bell-ringing Santa Clauses on the street. I dropped the twenty in one of their buckets, and I thought, 'Oh my god, I'm a whore.'" He laughed again, amazed. "But you know," he concluded, "I think I was looking more for affection than sex. I never found that while I was in the service. I never did."[20]

"It would be impossible to calculate the contribution of the Astor Bar to the war effort," Paul Forbes concluded after the hotel closed its doors. "Impossible to estimate the number of one-night romances which brought comfort to the tense fighting men and reassured them that the things worth fighting for were still with us."

The Astor Bar's fame extended well beyond "show people" and GIs. Composer Cole Porter, who, though technically closeted, was famously gay to those who knew him, wrote the song "Well, Did You Evah?" for the 1939 musical *Du Barry Was a Lady*. Composed as a duet between two men, the song contains many of the same kinds of coded exchanges with which gay men identified themselves to one another in the 1920s and '30s, such as "You know you're a brilliant fellow? / Thank you / Drink up, chap." And sure enough, there is the Astor Bar, in the line "Have you heard that Mimsie Starr? / Oh, what now? / She got pinched at the Astor Bar . . . Well, did you evah? / Never!"

The line not only memorializes the importance of the Astor Bar to gay life at the time, but also hints at the risks that gay men ran if they didn't adhere to the rules imposed on them in places like the Astor. "Mimsie" in the song lyric was arrested for drawing too much attention to himself, for behaving in an overly campy or "swishy" manner.

One historian writes that "Gay-bar patrons often blamed the swishes and the butches for raids, arrests, crackdowns, and even for society's hatred of homosexuals. 'They're the kind who make it so rough on the rest of us,' explains a technical sergeant to a lieutenant at a gay bar in the war novel *The Invisible Glass*."[21] Bud Robbins, who loved the Sinatra film *Anchors Aweigh*, might have appreciated that one of the best-known versions of "Well, Did You Evah?" was recorded by Bing Crosby and Frank Sinatra for the 1955 film *High Society*. But the song's queer subtext is legendary. The song was also recorded by Debbie Harry and Iggy Pop in 1990 as part of a project to benefit HIV/AIDS research.

The best memorialization of the Astor in song, however, is definitely "She Had to Go and Lose It at the Astor," by Harry Roy and His Band, also from 1939. The song opens with a spoken-word section describing Minnie, a young girl "about 18 years old," and her mother, who tells Minnie she looks beautiful and that, "above all I want you to be very, very careful." The song then launches into its refrain: "But she had to go and lose it at the Astor / She didn't take her mother's good advice / Now there aren't so many girls today who have one / And she'd never let it go for any price." The double entendre continues through several more stanzas, with Minnie searching from the penthouse to the cellar, in every room and under the beds, interrogating all the bellboys and the porter and blaming the chef and the doorman. Finally, the chauffeur finds "it"—Minnie's sable cape. "And she thought that she had lost it at the Astor."

Nominally, the song is, obviously, a winking account about a girl losing her virginity while on a date at the Astor Hotel. Even the choice of a "sable cape" for the lost item in question continues the allusion. But don't let the sex of the song's subject fool you. Even back then, it was not uncommon for gay men to use female pronouns *she/her/hers* and female names as a teasing, affectionate way to refer to other gay men. This practice has its roots in the multiple ways gay people had to try to escape notice from the straight world while still identifying themselves to one another. Gay service members did this as well, sometimes to avoid detection when sending letters to one another during the war. Writes one historian, "Gay male and lesbian GIs and their loved ones . . . used their own secret codes or gay slang, or changed the gender of names and pronouns. Ben Small's boyfriend's name was Don, he explained, 'so I addressed his letter to "D." When I used affectionate terms, there was no way [the military censors would suspect,] because I was just saying "My darling D." and then going on with the letter.'"[22] Another GI, Jerry Watson, told a correspondent of his, "Emphasize the word girls and no one will be the wiser. And if you mean Gene, say Jean, and Joan for John . . . etc."[23] When one knows this, and especially considering the importance of the Astor Bar to young gay servicemen in New York City for the first time and possibly free to explore their sexuality in public for the first time, the song assumes a totally different dimension.

But the final chapter of the Astor Bar was a dark one. In the 1960s, the bar that had been something of a safe space for generations of gay men became a hunting ground. Its reputation among gay servicemen, "show people," and others who had something to lose by being exposed attracted a well-organized and ruthless criminal extortion ring that operated there and in other hotels in New York, Chicago, and elsewhere, before being taken down by the FBI and the NYPD starting in 1965. In the ring's decade of operation, thousands of gay men were extorted in often complex schemes that netted the criminals behind the operation at least two million dollars. Among the victims were Army generals, a Navy admiral, a Republican congressman, a Princeton professor, and a popular performing artist (never identified but long rumored to be Liberace).[24]

The scam was elaborate. A young, sometimes underage, hustler—referred to as a "chicken" in the slang of the time—would zero in on a gay man at the Astor or another gay-friendly establishment and suggest that they go up to a room. Once the two were having sex or about to, burly men in suits claiming to be vice squad detectives—and known as "bulls"—would bust in. They looked the part of legitimate police, complete with badges and official-seeming arrest forms or warrants. Terrified of exposure, the mark would then be pressured to offer a bribe, or "bail money," to avoid being arrested for corrupting a minor, or worse.[25]

Sometimes the bulls would go so far as to "arrest" the mark, drive him to a precinct house, and pretend to go inside to check with the duty captain to see if the charges could be dropped in exchange for a payment. Sometimes the mark would even be taken to night court and seated in the back row. The victim, faced with the loss of his livelihood, reputation, and possibly family, would cave, and the bulls would wait with him until the banks opened in the morning. These brazen methods were chillingly effective. In some instances, the extortionists took men for all they had.

In one particularly tragic case, a married Navy admiral named William Church, who had his identification stolen by a hustler at the Astor Hotel and was shaken down months later, was approached by legitimate investigators who wanted him to help them make their case against the crime ring. Testifying in open court would have cost him his career and his reputation, in addition to opening up his family to shame. Admiral Church agreed to come to New York to speak to investigators off the record, but instead, he drove to a motel in Bethesda, Maryland, checked in, and shot himself in the head.[26]

The extortion scheme was so successful in large part due to rampant homophobia among the police, the press, and the public at large at that time. Scandal sheets like *Confidential* magazine delighted in outing prominent people, sniping about "tearoom arrests," "lavender stripes," and "forbidden satisfactions." For decades, police, too, engaged in entrapment schemes, sending good-looking officers undercover to bathhouses, public restrooms, and gay bars to proposition or tempt the men inside. Extortion by police to keep the secrets of closeted men was so common in the mid-twentieth century that it even had a name: "fairy shaking."[27] The marks at the Astor Bar would, therefore, have had no reason to doubt that the bulls bursting into their rooms were exactly what they presented themselves to be.

Perhaps what is most remarkable about the "Chickens and Bulls" case, as it was called by the NYPD, was that it became a case at all and one that was seriously investigated by the FBI and NYPD and prosecuted by the district attorney. As William McGowan, who uncovered this forgotten story in *Slate* magazine, pointed out, there are two likely reasons it was. The New York Police Department didn't like imposters posing as corrupt police, which hit a little too close to home. And the victims of the extortion ring were white, well-to-do or prominent gay men, people who had connections and were able to command official attention in a way that working-class gay men or men of color could not. It was one of the most publicized instances of law enforcement and prosecutors working to protect gay people from harm rather than punishing them for existing.

In a strange historical footnote, one of the leaders of the Chickens and Bulls extortion ring, a thirty-nine-year-old small-time crook and sometime wrestler named Ed Murphy, worked as the head of security for the Hilton hotel, where some of the extortion took place. Murphy would shave an inch off the doors of the hotel rooms the chickens used, so he could insert a dental mirror through the gap and see the moment when the mark was in a compromising position and the bulls could break in.

Ed Murphy was himself gay, and when he was arrested with a counterfeit detective's shield in his possession, he quickly turned informant, providing details that proved instrumental to bringing down the ring. Murphy would go on to play several other small roles in gay history—including as a bouncer at the door of the Stonewall Inn on the night of the 1969 police raid there that is popularly credited with launching the modern gay rights movement. Murphy was reportedly handcuffed by police to a drag queen named Blonde Frankie, but the two managed to flee in a taxicab to another gay bar farther downtown, where another drag queen, who was reportedly into S&M, and therefore had access to handcuff keys, freed them from their shackles.[28]

By the 1980s, Murphy had reinvented himself as a gay rights activist. He was a fixture at annual Pride parades in New York City and liked to call himself the "mayor of Christopher Street." He died of AIDS in 1989.

On the Astor Hotel's last morning, June 30, 1966, Jerry Buck of the Associated Press reported that the hotel, "which has stood along gaudy Times Square like a maiden aunt for nearly 62 years, calls it quits today." It's a funny image for an institution that famously hosted such frissons of opportunity, sexual possibility, relative safety, and then fear for so many generations of gay men. "It's sad. Any passing is sad," said manager Erwin Schel, who was probably tired of talking to reporters about the dreary old hotel—and of trying to find new ways to sound despondent.

On October 3, 1966, the auctioning of the hotel's interior furnishings began. Everything was on the block—from silver candlesticks to brass lamps to love seats to water boilers from the basement to the furniture from the "Du Barry Suite," which featured a handsome six-piece bedroom set complete with canopied bed that went for only two hundred dollars.[29] Also among the items sold off: a taxidermied moose head, five hundred gravy boats, crystal glasses with the Astor crest, and swizzle sticks by the hundreds. "For the man who has everything," suggested the *New York Times*, "why not the 150-foot-long, U-shaped Astor Bar (guaranteed to have supported George M. Cohan's elbows) or the hotel's registration desk?"[30]

What happened to the actual bar is anyone's guess. The wrecking ball finally swung in 1967, reducing the Astor Hotel to rubble and making way for the sleek glass-and-steel skyscraper that currently stands at One Astor Plaza. Still, for several generations, the bar had served as a gathering place for gay men from all over the city, the country, and even the world—the right side of an oval, which has no sides. It was a universally known queer space that was invisible to anyone unaware of the secret codes used by gay men before Stonewall. But for all those decades, all that time, the name "Astor" meant one thing for gay men: community. And after 1966, all that was left was a memory. "A memory," as Paul Forbes put it, "of what had been a landmark."

11

FERNCLIFF

1952

Of course she married Vincent for the money. I
wouldn't respect her if she hadn't. Only a twisted
person would have married him for love.

—Louis Auchincloss, *quoted in*
The Last Mrs. Astor, *Frances Kiernan*

On January 24, 1932, the front page of the evening edition of the *New York Times* painted a picture of a world teetering on the brink of chaos. Communists were revolting in Spain. The Third Reich had secured enough lines of credit in Germany to expand its economic influence on the international stage. Japanese Marines had landed on Chinese soil and seized several forts in Shanghai. Kidnappings for ransom were so widespread in the United States that the Senate voted to make them a federal offense, punishable by death. And Franklin Delano Roosevelt, governor of New York, declared in North Dakota that it was his "simple duty" to run for president of the United States.[1] He would run as a Democrat, which made him, in the eyes of many of the men he had known at Newport and Harvard, a class traitor. FDR was, after all, from a select stratum of New York society, with deep roots on Lafayette Place and long-standing ties to the Astors. Roosevelt's half brother, Rosy, had married Helen Schermerhorn Astor, one of Vincent Astor's many aunts.

But that January day, Vincent Astor was worried about none of these things. In Miami, far from the frigid New York City winter, he was preparing to depart on an extended cruise to the South Pacific aboard the *Nourmahal*, a voyage he claimed would be in the interest of science. On a similar cruise in 1930, Vincent had brought along Dr. Charles Haskins Townsend, director of the New York Aquarium. They had arrived back in port with passengers that included four-feet-long lizards, a three-hundred-pound turtle, some charming but loud baby sea lions, a flightless cormorant, and many species of tropical fish that had never before been successfully transported alive. In addition to Dr. Townsend, Vincent's guests on that earlier cruise had included scientists from the American Museum of Natural History, the Brooklyn Botanical Garden, and the New York Zoological Gardens. The newspapers had gushed over the trip, and Vincent had basked in their conviction that he really had something to offer the world, something more substantial than his money.

Vincent felt certain this cruise would be even better. They planned to journey first to Havana, and then to traverse the Panama Canal, passing through the Galapagos Islands and into the Pacific Rim, hunting for scientific specimens along the way. But science wasn't the only aim—what Vincent had in mind appears in the log he and his friends kept as the journey began. The log opens with a cartoon about the suspected aphrodisiac Spanish fly and a poem titled "Dr. Holden's Rape Remedy," named for guest Milton "Doc" Holden, Vincent's best friend from childhood. The other passengers included Priscilla "Pris"

Preston, Gertrude Lewis Conaway, and Eleanor Barry, who would keep most of the high-spirited notes of the trip.[2] Not included? Helen Huntington Astor, to whom Vincent had been married for almost two decades.

This was not the first *Nourmahal* to carry Astors, their friends, their pet scientists, their presidents, or their mistresses on voyages to exotic locales. The first *Nourmahal* had belonged to Vincent's grandfather William Backhouse Astor Jr. and was a triple-masted combination sailing and steamship that was notorious in its day for being a place on which William Junior's wife, *the* Mrs. Astor, never deigned to set foot. Their son, Vincent's father, John Jacob "Jack" Astor IV, later owned his own steam yacht the *Nourmahal*.

When Jack Astor went down with the *Titanic*, Vincent became the youngest man in the family's history to assume the role of figurehead to the house of Astor. He was an undergraduate at Harvard when his father died, but he wasn't much of a scholar. An article in *Time* magazine from 1928 remarked that Vincent "tutored valiantly" to enter Harvard, where he was "undistinguished scholastically" and "socially tranquil." His cosseted upbringing had rendered him awkward to the point of being almost socially stunted. One historian quoted a friend of Vincent's who pitied him somewhat. "It's hard to be so rich," the friend said. "His friends were wealthy, but not on the same level. Most people wanted something from him. Even if they had money themselves, they welcomed a free six-month trip on his yacht. . . . Vincent saw this and it made him suspicious of everyone, particularly his family. What could his relatives do right? If they ignored him, that was wrong. If they were nice to him, he wondered if they were after something in his will."[3]

By the time of Vincent's birth in 1891, money had already wreaked its inexorable influence on the Astors. His parents' marriage was famously unhappy, and according to one historian, "Vincent realized early on that his mother could hardly bear the sight of him."[4] In turn, Vincent settled all his filial affection on his father, but Jack was an unpredictable object of his love. When Vincent misbehaved, his father would beat him with a shoe or a strap.[5] Like many of the men in his family, Jack was a poor communicator, with an inclination toward solitude, replacing the normal human interactions of everyday life with retreats into an arcane world of his own invention and largely under his control. Jack's love for his yacht, however, was never in doubt.

Vincent endured a lonely, painful childhood, raised first by an Irish nurse and then by a German governess. He was kept out of the way and always aware of being unwanted. His parents were so choosy about whom he should associate with that he had almost no playmates. He didn't have the boisterous relief of siblings his own age and barely knew his sister, Alice, who was ten years his junior. They never developed a good relationship, even when, as adults, they lived next to each other in Rhinebeck, New York. Vincent always secretly suspected Alice wasn't an Astor but was the product of one of his mother's affairs; by some accounts, he suspected that Alice's father was a Cuban polo player with whom their mother had been involved.[6]

Vincent grew into an awkward young man in his body in addition to his soul. He towered over almost everyone he knew, standing six feet, four inches in his socks, but rather than strapping, he was skinny and hollow-chested, with a receding hairline and an unfortunate upper lip. One of his contemporaries characterized his ungainly physiognomy as an "elongated Neanderthal man."[7]

When, in 1909, Jack Astor announced that he and Ava were getting a divorce and that he intended to marry a woman two years younger than Vincent, the Astor heir responded with something akin to blistering sibling rivalry. He couldn't stand his future stepmother, Madeleine.

He agreed to serve as his father's best man when the wedding finally took place in 1911, perhaps because he knew that if he refused, the only parent whom he had ever really loved would be lost to him.

Sometimes, it may have seemed to Vincent that the ocean had it in for his father. Shortly after his parents finalized their divorce, he went on a cruise with his father on the *Nourmahal*, together with his father's friend H. V. Kaltenborn, through the West Indies. While they were under way, a hurricane tore through Jamaica, and the *Nourmahal* was feared lost. For over a week, newspapers reported breathlessly on the missing yacht, as an entire fleet of ships, including U.S. revenue cutters, a Royal Navy cruiser, a German Navy cruiser, and a few banana boats trawled the waters looking for them. Father, son, and company, it turned out, had docked safely in San Juan, Puerto Rico, cut off from cable communications and blithely unaware that anything was amiss. They'd enjoyed exploring the historic fort and winding streets of Old San Juan in a giant touring car Jack Astor had shipped from New York for that purpose.[8] But in 1912, Jack's oceangoing luck would finally run out.

When news of the *Titanic* disaster hit the wire services, the newspapers reported that Vincent was seen leaving the White Star Line offices weeping. Not yet twenty-one, he was the new scion of the Astor family fortune: immature, unready, and afraid. More than one observer wondered if the strain of the sudden assumption of responsibility was too much for Vincent. On his twenty-first birthday, crowds of people gathered around the Astor family offices to observe the awkward, self-conscious young man who had just become the richest person in America.

Like his father, Vincent found succor in mechanical tinkering, projects well suited to a solitary nature in possession of a big bank account. While still a teenager, he bought himself a Franklin Speedster with an air-cooled engine and devoted himself to its maintenance. "Cheerfully greasy," *Time* magazine recounted, "he dismembered it and screwed it together again."[9] In 1914, when he was twenty-two, he married Helen Dinsmore Huntington, a union that looked right from the outside—she was a society girl who would go on to be a political hostess and patron of the arts, including the opera and the ballet. But the marriage proved to be an unmitigated disaster, not all that different from the pairing of Vincent's parents. The reason for their being so ill-matched is hard to know, though one novelist contemporary of theirs described Helen in his private papers as "a grand, old-fashioned lesbian."[10] Elsewhere, it has been suggested that Vincent married Helen because they had grown up together in Rhinebeck and because he was particularly close to her father. In a family as cold and forbidding as his own, and as lonely, perhaps he was looking for something simple: a surrogate father.[11]

During the wedding ceremony, Vincent began to feel unwell. He was exhausted, feverish, and achy. His jaw felt tender and sore. It's tempting to read in the rebellion of his body some kind of expression of anxiety, or reticence, or unfitness. In the end, his ailment was more mundane; he was diagnosed with the mumps. But the mumps can have a brutal side effect, and it rendered him sterile. On his wedding day, the ominous aches in his body foretold the end of the line for the American Astors. The couple honeymooned on Jack Astor's *Nourmahal*, a feverish and achy journey on a ship owned and loved by Vincent's dead father, on which no more Astors would ever sail.

When the Great War broke out, Vincent turned his attention more deeply to ships, serving in the U.S. Navy as an ensign and then rising to lieutenant. The *Nourmahal* was designed for sleekness and speed, and so Vincent loaned it to the U.S. government to aid the war effort while both he and Helen volunteered.

After the war, he and Helen settled into the uneasy social prominence they had inherited along with Beechwood, the Newport summer palace, from his grandmother Caroline Astor. They didn't take as
full advantage of that prominence as one might expect, though; they
were almost never seen in their designated box—Number 7—in the
"Golden Horseshoe" at the Metropolitan Opera.[12] They lived in Mrs.
Astor's old house on Fifth Avenue, which was still done up entirely in
her style, and passed their weekend days at Ferncliff, the rolling estate in
Rhinebeck that had been built by Vincent's grandfather William Junior
not far from Rokeby, the house his great-grandfather William Senior
had bought. Vincent kept the *Nourmahal* moored close to Beechwood
in Newport, but he began freeing himself from the landlocked ways of
all the Astors before him. He did something that would have been un-
thinkable to the first John Jacob Astor: he started selling off real estate.

Vincent's upbringing was so cloistered that, by some accounts, he
hadn't even known that slums existed in New York City, much less that
Astors owned so many of them. When he discovered the conditions of
so many of the tenants living in properties his family owned, he was
disgusted—becoming the first Astor in four generations to display an
apparent sense of guilt. His agents and property managers, of course,
were surprised by his dismay. But Vincent's awkward exterior concealed a nerdy, perhaps even sentimental soul. He built a playground in
Harlem on Astor land valued at a million dollars. He also provided for
another playground to be built in Central Park, saying it was "better
to have dead grass in the park than sick children in the tenements."[13]

Supposedly, when he heard a rumor that some of the apartment
blocks in his holdings on the West Side were being used as brothels,
he went knocking door-to-door, trying to figure out where they were
so he could shut them down. He even enlisted the premier architecture
firm of fin de siècle New York, McKim, Mead, and White, to build

a convalescent home for children in Dutchess County; it still exists today: the Astor Home for Children.[14] Kids were provided with train fare from Grand Central Station to Rhinebeck and given free clothes and supplies while they stayed in the countryside, breathing healthful air and being taken on boat rides. Vincent served as president, and Helen as secretary.

Within ten years, Vincent had liquidated about half his considerable real estate holdings from the Astor offices.[15] He even unloaded his portion of the Waldorf-Astoria, which he co-owned with his English cousins who had descended from Will Astor. Each branch received $7.56 million in the sale.[16]

Later, according to the *New York Times*, "during the administration of Mayor Fiorello H. La Guardia[,] Mr. Astor sold his remaining slum holdings to the newly organized Municipal Housing Authority for little cash and a long-term low mortgage."[17] The MHA was the forerunner to today's New York City Housing Authority, the administrator of public housing projects in the city.

In the mid-1920s, Vincent decided that Caroline Astor's Fifth Avenue palace was hopelessly outmoded, so he sold it—though he and Helen held a grand farewell ball for descendants of the original Four Hundred, and other guests, including the mayor. The house and the land it stood on sold for $3.5 million, around $60 million in 2022 money. Temple Emanu-El now stands on the site of the last scene of the Astors' Gilded Age splendor.[18]

Vincent and Helen moved into an elegant new house at 130 East Eightieth Street. Inside, Vincent had an exact replica of his father's bedroom constructed, and he transferred the identical bathroom fixtures, changing only the bathtub. (In later years, after the final disappearance of the Astors from the New York scene, this house would be transformed into the headquarters for the Junior League.)

Though Vincent and Helen both had more philanthropic natures than any previous Astor, they otherwise had very little in common with each other and lived completely separate lives. Longtime New York gossip columnist Maury Paul, who wrote for years as "Cholly Knickerbocker," was friendly with Vincent but couldn't stand Helen. His biographer noted that Paul "considered her as cold as marble and as hard to understand."[19] But out of respect for Vincent, he devoted a lot of column space to debunking the rumors that the two were effectively separated, even though everyone knew they were. It was Paul who insisted that all the time the couple spent apart was due to Vincent's love for the *Nourmahal* and Helen's distaste for yachting—not unlike the lie Caroline Astor had told two generations before.

Vincent withdrew into the arcane interests that only those with great wealth can afford. At one time, he maintained a collection of more than thirty automobiles at Ferncliff. He also built his own private miniature train line there, a pleasure project that could carry up to twenty passengers. He loved his train so much that he had a different version constructed at a home he owned in Bermuda. In later life, he built a sprawling, elaborate electric train set in his Manhattan home, and he would play with it after dinner.

In 1928, after reaping some profits from his investment in the 1925 silent MGM film *Ben-Hur: A Tale of the Christ* (at the time, a production with the biggest budget Hollywood had ever seen), Vincent decided it was time for his own *Nourmahal*. He ordered that she be built by the Krupp Iron Works in Kiel, Germany[20] at a cost of about $1 million, or about $17.5 million today. That probably sounds like a lot, but at the time of this writing, Jeff Bezos has just launched a triple-masted, 417-foot sailing yacht at an estimated cost of $500 million. (Truly, we are living in a second Gilded Age.)[21] Even so, Vincent's *Nourmahal* was nothing to sniff at. The plan of the ship sprawled over three decks, one of which even had places for gun mounts in the event of travel to politically unstable areas.[22] When she was finally completed, Vincent's *Nourmahal* would be the biggest oil-burning yacht in the world. Clocking in at 263 feet long, the vessel boasted diesel engines, a top speed of sixteen knots, and a cruising radius of a staggering 19,000 miles.[23] Inside, *Nourmahal* offered her privileged few guests eleven elegantly appointed staterooms, a wood-paneled library, multiple lounges, a dining room that could seat eighteen, and even an emergency operating room. The *Nourmahal* also had full cabins for the officers of the forty-two-man crew that was required to operate and maintain the yacht.[24] A photo album from the yacht's launching in 1929—the same year as the stock market crash that ushered in the Great Depression—shows deep bathtubs, toile curtains, shield-backed chairs, and crystal candlesticks. Behind the double wheels in the stern stretched a semicircular upholstered sofa, perfect for lounging when steering got too arduous.[25]

Unlike the Vanderbilts, whose "Commodore" had gathered his first fortune from plying the waters between Staten Island and Manhattan before he moved into railroads, the Astor wealth had always been tied to the land, either from the animals foraging upon it or from the rents wrung out of its ownership over the centuries. But early on, Vincent had discovered the distinct pleasures of the sea, especially for a man like him: born into a public profile for which he had neither inclination nor, apparently, facility.

"Reporters cannot infest the oceans," *Time* magazine wrote of Vincent's elegant new yacht. "The strain of question and answer to which a public figure is eternally subjected is particularly distasteful to the new commodore [of the New York Yacht Club]."[26] Vincent's new *Nourmahal* would provide the perfect escape. When he was aboard her, no one would take his picture. No one would want anything from him.

Anyone on board with him would be there by his express invitation. She would be his domain, his purview, his floating castle.

The log of Vincent's 1932 cruise makes the whole jaunt sound rife with hijinks, which is in keeping with his sense of humor when in private with his friends. He had a taste for practical jokes that bordered on the pathological. According to one historian, his elaborate preparations for a joke often began long before the scheduled visit. Once, a wealthy businessman joined Vincent for a cruise on his yacht, and when they were three days out at sea, a stock market report came through on the *Nourmahal*'s wireless set: the guest's stocks were plummeting in value. The man spent the next few days in black despair as each report, worse than the one before, revealed his utter ruin. Back on dry land, he discovered that he had been a victim of one of his host's favorite jokes. Vincent, it seemed, had prepared by getting an exact list of his friend's holdings.[27]

At last, all the preparations were finally in place, and the yacht—which Vincent and the merrymakers on board referred to as "Nourmy"—left Miami bound for Havana. While at sea, the guests played a game that likely involved copious amounts of alcohol; they called it "Nourmy tennis—very good for the lungs and the liver."[28] When they arrived in Cuba, the party attended a dinner at an American-run nightclub called Sans Souci after spending the afternoon sunbathing on the yacht club beach. "Lunch at the Country Club was usual," the log remarks, the only unusual thing being the conversation, which only twice wandered from "topic A"—which was probably sex, given the context. Sans Souci, seven miles outside Havana, featured dancing, floor shows with imported American talent, and a side room with a quasi-illegal casino featuring roulette and chemin de fer.[29] The party stayed out dancing until three in the morning. In

Havana, at the time a sexual playground for the yacht-borne American rich, one might never have known that the world outside was on fire.

The *Nourmy* left Havana on January 27, headed for Haiti, which was in the final years of occupation by U.S. Marines. Vincent and his shipmates made it through heavy seas that sent many of them green-faced into their bathrooms. They put in at Port-au-Prince on January 30, where they went ashore to take in some of what they termed "native dancing." "At least that's what they called 'it,' it being a matter of shaking every part of one's anatomy to the beating of two native drums," snarked Eleanor Barry, the writer of the ship's log.[30]

On the last day of January 1932, Vincent and his friends set out for the Panama Canal, following an aircraft carrier that, they noted, was "bound for the Japanese fray," and they arrived in the Galapagos nine days later. Vincent went onshore with Will, Doc, "Gertie," and Eleanor, and the lot of them went scrambling over the island and captured one of the famous swimming iguanas. They whiled away their time shark fishing and then they met and dined with Dr. Friedrich Ritter and his mistress, Dore Strauch, on Floreana Island.

If Vincent's love for the *Nourmahal* was due in part to her distance from all the attention and cares of his landbound life in New York, then he would have been particularly intrigued to meet this odd couple. Dr. Ritter was a married German physician who, in 1929, fell in love with Strauch, who was both married and one of his patients. They ran off together and set themselves up on Floreana, one of the few islands in the Galapagos with a steady supply of potable water, where they built a hut out of volcanic rock and driftwood and lived a hard subsistence life, rarely wearing any clothing. Dr. Ritter claimed that living simply, off the land, away from the corrupting influences of the modern day, would make a person strong. One wonders what he thought as Vincent and his friends and his mistress, all in pith helmets, arrived at Floreana in his yacht with her crew of forty-two.

Vincent's encounter with Dr. Ritter would be one of the most exotic elements of his 1932 voyage. Reported all over the world, it may even have encouraged others to make the journey. Another couple, Heinz and Margret Wittmer, arrived from Germany shortly thereafter and settled on the island as well, bringing along their son. Then came the "Baroness," an Austrian named Eloise Wehrborn de Wagner-Bosquet, who appeared with her two German lovers and an Ecuadorian servant in tow. Perhaps mindful of the *Nourmy*'s recent visit, she planned to build an elegant hotel on Floreana, but in March 1934, the Baroness disappeared with one of her lovers. One of the Wittmers claimed the two had left on a yacht bound for Tahiti, but no such yacht was registered arriving in the Galapagos. A few months later, Dr. Ritter died. The apparent cause was food poisoning, but on his deathbed, he accused Strauch of poisoning him.[31]

In 1932, though, Vincent and his friends might have found the couple romantic. A few days after meeting them, with nothing but the blue horizon on every side, he and his guests celebrated Valentine's Day. Vincent's handwriting appears in a silly joke on a telegram form in block letters: "Miss Barry Curly head—eyes so blue / Figure, Form Divine / Just save up all your vermin / And I'll be your Valentine." He doodled drawings of a spider, a caterpillar, and a bug alongside this goofy love note. They were still at sea, out of sight of land and reporters and news wires, when Doc Holden's birthday rolled around on February 19. They celebrated with a cannibalism-themed party. The celebrants all wore paper hula skirts, and the dinner menu, pasted into the log book, lists "Babies Faces à la Bilge, Sacrificial Blood, Pre-digested Galapagos Tortoise, Roast Rump of a Broker, Old

Corns—Boiled Yahoo, Iced Poo-Poo, and Essence de Negra."[32] Nothing like a little sexually charged racism to liven up a birthday party on a mega-yacht! On February 20 they spent their days bopping around Tahiti, visiting the grave of Gaugin, and Pris Preston broke her arm falling out of a car. The cruise ended in California on March 21, lacking some of the public acclaim Vincent may have dreamed of. It was, in the end, a pleasure cruise for a wealthy forty-one-year-old playboy made "scientific" by "the penguins swim[ming] blithely around Mr. Colson's bathtub." This was how Vincent Astor spent his time in the opening years of the Great Depression.

The following February, a month before he was to be inaugurated for his first term as president, Franklin Delano Roosevelt took a ten-day cruise with Vincent, his cousin by marriage, on the *Nourmahal*. The two men were very close—their Hudson Valley estates bordered one another, and after FDR's bout of polio, he would often use the swimming pool at Ferncliff to exercise. On this particular cruise, they stopped over in Miami, so the president-elect could make a speech. Vincent had a bad feeling about this stopover, but he couldn't put his finger on why.

He and the president rode in a motorcade from *Nourmahal*'s berth to the president's speaking engagement in Bay Front Park, together with several other visiting dignitaries, Vincent two cars behind Roosevelt. While the president-elect was speaking, a bricklayer named Giuseppe Zangara pulled out a gun and shot at him. The bullet missed Roosevelt but struck and instantly killed Chicago mayor Anton Cermak and wounded four onlookers.[33] Zangara was tackled by police, wrestled into submission, and then put on the trunk rack of Vincent's car, with one police officer riding next to him and another standing on the running board. One of the injured men was loaded into the car with Vincent. "Vincent held his head," a historian wrote later, "put a cigarette in his mouth, and tried to soothe him. The wounded man could only mutter over and over again that his wife would not be able to get home, as the car keys were in his pocket."[34]

Despite not being especially suited to politics, Vincent nevertheless found himself interested, perhaps because of his proximity to Franklin Roosevelt's growing political power. Taking a page from Will Astor and his English cousins, Vincent decided to start a newsmagazine to compete with Henry Luce's *Time*. Roosevelt was even his first subscriber, handing over one dollar.[35] The first issue of *Today* was published in October 1933. Not long after that, one of Vincent's partners in the magazine was killed in a riding accident. Vincent took over sole ownership and then absorbed a largely defunct periodical called *News-Week*, eventually merging it with *Today* to make *Newsweek*. It wasn't long, however, before he and his magazine were no longer aligned with FDR's politics. The magazine became known for its harsh criticism of the New Deal.[36] Part of the political falling-out between the two men might even have been traced to the *Nourmahal*. Vincent spent $125,000 a year keeping her crewed, maintained, and ready year-round, and this was during the depths of the Great Depression. When he invited FDR on another cruise later in the 1930s, FDR told him that "if the rich could afford such unnecessary extravagance, perhaps it was time to 'soak the rich.'"[37]

By the end of 1940, Vincent and Helen had finally thrown in the towel on their marriage and divorced. Shortly thereafter, Vincent married Mary Benedict Cushing, called "Minnie," one of a trio of society belles known as the Cushing sisters, but that proved to be as unfortunate a mismatch as his first marriage. By the early 1950s, he was ready to divorce Minnie, but only on the condition that she find him another wife. The first candidate she suggested was Janet Rhinelander Stewart, who had recently divorced her third husband, James Smith Bush, great-uncle to President George W. Bush.

The problem with Janet, however, was she had money of her own and, therefore, no interest in Vincent's proposal. She turned him down with a rejection that lives on in social infamy: "Marry you? I don't even like you."[38] Vincent informed her that he was in poor health and that doctors had told him he was unlikely to live more than three years—to which she reportedly replied, "But, Vincent, what if the doctors are wrong?"[39]

What then, indeed?

Not to be daunted, Minnie soon hit upon another idea. In 1952, a dinner in Manhattan was arranged by some friends, who invited a well-liked widow named Brooke Marshall. Her husband of twenty years, Buddie Marshall, had died just six months before, and this was her first outing since. Brooke was heartbroken over Buddie's death but also fearful about her financial future. Buddie had left her some money, but not enough. She was fifty, and though she had a job—working as an editor at *House & Garden* magazine—it didn't pay well. She would have to sell the house they had lived in and economize. Or, she could find a man with money to marry.

Vincent was, not coincidentally, seated across from her at the dinner, and Minnie was at another table. Brooke was acquainted with Vincent a little bit. They had mutual friends and had crossed paths over the years, but by no means was she in the Astors' inner circle. For instance, neither Vincent nor Minnie had reached out to Brooke to offer their condolences when Buddie died. But as the dinner got under way, over the tinking of silverware against china and the pouring of the wine, Brooke noticed that Vincent was staring at her. "Every time I looked across the table, I found him looking at me in an intense way,"

Brooke wrote later in a memoir. She started to grow alarmed. "I could not understand why he was concentrating on me. What had I ever done to him? I wondered what was wrong with him."[40]

After dinner, he made a beeline for her and asked to speak with her privately in a corner of the room. And so began what has to be one of the looniest courtships in modern history. Vincent apologized for not sending Brooke a condolence note after Buddie's death. "If we were alone I would kneel at your feet," he told her. "Tell me about yourself and Buddie." She did the best she could, describing her marriage matter-of-factly to this man she didn't especially know.

Then Vincent's wife, Minnie, sauntered up and suggested, as the evening was winding down, that they drop Brooke off in their car. As they headed toward Brooke's apartment building on Sutton Place, Minnie brightly offered another suggestion. Why shouldn't Brooke come to Ferncliff for the Memorial Day weekend? Brooke began to feel as though she were caught in a web spun by two rather desperate spiders. *Perhaps they are just rich and bored and looking for new friends*, she thought. She hadn't yet accepted the invitation when they reached her home, but that didn't seem to faze the Astors. "They both called after me as I dashed across the street. 'We will ring you in the morning.'"[41]

Sure enough, the desperate Astors called Brooke bright and early—one right after the other. First was Vincent, who insisted on having tea with Brooke if not that same day, then the next. Then her phone rang again, and it was Minnie, who insisted Brooke also come for the weekend. "The Astors were not close friends, and at the back of my mind I wondered why they were both so keen to have me," she recalled later.[42] She didn't have to wait long to find out.

When Brooke arrived at Ferncliff, she wasn't impressed. Not by the sheer size of the estate, nor by the indoor tennis court where they played croquet, nor by the big hall where they gathered for drinks.

She found it all depressing. "It was really quite hideous," she later wrote, "the furniture was uninteresting . . . the fireplace was filled with ashes and no wood." Her private criticisms didn't stop there. "The only flowers were Easter lilies and hemlock boughs stuffed together in a huge vase on a large table in the middle of the room!" Brooke was shocked, expecting more from an Astor country estate. "I could never live in such a depressing place," she thought.[43]

No sooner had she gone to her room and freshened up than Vincent invited her for a short drive, then quickly pulled over, and proposed. "Minnie wants to leave me," he told her, "and up to now, I have refused to give her a divorce, but now that I have met you, I will give her a divorce if you will marry me."

Brooke couldn't believe her ears. "You hardly know me," she wisely pointed out.

But Vincent had decided he knew enough. "I have never known anyone to have more friends and be more loved and admired than you; and I can swear on the Bible that if you marry me, I will do everything I possibly can to take care of you and make you happy—and earn your love."[44]

Brooke didn't know what to say, but she didn't say no. She asked for some time to think about it. Meanwhile, Vincent left for Japan for two months and began a letter-writing campaign to wear Brooke down. Brooke talked to her friends about Vincent and heard all the tales of his morose behavior, his constant drinking and smoking, and his extracurricular sexual activities on the *Nourmahal* and elsewhere. But then of course there was the money.

Astor told Brooke she'd get $1 million just for marrying him, and another $5 million after the first year.[45]

Brooke would later insist that she wasn't convinced by the money.

She was, she claimed, charmed by the ardent letters Vincent wrote her, sometimes five a day, each of which he would mail to a different post office in the Berkshires, where Brooke had a home. He explained that this had something to do with his having worked with the FBI and Naval Intelligence.[46] Despite the inconvenience of having to drive around all day picking up mail, Brooke said she found his missives "beguiling." "I don't think I would have married Vincent if it had not been for these letters," she later wrote.[47] Even her closest friends, however, had their doubts.

"She was too much of a lady to take all that from him and then say he was a real monster, so she couldn't do that," Annette de la Renta told me recently, "but I never heard anyone say a nice word about Vincent Astor."[48] *Repulsive* was the word her friend, writer Louis Auchincloss, used when describing Vincent to a reporter from *New York Magazine*."[49]

Vincent's letters may have eased Brooke's doubts, but the prospect of his money certainly helped. It usually does. Vincent didn't have to wait long for her answer. Brooke accepted his proposal by mail, and months later he changed his will, giving her five million dollars and Ferncliff, the house she had found so depressing.[50]

Vincent's largesse, however, did not extend to Brooke's only son, to whom he took an instant dislike. His name was Anthony Marshall, but he was known as Tony, and at twenty-nine was already a grown man. "Vincent was very jealous of me and any time I would spend with her," Tony later recalled. "He didn't want us to see each other."[51] And what Vincent wanted, Vincent got. Tony was allowed to attend their wedding in 1953, but he saw his mother only two more times in the five and a half years she and Vincent were married.[52]

Brooke Astor would later write that the long separation from Tony was hard on her, but that pleasing Vincent was paramount. "I concentrated on Vincent. It was what he longed for and needed desperately and it was what I had to give. I made that gloomy house into a cheerful, attractive *home*."⁵³

There was one bright spot, as Brooke saw it. Vincent took a shine to Tony's young twin sons, Philip and Alec, who were born the same year Brooke and Vincent married. As the twins grew from babies into rambunctious little boys, they were often invited to visit without their parents. Vincent, perhaps feeling keenly the lack of any Astor heirs, apparently liked the children so much that he wanted to take them from Tony and their mother and raise them with Brooke. "He said that he thought that we should adopt them as we 'had more sense than their parents,'" Brooke wrote, "but I never broached this subject to Tony or his wife as I knew quite well what the answer would be." She may not have wanted to offend her son and daughter-in-law by bringing it up, but she did include the anecdote in the memoir she published in 1980, when Philip and Alec were twenty-seven and old enough to read it.⁵⁴

By marrying Vincent Astor, Brooke was suddenly catapulted into a world of wealth unlike anything she had ever imagined. Private planes, serious jewels—there were few limits to the things and people she could collect. But she was often lonely, and catering to the whims and moods of America's richest man was exhausting.

Vincent's difficult and awkward character frequently expressed itself as paranoia. He didn't permit Brooke to speak on the telephone when he was home, which was most of the time. Brooke loved parties, but Vincent hated them, allowing her to throw only one big bash, when they were married. He was also extremely jealous, although Brooke quickly learned that Vincent, in her words, "sought solace" with other women, which she naturally found "upsetting and humiliating." Upon this discovery, she went to her room and wept, writing "how foolish I had been to believe in those love letters!" She said nothing to Vincent, however. "I had the sense not to make a scene; Vincent would neither have forgiven nor forgotten."[55]

Brooke was, it seems, willing to put up with anything. Vincent drank constantly. Tony's first wife, Elizabeth Cryan, described what she had seen on one of her few visits to Ferncliff. "At ten-thirty a.m. the sherry came out. Before lunch the martinis came. Wine with lunch. At five o'clock the scotch came out, and then everyone went and changed for dinner. Dinner was martinis and wine, and liquor afterward." She pointed out that this was on top of all the medication Vincent was taking.[56]

Despite the copious amounts of alcohol and cigarettes Vincent consumed, he did manage to live longer than the three years he'd predicted to Janet Newbold. Brooke had to put up with Vincent for five and half years before he suddenly died of a heart attack in their New York City apartment in 1959. He was sixty-seven.

All of Brooke's hard work was, in the end, amply rewarded. There had been rumors the two were considering divorcing, but his will was clear. Vincent's estate was worth about $130 million, and Brooke got nearly everything. His bequests to her included a $60 million trust fund, the income from which could be used for her living expenses. She was also named president of the $60 million Vincent Astor Foundation, which he had started in 1948 with the vague mission of "the alleviation of human misery" and the specific mission of avoiding inheritance taxes.[57] Brooke also received $2 million in cash, together with Vincent's valuable real estate portfolio: their apartment in New York City, Ferncliff, and houses in Maine and Arizona. According to Alice Perdue, who worked in Brooke Astor's office for years, "the cash and personal property are what grew into what was in 2007, at the time of her death, her estate of about $130 million (investments and property)."[58]

Vincent's death was an extraordinary turn of events, not just in Brooke's life, but also in the history of the Astor family. The fortune that had been watched over and cultivated by generations of Astor men—that had been created by John Jacob Astor, who'd callously torn it out of the wilderness and the hands of debtors who held leases on his New York properties—had been handed over entirely to a woman, someone who was not even an Astor by blood.

But before Brooke could begin to reinvent what the name "Astor" meant in the minds of many New Yorkers, she had to rid herself of one more actual Astor: John Jacob "Jakey" Astor VI, Vincent's half-brother, the famous "*Titanic* Baby." Vincent did not leave Jakey anything in his will; nor did he give anything to Jakey's son, Vincent's only nephew, William Backhouse Astor III. Jakey sued Brooke in surrogate court, demanding half of Vincent's fortune. Brooke, however, did not blink. To her way of thinking, she'd earned that money by staying married to a difficult and demanding man, and she wasn't about to give any of it up. She'd had too many reversals of fortune in her life to do that again. She was Mrs. Vincent Astor, and his money was now hers.

If you are wondering why Jakey Astor needed money, it turns out he hadn't been in his father's will—not by name, anyway—when the *Titanic* sank. When Jack Astor married his young wife, Madeleine, he set up a five-million-dollar trust for any children he might have with her. Had he lived to see the birth of his second son, he might have rewritten his will to divide his estate more equitably between the two boys—or so Jakey asserted. Jakey had inherited the five million dollars, but that was nothing compared to what Vincent had gotten. He had no legal right to Vincent's money, but that didn't mean he couldn't try to claim one.

Jakey said that Vincent was "mentally deficient" and "suffering from senility and was lacking in testamentary capacity" when he changed his will while in a hospital in 1958. He accused Brooke of using "improper conduct and undue influence" to manipulate his half-brother.[59] In surrogate court in Poughkeepsie, New York, his attorneys accused Brooke Astor of enabling Vincent's alcoholism and even supplying her husband with liquor while he'd been hospitalized, which Brooke readily admitted to under oath.

"Did you know that Vincent had liquor in his room at the New York Hospital?" Jakey Astor's attorney asked her.

"Yes, I did." she said, "I brought it there. We always had a drink in the evening."[60] Brooke insisted that her husband was not senile and knew exactly what he was doing with his money. She was also quite clear during a pretrial hearing why she thought Vincent had left nothing to Jakey. "He thought he was the most useless, worthless member of society and he despised him because he was a slacker and a draft evader,"[61] she said.

Before the case ever went to trial, both sides agreed to settle. She gave Jakey $250,000, which was nothing to her and he was quick to take. History doesn't record much about him after the lawsuit, though. He lived another forty years and had a series of messy marriages and divorces. He died in Miami in 1992. "People say that the British Astors are a branch of the family," Jakey Astor was quoted as saying after his battle with Brooke was settled. "That is no longer true. Today they are the trunk and we are the branch."[62]

With John Jacob Astor VI bought off, Brooke now had the name, the fortune, and the foundation, and she set about remaking all three as her own. The last act of the Astor family drama in America was about to begin.

12

THE LAST ASTOR

2013

Altogether the American Astor Family in its fifth generation
would have made the original John Jacob turn in his grave.

—Cleveland Amory, Who Killed Society?

"I miss home," Tony Marshall said faintly, though it wasn't clear if he was speaking to himself or to one of the three parole board members gathered by his hospital bed. A tube was pushing oxygen into his nose to help him breathe. He couldn't remember exactly how long he'd been locked up at the Fishkill Correctional Facility. A month? But then he'd fallen and was brought here, to a real hospital. That had been, what, maybe three weeks ago?[1]

It was August 21, 2013, and this meeting was important. Tony's lawyers had made that very clear. This was his chance to get out, to stay alive. No one thought he would survive his sentence. One to three years—they might as well have given him life. He was eighty-nine years old. When his mother, Brooke Astor, was that age, she was still going out every night to dinners and parties, but Tony—as had been

made clear to him by everyone his whole life, including his mother—
was no Brooke Astor.

He had quadruple bypass surgery in 2008, and during his trial in
2009, he suffered a stroke. Now he was racked with Parkinson's, con-
gestive heart failure, and an endless list of aches and pains.[2] He couldn't
stand without support or walk more than a few paces without getting
dizzy. His damned fingers couldn't even manage the buttons on his
shirts without help.

His attorneys had filed a request for "compassionate release," a
medical parole, soon after he was locked up.[3] That's why this man and
these two women from the parole board were there, gathered around
him. They'd read his file and the letters his friends had sent on his
behalf. Now he had to answer their questions.

"Do you recall the allegations that led to your conviction?" one
of them said.

"I remember it," Tony said without hesitation, "all too well."[4] He
still had some fight left in him.

He bitterly remembered the allegations made by Philip, his own
son, and the betrayal by his other boy, Alec, who had done nothing
to warn him about the forces Philip was marshaling against him.
Philip, backed by Brooke's wealthy friends, had filed a legal petition
for guardianship, claiming that Tony was taking advantage of his
mother, stealing her money, forcing her to live in filth. "Elder abuse"
Philip's lawyer had called it.[5] The headlines had been awful. Tony was
the "'Evil' Son,"[6] his wife, Charlene, "Astor's Hayseed Daughter-In-
Law."[7] Wherever they went, they were chased by packs of reporters
and photographers.

Tony had looked after his mother's money since 1979 and thought
he'd done a damn fine job of it. He often told people the only thing
Brooke knew about money was how to spend it or give it away.

According to him, when he started managing her affairs, she had only $19 million, and she now had $82 million.[8] Not exceptional given the length of time he'd been overseeing her personal account, but he claimed that no one appreciated how much he had saved her. He'd been paid only a fraction of the fee a professional money manager would have charged, and he had caught all sorts of waste. There was that famous designer who, Tony claimed, had double-billed his mother for a dress, just to choose one example. It took Tony months of letters back and forth, but he'd gotten her money back, and he was proud of it.[9] How could they think he would ever do anything to hurt her?

"My mother loved me," he had tried to explain to a reporter from *New York Magazine* shortly before the indictments against him were announced, hoping perhaps to influence public opinion, if not the district attorney. That's why, in 1998, she had given him a duplex apartment of his own, on Seventy-Ninth Street, not far from hers.[10] Also the car and driver, and then the cash bonus, five million dollars, in 2003, and Cove End, the house in Maine that she loved, which she signed over to him. It was only natural that his mother would want to reward him for his hard work on her behalf. Why wouldn't she want to make up for all the time they had lost over the years, time she'd given to Vincent, or her foundation, or her causes?

"She loved me in many different ways throughout the years," Tony insisted to the skeptical reporter. "She loved me by giving me gifts, whether monetary or an object or Cove End. She also loved me because she included me in trips."[11] But the more he tried to explain to the reporter, the sadder it sounded. The more he protested that his mother had loved him, the more he couldn't escape the truth that most sons don't even have to ask.

"Do you want to explain what happened?" one of the parole board members asked him.

Tony said, "No."

He hadn't spoken at the trial or the sentencing. They had just wanted to see him grovel. His wife, Charlene, was his rock. She sat there in court every day, in the second row, behind him, trying to keep her composure while listening to prosecutors and witnesses recount all those terrible things his mother had said about her to her friends, calling her "that bitch," saying she had "no class and no neck."[12] And then there were the snide things Brooke had whispered about Tony. He'd been stoic and silent. You just have to press on. That's what he'd always done.

His son Alec had written to the sentencing judge about his concerns for his father in prison, and the judge urged Tony to "receive your son back into your life, before it is too late."[13] But Tony couldn't do it. He hadn't spoken with Alec or Philip in years. He had written them out of his will, and their children, too. Some betrayals are too deep to heal. Now, lying here alone in this horrid hospital bed, he had no one except for Charlene.

"If you had to do it all over again, would you have done things differently?" one of the parole board members asked gently.

"Quite," Tony replied.

Of course he'd made mistakes. He should never have given himself that bonus in 2005. How much had it been for, $2.4 million over two years? Well, as he recalled it, his mother's accountant had come up with that number, not him.[14] But still . . .

"In retrospect . . . it doesn't look good," Tony had confessed to the reporter. "If mother was interested in financial details," he'd continued, "I'm sure she would have agreed."[15] He shouldn't have said that last bit; it didn't sound right. But it was true: he hadn't talked with her about it. She was never interested in financial details, even when she was still able to speak. But she wasn't really able to talk much by then.

Did they think he had wanted to end up like this? Disgraced.

Shamed. It seemed incredible, now that he was a prisoner both of the state and of his own failing body, that there was a time when he was young and healthy and almost free. But with a mother like Brooke, Tony was destined never to be quite free.

He had tried to create a meaningful life for himself. He'd done everything a young man of his generation and class was supposed to. He'd prepped at the Brooks School. Joined the U.S. Marines in 1942. Stormed the beaches at Iwo Jima and had a Purple Heart to show for it. Then he'd gone to college at Brown, and later, he became an ambassador. No matter how the press tried to minimize his accomplishments, they couldn't take that away from him.

"Do you have any regrets about what you did?" another parole board member broke in. Even after all that had happened, on some level Tony still couldn't believe that when these people looked at him, they didn't see a gentleman with a distinguished career in public service. They saw a swindler.

"Well, regrets, naturally," he allowed.[16]

He had played the hand he was dealt. And if he was honest, Tony would say that his hand hadn't been as easy as it probably seemed. His father, Brooke's first husband Dryden Kuser, had been a mean and abusive drunk. Tony was relieved when Brooke divorced him and married Buddie Marshall. Tony liked his stepfather, even taking his surname when he turned eighteen. But Buddie didn't have much time for his stepson. And Tony's mother always put whichever man she was seeing ahead of him. She certainly seemed to have no problem ignoring Tony for the five and a half years she was married to Vincent Astor.

He would never say so to anyone, except maybe Charlene, but Tony knew that while his mother certainly loved him in her own way—didn't she?—she maybe hadn't *liked* him all that much. Even now, as an eighty-nine-year-old man, a grandfather to grandchildren he refused to see, some part of Tony was still a sad, lonely little boy wondering why he couldn't have gotten even a fraction of the attention his mother had so willingly lavished on men who didn't deserve it.

The judge had seemed sympathetic at the end. "I do believe that she did love you, Mr. Marshall," Justice A. Kirke Bartley Jr. said in court, "and your acts notwithstanding, I do believe that you loved your mother."[17]

Tony told the parole board members gathered around his hospital bed the same thing he had told that *New York Magazine* reporter. He loved his mother. He told them she was an "extraordinary person"— which was certainly true, but extraordinary is rarely easy, and being Brooke Astor's son had been many things, but easy was not one of them.

For Brooke, nothing with Tony had been easy, either. She was only twenty-two years old and had already been unhappily married to Dryden Kuser for five years when she gave birth to her only baby in 1924. She'd met Dryden when she was seventeen, at his Princeton prom, and was smitten. He looked into her eyes as they held each other nervously on the dance floor. None of the other boys had done that. It was enough to make up for his atrocious dancing.

"I should have been warned by this," she wrote later. "He lacked rhythm—a very important lack."[18] Somehow, Dryden and his parents convinced Brooke's mother that marriage was a good idea. The fact that the former were wealthy and prominent, and Brooke's family was only respectably middle class, no doubt helped. But the marriage was a disaster. Brooke had no idea how sex was supposed to work, and Dryden was demanding and demeaning. He also turned out to be a gambler, a philanderer, and an abusive drunk. When she was six months pregnant, Dryden broke her jaw.[19] It was Dryden who finally asked for a divorce. Lucky for Brooke, he'd fallen in love with someone else. Tony was just five, but his father had never shown any interest in him, and after the divorce, he rarely saw his son at all, reaching out only when he wanted something. Tony's defense lawyers told the court that "Mr. Kuser called his son from his deathbed—to ask for a bottle of Scotch."[20]

The ten years Brooke spent with Dryden Kuser were unspeakable, but then came stockbroker Buddie Marshall, and as Brooke later wrote, "It was a revelation to me that life could change from complete chaos to order and serenity."[21] They would be together for twenty years, a period Brooke described as the happiest of her life, especially once they unloaded eleven-year-old Tony at boarding school.[22] Brooke claimed Tony was "getting spoiled" living in the enormous penthouse apartment she and Buddie had moved into at 10 Gracie Square and summering with them in Portofino.[23] Boarding school, she decided, would be the solution, and Buddie wholeheartedly agreed. Brooke didn't write much more about her son in her memoir, but she did mention, more than once, that he was a "wretched" student.[24]

Brooke knew on some level that Tony was lonely and unhappy. But as journalist Meryl Gordon has pointed out, Brooke's "feelings toward her son were blunted by her rage toward his father. She knew it and felt guilty, but she could not help herself."[25] She hated Dryden Kuser.[26] The specter of his physical violence and emotional and sexual terror overwhelmed Brooke whenever she thought about Tony, the one tangible reminder of that wretched period in her life. The only way for her to leave all that behind was for her to bracket Tony off, treating him as an afterthought.

The two didn't even spend school holidays together. Instead, Tony often went to stay with Brooke's parents, whom he adored. He especially loved Brooke's father, who'd been commandant of the U.S. Marine Corps. In his last year at boarding school, when Tony chose to follow in his grandfather's footsteps and enlist, he used his stepfather's last name, "Marshall," instead of his legal name, "Kuser." Brooke said Buddie Marshall was touched by the gesture, but apparently not enough to go ahead and adopt Tony.

Initially, it seemed to Brooke that whatever her shortcomings as a mother might have been, Tony was turning out just as he ought. While at Brown, he'd married a perfectly nice girl from Pennsylvania, had the boys, and then served with the CIA for a few years. Luckily for him, he was not wholly dependent on his salary to make his life. When Brooke divorced Dryden Kuser, her attorney insisted on a trust fund for Tony as part of the settlement. Brooke received alimony payments from Dryden, and when she remarried, the alimony was directed into the trust for Tony.[27] Both Dryden and Brooke, however, came to regret the arrangement.

Dryden gambled away much of his money and ended up suing Tony to get the trust fund back; he failed. And when Buddie Marshall's career took a downturn, Brooke repeatedly pressured Tony to give her money to buy jewelry, and, once, to install a swimming pool at their country house.[28] Nevertheless, with the help of the trust fund, Tony was able to begin to step out from under his mother's considerable shadow.

But then Buddie died, and Brooke married Vincent, and quite unexpectedly, her shadow lengthened.

With Vincent's fortune, and the help of some talented public relations and philanthropic advisers, Brooke reinvented herself and her life—and rehabilitated the meaning of the name "Astor." By the late 1960s, she had established herself as *the* Mrs. Astor redux.

Tony, however, felt thwarted. He had left the CIA and tried his hand at some businesses in Africa, but nothing much had come of that, and he turned to his mother for help to kick off what he hoped might be an exciting new diplomatic career.

Brooke reached out to her friend Nelson Rockefeller, who was then governor of New York and who would go on to serve as vice president under Gerald Ford in 1974. Brooke had backed Rockefeller and donated heavily to Richard Nixon's 1968 campaign as well, so as a favor to her, Tony was appointed ambassador to Madagascar in 1969. It was not exactly a plumb posting, but at least it was out of the way, and how much damage could he do?

Apparently, quite a bit. Tony was accused of plotting a coup and was declared persona non grata by the Madagascan government. He was hastily reassigned to the U.S. embassy in Trinidad and Tobago, which was certainly pleasant—the islands were sunny and warm—but not a sign that he was on the diplomatic fast track. After a few years in the Caribbean, and more costly donations by his mother and Tony to Nixon's reelection campaign, he was given a higher-profile posting, in Kenya. But it all ended when Gerald Ford failed to win reelection, and in 1978, a fifty-three-year-old Tony washed ashore in New York looking for something to do. And once again he leaned on his mother and her connections.

Brooke tried to get him a position in charge of the Bronx Zoo, but that didn't happen. Next, she called in all her considerable social favors to pressure the trustees of the Metropolitan Museum of Art to name him the museum's president. She had recently made a big donation to the Met, with the creation of the Astor Chinese Garden Court, but even that wasn't enough. The board wanted nothing to do with Tony.

"She was furious at us, at all the board, when we said no, furious, furious," Annette de la Renta, who at eighty-three still serves on the Met board, told me when we met recently to talk about Brooke and the

Astor legacy. "She'd just given the Chinese galleries, and she thought, 'Maybe I'll put him there, and it will make him happy,' but nothing would ever make him happy. He was just an unhappy person. He was whiny all the time. And he was bitter because he felt his mother really only ever loved one man. She loved Buddie Marshall."[29]

Unable to pawn him off on a cultural institution, Brooke finally asked Tony to oversee her personal investments. She gave him an office he could go to in the suite used by her bookkeeper, Alice Perdue, and the employees of the Vincent Astor Foundation. For Tony, it was a strange position to be in. He'd seen combat, worked at the CIA, and headed embassies around the world, and now here he was, without an identity of his own. No man wants to find himself in his mid-fifties, still beholden to his mother, sometimes invited to her cocktail parties (though rarely to her intimate seated dinners for friends) or asked to fill a seat at this or that charity event, always one step behind Brooke, like a courtier to a queen. It was emasculating—and only made more so by his mother's constant belittling of him.[30]

Others saw how Brooke spoke to Tony. Alice Perdue later wrote, "As much as I revered Mrs. Astor, I certainly saw many instances of her disregard for her son's feelings. She didn't seem to realize how hurtful she could be to him. It was uncomfortable, for instance, to hear her say . . . she couldn't spend Christmas with her family because they all were in heaven—while Mr. Marshall was sitting there listening to her. He was family, wasn't he? He must have resented that. . . . Couldn't she have cushioned that and many other comments about him?"[31] Apparently, she could not.

By 1981, when I first met her at Mortimer's, Brooke Astor was relishing her role as the society doyenne par excellence. As head of the Vincent Astor Foundation, she doled out money to all manner of New York institutions and charities, large and small. "You are going to have a hell of a lot of fun running it, Pookie," Vincent had promised her before he died in 1959, and she certainly did.[32] Always perfectly dressed in Chanel suits with her wide brimmed hats, her gloves and pearls, she'd invite the press to ride along as she dropped in on housing projects and homeless shelters to check on how her money was being spent. Sometimes her friends would express mild surprise that Brooke dressed in the same Upper East Side suit of armor for a trip to an uptown housing project that she would have worn for a board meeting at the Metropolitan Museum of Art, but she dismissed these concerns out of hand. "If I go up to Harlem or down to Sixth Street, and I'm not dressed up or I'm not wearing my jewelry, then the people feel I'm talking down to them," she told a reporter. "People expect to see Mrs. Astor, not some dowdy old lady, and I don't intend to disappoint them."[33]

By the late 1980s, Tony had divorced the mother of his two children, Elizabeth Cryan, and was married to his second wife, Thelma Hoegnell, who had been his secretary, but their marriage had been rocky for some time. In 1989, however, something quite amazing happened. Tony Marshall fell wildly in love while summering at Cove End, his mother's house in Northeast Harbor, Maine. He was sixty-five, and the woman he'd fallen for, Charlene Gilbert, was forty-three. To complicate things, Charlene was already married and had been for more than twenty years—to the minister of Mrs. Astor's church in Maine. When her and Tony's affair was discovered, the small town was engulfed with the scandal, which only intensified when they both filed for divorce from their spouses, and Charlene left her three teenage children behind to move to New York. Tony and Charlene married in 1992, and by all accounts he adored her, but Brooke could never stand her.

Over the next few years, some friends began to notice that Brooke was forgetting things. She was in her early nineties, so this was to be expected, but Brooke noticed it as well, and it concerned her enough that when she was ninety-four, she decided to step back from the foundation. By then she'd handed out some two hundred million dollars to charitable organizations all over New York City, which only seemed right, as that was where John Jacob Astor had clawed out the family's fortune. The Astors had made New York, just as New York had made the Astors. Their rise and the rise of the city were inextricably linked, a marriage that had lasted for more than two hundred years. And with her largesse, Brooke Astor paid the city back for at least some of the misery from which so many generations of Astors had profited.

But it wasn't clear what she would do with the foundation.

According to Meryl Gordon, "for decades [Brooke] had dangled before her son the possibility that he would inherit her role."[34] Brooke knew that handing Tony the reins of the Vincent Astor Foundation would have given him tremendous social cachet; the purse strings were considerable and connected to every cultural institution in New York that mattered. As the foundation's head, Tony would no longer have been in his mother's shadow. He would have been the one courted and fêted just as Brooke had been. As for his wife, Charlene would have achieved the social prominence and access Tony wished for her. Their positions would have been secured.

Brooke decided not to let that happen.

The truth was Tony had always been a disappointment. "He was so unfortunate that I decided not to have any more," she had once confessed to a friend, and not a particularly close one.[35] Any more *children*, she meant. And she didn't. One and done. "My son is nothing like me," she had complained to another friend, "All he wants is money, money, money, and I don't know what he's going to do with this money."[36]

In 1996, Brooke announced she would dissolve the Vincent Astor

Foundation entirely. She gave an interview to the *New York Times*, with Tony by her side, and explained to the reporter why he was never going to be good enough. "My son is not an Astor," she said. "There is no family to leave it to. If you have children, like the Rockefellers did, you leave it to your children. If you have no children, I think it's a nice idea to close it."

The reporter asked Tony how he felt about that.

"I would hate to second guess 'Is this something that my mother would like to give to,'" Tony said.[37] It was, at best, a diplomatic answer, but the words must have tasted bitter on his tongue. By December 1997, she had given away the foundation's remaining $24 million.

Had she ever planned on rewarding Tony with the foundation? "No!" Annette de la Renta told me emphatically. "She wanted him as far away from the Astor legacy as she could possibly keep him."[38]

His mother did buy him a $2.9 million duplex apartment on East Seventy-Ninth Street, however, and over time, his salary as her financial manager had grown to about $450,000 a year.[39] But he was rubbing shoulders with people who had much more than he did, and he had serious concerns about what would be left for Charlene should anything happen to him. He also knew exactly how much his mother had and that the majority of her money was going to charity, not to him.

Tony was set to receive plenty, but he would never touch what remained of the Astor fortune. According to Meryl Gordon, he was to inherit Brooke's "Park Avenue apartment (later valued at $46 million); Holly Hill, a sixty-five-acre property in Upstate New York, that could be developed; Cove End (worth $7 million); a $5 million bequest; and a yearly payment of $4.2 million for life, which represented a percentage of a trust."[40] But there was no telling if he would outlive his mother. The two were, after all, only twenty-two years apart in age, and Tony wasn't young. He'd already had a heart attack, and he was well aware—and his wife no doubt reminded him—that if he died before his mother, everything she'd willed to him would go to charities instead. Charlene would get nothing.

When Brooke was ninety-eight, Tony arranged for her to be tested by Dr. Howard Fillit, a geriatrician and neuroscientist at Mount Sinai.[41] She was reluctant to go, and when Tony showed up to accompany her to the appointment, she said, according to him, "You only want to come to see how soon I will die."[42] Unfortunately, her worst fears were confirmed: Alzheimer's. She couldn't copy a simple drawing of a clock, or remember a series of words in order.[43] "You have to have a pretty bad memory not to remember three words," her doctor would later testify in court.[44]

Tony only shared his mother's diagnosis with Charlene, his two sons, Brooke's butler, and her attorney, Terry Christensen. He did something else, however, that would prove to be a huge mistake when it was discovered years later during the legal battle over her guardianship: he wrote Dr. Fillit a seven-page letter about his mother's decline, going into detail about her struggles with writing, spelling, and math.

"I feel like I'm losing my mind," he reported Brooke telling him. "She is delusional at times having asked me, 'Are you my only child?'" he wrote.[45] Was he a son grieving his mother's decline, unburdening himself of the pain he was feeling to the only audience with whom he believed he was able to share it? Or was he a calculating man establishing a paper trail of concern regarding his mother's mental capacity, in the event that he needed to challenge any changes she attempted to make to her will that would further erode his inheritance? Perhaps he was both.

The letter, dated December 26, 2000, would become a crucial piece of evidence.

In January 2002, Brooke Astor did make a change to her will: Tony would still inherit Cove End, but his mother stipulated that she wanted him to give it to his son Philip when he died, not to Charlene.[46] The capriciousness of this worried Tony, and rankled him, too, as it ensured that everyone would be ever eager to stay in Brooke's good graces. When Tony got wind of that, Terry Christensen would later testify, he had been furious, saying, "I won't have [Philip] breathing down my neck and waiting for me to die. I'll do the right thing, but I can't have that."[47]

Despite her failing memory, Brooke maintained a busy social schedule, and she worked hard to keep up appearances. A lifetime of training had taught her well. Brooke always had amusing anecdotes at the ready if she got confused, and when she was stuck for a name, as she increasingly was as the years went on, an airy "Darling, so good to see you" would do just fine.

Tony told his mother she needed cash. He convinced her to sell her favorite Childe Hassam painting, *Flags, Fifth Avenue*, which she had bought in 1971. The painting had hung in her red lacquered library, above the marble fireplace, ever since. The room was designed by Albert Hadley, with brass-fitted bookcases filled with Vincent's collection of leather-bound first editions. The Hassam painting was the centerpiece, though, and she loved showing it off to visitors.[48]

Fifth Avenue had been the site of all the Astors' greatest triumphs, and Hassam had painted the work in 1918, shortly after the United States joined the fight in the Great War. The painting showed Fifth Avenue festooned with the flags of Great Britain, France, and the United States billowing over an excited crowd of people and a blur of automobiles on one of those perfect, crisp sunny days when everything in New York seems full of promise. Brooke was sixteen years old then, just coming into the bloom of her youth. She still remembered flashes of those intoxicating days, one year before her dreadful first marriage, globetrotting with her parents, whom she adored. Mrs. Astor had pledged the painting to the Metropolitan Museum of Art in her will. She'd told its director,

Philippe de Montebello, of her promise. The Met was counting on it, an American masterpiece, a vital portrait of New York City for the most important museum in New York. "Tony wanted me to sell the painting because I'm running out of money," Brooke confided to Annette de la Renta.[49] Brooke's son had gotten ten million dollars for the work from a dealer, who then sold it to someone else for a reported twenty million. Brooke didn't know about that, nor about the two-million-dollar commission Tony had given himself on the sale. To reduce the capital gains tax owed, he had also lied to the Internal Revenue Service about how much his mother had originally paid for the painting.[50]

Brooke replaced the Childe Hassam in the library with a portrait of her father in his U.S. Marine Corps uniform, and for a time, she continued to greet visitors there, under his watchful eye. Years after her death, and once the battle over her estate was resolved, the contents of this beloved room would go on the auction block at Sotheby's: Vincent's books, the Van Cleef and Arpels carved-ivory Indian elephant with inlaid emeralds and rubies, and even the Chinese bronze figurine of a buffalo were put on display for a standing-room-only sale that lasted for two days.[51] The money went to charity.

When in March 2002 Brooke turned one hundred, all of New York society, and much of the media world as well, unrolled like a red carpet at her elegantly shod feet. Her friends organized a gala for the occasion. It was held at David Rockefeller's estate, Pocantico Hills, in Westchester. The ballroom of the Playhouse, as the house was called, was lit with soft fairy lights. Elizabeth King Farrell, who, the *New York Times* had once said, could "make topiaries, vinegars, or petit fours that look like Wedgewood china as easily as others make instant coffee," was enlisted to prepare the food and took charge of filling the room with flowers.[52] Brooke wore the most exquisite ice-blue evening gown, designed by her dear friend Oscar de la Renta, with lavish pleated ruffles at the wrists. She chose jewels befitting an Astor: heavy, glinting diamond earrings and a double-stranded choker strung with pearls as big as Bing cherries. A diamond brooch winked from just below her collarbone.

Everyone was there: Henry Kissinger, Kofi Annan, Barbara Walters. The president, George W. Bush, wasn't able to attend, but his congratulatory letter was read aloud. The only photographer was the *New York Times*'s fashion beat reporter Bill Cunningham, whose discretion and gentleness Brooke had always admired. That evening, she loved sipping wine while listening attentively to all the speeches in her honor. Everyone laughed when she bossily told David Rockefeller to "Stand up!" so that he could be acknowledged. The Café Carlyle's Bobby Short played show tunes and Big Band numbers. Brooke's only regret was that her body wouldn't let her dance anymore.

She even gave a speech at the mic'd lectern, surrounded by delicate cherry blossoms, the perfect flower for spring. As she thanked all her friends, she told them one of her favorite anecdotes, about how her mother would always tell her, "Brooke, don't get beyond yourself." She thanked her friends in the polished, aristocratic tones they knew so well. "I'm just an ordinary person," she said, "who's had an extraordinary life." This remark of hers, meant in all candor, was nevertheless met with polite chuckles. No one would ever have called Brooke Astor ordinary. When she slipped and told the same anecdote again, about her mother's advice that she not get beyond herself, none of her friends seemed to mind. They didn't even mind when she told it a third time.[53]

The press reports couldn't have been more glowing. All in all, the evening was a triumph to rival her many social triumphs. Brooke could never have imagined that the video of that wonderful evening would one day be introduced as evidence at her son's criminal trial.[54]

Over the course of the next year, Brooke's world began to shrink considerably. Her close friends still came by, Annette de la Renta and David Rockefeller, and so did Tony's two sons, Philip and Alec. Both boys had grown up following their own idiosyncratic paths, far away from Fifth Avenue. Alec was a photographer, and Philip was a professor of historic preservation at Roger Williams University. But visits were increasingly hard for everyone. Brooke might be asleep when someone arrived, or disoriented and angry. Sometimes a visitor might try to make small talk, but her hearing was terrible, and after a time they would just sit with her smiling, holding her hand.

Tony increasingly began taking over Brooke Astor's affairs, or trying to turn her affairs into his, but at some point came to realize— which perhaps he had not thought of when he wrote that letter to Dr. Fillit—that to protect Charlene and hasten the transfer of funds from his mother's estate to his own, he would need Brooke *not* to be "losing her mind." Quite the contrary, he needed to be able to claim that Brooke was in full control of her faculties. And he needed to start making changes quickly.

He brought in his own attorney, Francis X. Morrissey, who referred to himself as an estate planner, and began firing loyal staff members and cutting costs in Brooke's household. His mother wasn't using all the rooms in her duplex apartment, so did she really need all those expensive fresh-cut flowers? Perhaps a few bouquets of daisies from the nearby deli would do. In 2003, according to bookkeeper Alice Perdue, some of the staff had asked to have a gate installed at the top of the stairs in Mrs. Astor's duplex, afraid she might fall. It was going to cost about two thousand dollars—a lot for a glorified baby gate, but certainly something Brooke could afford. Tony refused. Perdue wondered, "Why would he say no?"[55]

Annette de la Renta began to notice the changes in the apartment when she visited for tea with Mrs. Astor one afternoon. "It all started, I swear to you, like an Agatha Christie story. All of a sudden, an apartment that had been full of flowers and full of lights—one light was on, and there were no flowers, or some horrible daisy or something," she remembers. "Little things that made me and David [Rockefeller] go crazy. I picked up the phone and I said, 'David, did you notice how depressing that hall was getting to her bedroom?' and he said, 'Yes, I was going to talk to you about that,' and then, little by little, it got worse."[56]

In June 2003, Brooke fell and broke her hip. She would spend that summer in and out of the hospital in New York City. "She would never be the same again," Alice Perdue later wrote.[57] Nurses were hired to care for her round the clock, and they kept notes. "She is dead set against eating, saying she wants to die," wrote one nurse in September. "She ignores us," another nurse noted, "and covers her face with the napkin." She became convinced there was a man hiding in her apartment, waiting to kill her. She couldn't say who he was, or where in her fourteen-room Park Avenue duplex he might be, but she was terrified.

Nights were the worst. At night, she was alone, except for a nurse and her dachshunds, Boysie and Girlsie. Mrs. Astor would insist that the nurse check under the bed and use her cane to poke around in the shadows, just to make sure the man wasn't there.[58] She no longer wanted to take the sleeping pills her doctor had prescribed; she didn't want to let down her guard. "I want to be awake if anyone tries to finish me," she said.[59] She also refused to let the nurse remove her hearing aids. She wanted to hear the killer coming.[60]

There was a doorman always on duty in the well-appointed lobby of 778 Park Avenue, and it would be impossible for anyone to get into the elevator or the back stairwell and reach Mrs. Astor's front door, let alone break in unseen. But this was of little comfort. People can be paid to look the other way, can't they? And there had been any number of men coming and going whom she didn't recognize. Workers, no doubt, but those men in blue suits as well, who smiled and nodded and asked her to sign things: white papers with black letters and lines.

"A very restless night," one nurse wrote. "Had nightmares. Was not able to tell her dreams, only that someone was trying to kill her, and I showed her that the door was locked."[61] But Brooke Astor knew she wasn't safe.

The days were better: there were more people around, at least. The cook was there, making nice-smelling things in the kitchen; the housekeepers bustled around, although not as diligently as they once had.

Tony and Charlene were having some success as producers of Broadway shows, and Tony told Alice Perdue to cut two checks from his mother's account for nearly half a million dollars to help fund his production company, which they set up in Brooke's apartment.

"I felt that the Marshalls really had started to take advantage of her," Perdue wrote. "You've got to realize that before this decline set in, Mr. Marshall and Charlene were very deferential to Mrs. Astor— there was always, I assume, the thought that if you got on her bad side, she could pick up the phone, call her lawyer, and say, 'I want to change my will'—who knows what she might do?"[62]

Tellingly, around this time, a series of highly questionable changes were made to Mrs. Astor's estate plan. In August, while she was still recovering from her fall, her lawyer, Terry Christensen, who shared Brooke's power of attorney with her son, sent Tony a letter in his mother's name, gifting him five million dollars. The letter read in part, "This should provide you with enough money to assure Charlene's comfort assuming that she survives you."[63] The windfall was what *New York Magazine* later called Tony's "first real payday."[64] It wouldn't be his last.

Christensen also informed Tony in writing that Brooke was transferring ownership of Cove End, her summer house in Maine, to him. She had suggested in her 2002 will that the house should go to her grandson Philip after Tony's death, meaning that Charlene would not inherit it.

As soon as the paperwork was filed and Tony got the house, he signed ownership of it over to Charlene, which meant that Brooke also had to pay $3.5 million in gift tax on the transfer. But that was just the beginning.

In mid-December, Terry Christensen arranged for Brooke to sign a codicil to her 2002 will, amending it. Her trusted attorney personally presented it to her for her signature; he had titled it, somewhat oddly, "First and Final Codicil," wording later portrayed in court as a sign to Tony that the attorney was uncomfortable with Brooke making any further changes to her will. Christensen was one of the few people who knew that Brooke had Alzheimer's. He had been close with her over the years, but prosecutors later suggested that Christensen also wanted to continue representing Tony's interests after her death.

According to this new document, instead of giving most of her estate to charity when she died—as Brooke had always claimed she was going to do—she would now be leaving nearly half of it in a trust to create a new foundation for Tony, the Anthony Marshall Fund. This meant that thirty million dollars of Vincent Astor's money—the same Vincent Astor who had detested Tony and refused to let Brooke see him—would now be under Tony's control.[65] It was a startling reversal.

As Meryl Gordon noted, "Six years earlier, Brooke Astor had closed the Vincent Astor Foundation rather than turn it over to her son. Now she was making him a philanthropist for all the world to see."[66]

The codicil Brooke had signed for Terry Christensen in December may have been the "first and final" one that he would be involved with, but Tony had other attorneys ready to step in, most notably Francis X. Morrissey, who had an alarming history of befriending wealthy elderly people and winding up in their wills. In 1995, the New York Supreme Court suspended Morrissey's law license after he took $960,000 out of a client's account without permission. After getting his license back, according to *Vanity Fair* reporter Vicky Ward, Morrissey had "been accused of 'undue influence and fraud' in the execution of wills of elderly clients who left him valuable real estate and artworks."[67]

On January 12, 2004, Morrissey showed up at Brooke's apartment with Tony and several other lawyers, this time to get her signature on another amendment to her will. This one would give Tony all the money from Brooke's personal estate that had previously been earmarked for her favorite charities, more than sixty million dollars—a staggering sum. And when Tony died, Charlene would get it all.[68] The second codicil also named Tony the sole executor of his mother's estate and allowed him to name successors and co-executors— which he promptly did once Brooke signed the document. Terry Christensen was out, Francis Morrissey was named co-executor of Brooke's will, and Charlene would one day succeed Tony as her estate's trustee.[69]

Morrissey and the other attorneys swore that Mrs. Astor was fully aware of what she was doing. But given the accounts of her nurses on that day, who saw her interact with her son and Morrissey, this seems hard to believe. One nurse, Pearline Noble, wrote later that "Mrs. Astor didn't know if she was coming or going. She told Mr. Marshall she don't want to be pushed in any business and she reiterated 'do you hear me' with a bang on the floor with her walking stick. She was having a hard time walking."[70] Noble would later testify under oath that Brooke's "legs started buckling" and that Tony and Morrissey "dragged" her down the hall and "pulled her" into the library to sign the codicil. Noble wasn't allowed in the room with them, but afterward, she said, Mrs. Astor seemed confused and asked her, "What just happened? Who are those men?"[71]

Most heartbreaking of all, later that night, another nurse noted that Mrs. Astor was scared. She believed "four men are in the house who know everything about her and she doesn't know them. Also that the men want her to do things. Very hard on herself. Referring to self as a 'dam(n) fool.'"[72]

Annette de la Renta knew nothing about what Tony Marshall was doing but had been growing increasingly concerned about her friend. It wasn't just the changes she saw in Brooke's apartment; Mrs. Astor expressed fear to her directly. "She said she had horrible nightmares," Annette recalled to me. "'The man was coming to get me, the man!' And I said, 'Who is the man?' She said, 'You know, the man,' that's all she'd say." David Rockefeller was worried as well. Brooke Astor had shown up at his house for lunch one weekend and, disoriented, refused to get out of her car, telling Rockefeller, "It's the men in blue suits, they make me sign things."[73]

She wasn't wrong about that. Mrs. Astor dined alone most nights, but rituals still mattered to her. She was, after all, still Brooke Astor. She had standards to maintain. Dinner was served promptly at seven o'clock every evening. The formal dining room was too much of an effort now, and the housekeepers had turned it over to the dachshunds, who romped and relieved themselves there, saving the staff the trouble of taking them out for a walk. Now Mrs. Astor took her dinner in the small sitting room next to her bedroom.[74]

She still insisted on dressing up for dinner. This meant carefully putting on her wig and her makeup, with a sequined caftan and shoes to match. Then there was the jewelry, which was always her favorite part. Brooke, like many a Mrs. Astor before her, loved important jewels. She would even bring a small evening bag to dinner,[75] which was served on a tray in front of the television.

The woman who had dined for decades with presidents and New York power players now spent evenings alone, quietly chewing on the pureed food that was easier on her fragile teeth, lost in thoughts she couldn't hold on to for very long.

Incredibly, just before she turned 102 years old, Mrs. Astor's signature appeared on a third codicil to her 2002 will, dated March 3, 2004. This one allowed Tony, as executor, to sell off her real estate portfolio as part of her estate, thereby getting a tax deduction.[76] The following year, Tony fired his mother's bookkeeper, Alice Perdue. The retinue of loyal attendants was disappearing. He also gave himself a bonus and bought a yacht—not on the scale of the *Nourmahal*, but big enough that she required a full-time captain, whose salary, like nearly all Tony's other expenses, would be billed to his mother.

Tony would probably have gotten away with the changes he made to his mother's estate were it not for his son Philip. Around this time, Philip, who has since devoted his life to ending elder abuse, learned that his father had helped his grandmother make changes to her will, though he did not know the full details of the changes. He also talked with his grandmother's nurses. When he learned the extent of Brooke's decline, he checked in with Alice Perdue and other former staffers whom his father had fired, and everything he heard from them set him on edge. He knew he had to do something to help his grandmother, but he didn't know what. Tony had sole power of attorney, and Terry Christensen was no longer working for Mrs. Astor.

In May 2006, Philip met with David Rockefeller and Annette de la Renta to discuss his concerns, and within a month, the three decided to file a petition for guardianship. This was a drastic action, but they hoped it would remain secret. "Philip was never in it for the money," Annette de la Renta told me. "He was a really nice boy, really decent. Mrs. Astor loved him."

In fact, in 2015, the *New York Post* revealed that Philip's decision to challenge his father's management of his grandmother's affairs wound up costing him and his twin brother, Alec, nine million dollars each, because their father disinherited them. But Philip insists he would have made the same choice if he had to do it over again.[77] He and his attorney filed the lawsuit, and Annette de la Renta, David Rockefeller, and Henry Kissinger signed affidavits on Philip's behalf.[78] The very next day, New York Supreme Court justice John Stackhouse agreed to temporarily make Annette de la Renta Mrs. Astor's guardian and named the bank JPMorgan Chase guardian of her assets.[79]

Their hope of discretion, however, was quickly squashed. The story broke on the front page of the *New York Daily News* on July 26, 2004. "Battle of New York Blue Bloods," the headline screamed.

The allegations leveled by Philip and his attorney exploded into the midsummer news cycle like a hurricane. The story was an epic family drama, made even more dramatic because it was the culmination of two hundred years of attention to the name "Astor" and everything it stood for. Fame, fortune, deceit, good and evil, old money, and new ambition. It offered a peek into the kind of Park Avenue apartments rarely even photographed for the pages of *Architectural Digest*. The tales of elder abuse were sordid and shocking, with grand and gracious Mrs. Astor reduced to a threadbare nightgown and forced to sit on a urine-stained couch in a once-glorious duplex gone to seed. No detail was too small to be recounted, no character too tangential to be unworthy of paparazzi attention.

With the abrupt change of control over Mrs. Astor's affairs, Tony was no longer allowed to access his office or receive his regular salary. He and Charlene vehemently denied all the allegations against them, but the attorney appointed by the city as Brooke Astor's advocate found Tony's actions suspicious. The most glaring red flags were the changes to her 2002 will, all of which drastically altered Brooke Astor's wishes as she'd expressed them in every previous will and to anyone who would listen.

Annette de la Renta and David Rockefeller shared one wish: that whatever time Brooke Astor had left would be spent as comfortably as possible. By October 2004, wilting under the glare of the press, and increasingly anxious about what might emerge in the event of a civil lawsuit over guardianship, Tony and Charlene were willing to make a deal. Tony agreed to give up his mother's guardianship and the salary that came with it. Everyone concerned agreed to hold off on legal challenges to the will changes, but Tony and Charlene had to return $11 million in cash, art, and jewelry and put up Tony's yacht and Cove End as collateral.[80]

The judge granted guardianship to Annette de la Renta and JPMorgan Chase on October 13, 2006. Tony and Charlene may have breathed a sigh of relief, but the real battle was just about to begin. Unbeknownst to them, prosecutors in the office of the Manhattan district attorney were about to launch their own investigation, focusing on allegations of fraud by Tony and others involved in the changes made to Brooke Astor's will.

Tony did get some good news that December, when Judge Stackhouse noted that "the allegations in the petition regarding Mrs. Astor's medical and dental care, and other allegations of intentional elder abuse by the Marshalls, were not substantiated."[81] Those allegations had been the most damning in the press, driving many of the most salacious headlines, but by then, the dismissal of charges of abuse didn't really matter. All sides were preparing for the bare-knuckle fight over Brooke Astor's estate, and the district attorney's office was moving forward with its criminal investigation.

Brooke spent the final year of her life attended by nurses and her beloved butler, Chris Ely, whom Tony had unceremoniously fired, but who was later summoned by Annette de la Renta to return to his trusted post.

Then, at long last, on August 13, 2007, Brooke Astor died. She closed her eyes for the last time at Holly Hill, the home in Westchester she loved and that Tony and Charlene had, years before, banned her from visiting, hoping to sell it off. Tony wasn't there when his mother died, though he did arrive shortly after. Charlene wasn't allowed in the house by court order, because Annette's attorney had told the court that Brooke's daughter-in-law had made some unpleasant scenes with the staff. The last Mrs. Astor to rule New York died with her caregivers, butler, and Annette de la Renta, her closest friend and fiercest protector, by her side, telling her she was loved.

The very next day, lawyers for her guardians, de la Renta and JPMorgan Chase, filed papers in Westchester contesting Brooke's will and its many codicils, alleging that Mrs. Astor "was not competent to execute" the changes and had been pressured to make them "under undue influence and duress."[82] Tony and Charlene continued to profess their innocence, insisting that Brooke had been fully competent to make all the bequests she had. Charlene explained her mercurial mother-in-law's alleged changes of heart to a reporter from *New York Magazine*, saying, "I think a certain amount of guilt came into her decisions for not being the best mother"[83]—though few people around Brooke Astor believed this. Just a few months after her death, however, the battle over her estate would once again be put on hold, when criminal charges were filed against Tony and Francis X. Morrissey, who had overseen two of the contested codicils to Brooke Astor's will.

Just days after Thanksgiving 2007, Tony and Morrissey were summoned to 100 Centre Street for their arraignment. Tony appeared shaken as he sat before the judge hearing the eighteen-count indictment against him read aloud. Two of the indictments would later be dropped, but he and Morrissey were being accused of taking advantage of Brooke's "diminished mental capacity" to swindle her out of $14 million in cash, stocks, and property.[84] Charlene was overheard trying to comfort her husband in court, reassuring him, "We'll be all right."[85] But the charges were serious. If convicted of first-degree grand larceny, former ambassador Anthony Marshall would be facing up to twenty-five years in prison.

After pleading not guilty, both men were arrested, fingerprinted, and released after paying $100,000 each for their bail. The following day, a haggard-looking Tony appeared on the front page of the city's tabloid of record, the *New York Post*. "Bad Heir Day" was the headline.

"This case is about greed," Assistant District Attorney Elizabeth Loewy explained in her opening remarks to the jury seventeen months later. "The greed of two men, Anthony Marshall and Francis Morrissey, to increase their own wealth."[86]

Loewy had been a prosecutor for two decades and had risen through the ranks to become head of the Elder Abuse unit. She opened her case by reading aloud from the letter Tony had sent to his mother's neurologist, Dr. Howard Fillit, at the end of 2000, a letter that made it clear that Tony knew his mother was losing her mind. In it, he called her "delusional at times" and said she no longer understood basic math. He wrote that numbers were "incomprehensible" to her. Loewy's message to the jury was clear: If Tony knew that Brooke was delusional then, and that numbers made no sense to her, then how could he pretend she was competent three years later to drastically change her will multiple times?

Prosecutors don't have to give juries a motive for crimes, but it certainly helps when they can, and Loewy explained why Tony, who already had millions of his own, had become so greedy. She pointed to the woman sitting two rows behind him in the courtroom: his wife. "Charlene was behind the scenes pressing her husband to get more from his mother," Loewy said.[87] "Anthony Marshall's preoccupation for getting money for Charlene was actually [the] motivation for the scheme to defraud."[88]

Charlene fiercely defended her husband to reporters. One day, she approached Meryl Gordon, who was in the courtroom covering the trial for *Vanity Fair*. "He did not do one thing wrong. He did zero wrong. We believe in the truth with a capital T," Gordon reported Charlene telling her.[89]

The trial dragged on for more than five dizzying months as a cavalcade of witnesses, more than a hundred of them, mostly for the prosecution, took the stand. Believing it would be prejudicial, Justice A. Kirke Bartley Jr. did not permit any details of the previous guardianship case to be presented to the jury.[90]

The questioning and cross-examinations were slow, even plodding at times, and often highly acrimonious. Spring turned to summer, then fall. The jury, made up of four men and eight women, grew restless. According to Meryl Gordon, some jurors invented a game, trying to guess who might play all the characters in a movie version of the case. Elizabeth Loewy should be played by Laura Linney, some jurors thought, and Charlene by Kathy Bates.[91]

Prosecutors spent days grilling Mrs. Astor's former attorney Terry Christensen, whom Elizabeth Loewy accused of enabling Tony and giving in to his demands. "Terry Christensen failed to protect Brooke Astor's interests," she told the jury, "Instead, he gave in to defendant Marshall's demands one by one."[92] Christensen's allegiance was divided, Loewy alleged, between his elderly client and the son who would likely soon replace her in importance to his firm. Christensen denied any wrongdoing.

As for Tony, he and Charlene attended court every day, though he remained silent throughout the proceedings, staring into the middle distance. With each passing day, he appeared frailer, weaker, his right hand often shaking, though some observers found themselves wondering if he wasn't playing up his appearance as a dignified but deeply diminished elderly gentleman to garner sympathy with the jury.

Once the prosecution rested its case, Francis Morrissey's attorney called just two witnesses, both handwriting experts, who claimed the signature Morrissey was accused of forging on the third codicil could in fact have been made by Brooke Astor. Tony's attorneys called no witnesses of their own, and Tony did not testify in his own defense. As Michael Wilson wrote in the *New York Times*, "He had become a silent spectator to the dark rehashing of his life, a mute figure in court these months . . . until the end, declining on Monday to add to this latest version to be told."[93]

It took the jury twelve days to reach a verdict.

According to jurors who gave interviews after the trial, they had disagreed over when Brooke Astor was no longer competent to make her own decisions. Some thought it was in 2002; others believed she still had moments of lucidity up until 2005.[94] Of course, it's an impossible question. Alzheimer's doesn't work like a switch, where one day the lights are on and, the next day, everything is darkness. The disease is much more insidious than that. The darkness creeps in gradually, one shade at a time. Many patients move in and out of shadows for a long while before they disappear entirely.

But the jury had to make a final determination, one that mattered not only for the criminal trial, but also for the estate battle ahead. Paul Saunders, Annette de la Renta's attorney, told the *New York Times*, "[Brooke Astor's] mental capacity is the central issue in the will contest."[95]

Tony was acquitted on two counts—a first-degree larceny charge for selling his mother's favorite painting and pocketing the two-million-dollar commission and another charge of falsifying business records. But he was found guilty on fourteen other counts and faced between one and twenty-five years in prison.[96] He showed no reaction as the verdict was read.

As for Francis Morrissey, his handwriting experts failed to convince the jury. He was found guilty of forging Brooke Astor's signature on the third codicil and of several other fraud and conspiracy charges.[97]

According to the *New York Times*, both men "staggered ashen-faced out of the courtroom without comment."[98] They were allowed to remain free pending appeals, which in Tony's case would drag on for years. At the same time, Tony was fighting in surrogate court in Westchester County for the money he had worked so hard to steal. That battle over Brooke Astor's $185 million estate, which commenced when her grandson Philip filed the petition to change her guardianship in 2006, finally wound to its long-awaited conclusion in March 2012.

Annette de la Renta and many of the charitable organizations with which Brooke had been involved wanted the court to recognize her 1997 will, which bequeathed the bulk of her fortune to the charities.

But after years of court battles and millions spent on attorneys' and bankers' fees, in the end, the court ruled that Brooke Astor's 2002 will would remain in effect, though all the questionable codicils and letters she had signed in 2003 and 2004 were ultimately reversed.

Tony Marshall's $31 million inheritance was sliced in half, and he no longer had a say in which charities should get bequests from his mother's estate or how those bequests could be used.[99]

Charlene got to keep Cove End, which Tony had given her, and some of the jewelry she'd been given by Brooke in her 2002 will. She also received two mink coats Brooke Astor had specifically bequeathed to her, though it's hard to imagine enjoying wearing minks that belonged to someone who held you in obvious contempt. Not that Charlene would ever be able to wear them. Some of Brooke's friends smiled when they learned about the gift of the furs—not just because John Jacob Astor had built his fortune on animal pelts, but because both coats were a size six, and as Brooke Astor had been keenly aware, they would never fit her daughter-in-law.

Tony remained free for a little over a year after the final financial settlement, while his appeals continued to wind their ponderous way through the courts, but by June 2013, he had delayed as long as he could. He arrived back in criminal court at 100 Centre Street in Manhattan, dressed in a light-blue sweater and blue sweatpants. According to the *New York Times*, his wife "wept as court officers scanned him with a metal detector."[100]

When Justice A. Kirke Bartley Jr. pronounced Tony's sentence, he began by telling him, "I wish to say I take no pleasure in following my duty. I am, in point of fact, fulfilling my oath. I know it is not dissimilar to the oath you took when you became a Marine officer."[101]

Tony Marshall appeared as a shadow of his former self as the judge sentenced him and Francis Morrissey to one to three years in prison.

Tony was wheeled out of the courtroom and delivered to the New York County Jail at Rikers Island, where he would be held for three days before being transferred upstate. For the first time in his life, Tony Marshall was no different from anyone else. All his special privileges, all his access, had been stripped away.

Charlene left the court with her attorney and her minister, telling reporters, "My heart has been ripped out of my body."[102]

The Manhattan district attorney, Cyrus Vance Jr., said in a statement, "I believe that the legacy of this prosecution will be that it raised public awareness of the silent epidemic of elder abuse."[103]

Tony's time at Rikers was brutal. Charlene would later file a Freedom of Information Act request to uncover details of his brief confinement there.[104] She claimed the guards didn't administer any of Tony's multiple medications. He was left overnight in his wheelchair, unattended, and could not stand or maneuver himself into a cot to lie down. Unable to go to the bathroom without help, he had urinated on himself and been forced to remain sitting in his own filth. After his three days at Rikers, he was remanded to Fishkill Correctional Facility, a medium-security prison in Beacon, New York. But he was there only about a month before his health deteriorated so much that he had to be taken to a nearby hospital.[105]

To be eligible for medical parole, "inmates must be 'so physically or cognitively debilitated or incapacitated that there is a reasonable probability' that they no longer present any danger to society."[106] When the three members of the parole board gathered around Tony Marshall's hospital bed that afternoon in August 2013, they were all in agreement. Looking down on the withered figure under thin hospital blankets, unable to take a full breath on his own, they saw a broken old man, a man being crushed by time and his own collapsing life. They may also have seen, as many did who followed his trial, the wasting away of the towering Astor legacy: gutted, made petty and small, and coughing its slow way to its inevitable end.

His parole was granted immediately. Anthony Marshall served just eight weeks of his prison sentence.[107] A little over one year later, Brooke Astor's son was dead.

In 1960, writer and self-described "proper Bostonian" Cleveland Amory wrote a bestselling book skewering society and all its various dramas and pretensions. In *Who Killed Society?*, Amory notes many of the Astor peccadilloes over the preceding hundred years and concludes that "whereas fifty years ago, in 1908, a financial prophet predicted that the Astor fortune would snowball until it reached, by the year 2000, exactly $80,000,000,000, actually the prophet was not only wrong, he was, judged at the halfway mark, almost totally wrong. For if the Astors had, by 1908, well disproved the old American adage of 'shirtsleeves to shirtsleeves in three generations,' they had also, as of 1958, rather well proved that by six generations an American Family is about ready to start all over again."[108]

EPILOGUE

Never admit anything to anybody.

—Mary Astor

The memoir of movie star Mary Astor, whose career spanned forty years and included an Academy Award for her role in *The Great Lie*, opens with a meditation on tomorrow, a day that never quite seems to come. "'Tomorrow we'll hear from Griffith. Lillian Gish said she'd talk to D. W. and set up the test for Friday.' 'Tomorrow we'll be on the train for Hollywood.' 'Tomorrow we have the interview with Jesse Lasky.' 'Tomorrow we meet Mr. Barrymore.'

"The 'we,'" she writes, "not being editorial or royal but familial, the unit that first put the product together that we called Mary Astor. Mr. and Mrs. O. L. Langhanke and daughter, Lucile."[1]

Because Mary Astor was not born "Mary Astor." She was born "Lucile Langhanke," called "Rusty" by her mother on account of her voluminous reddish hair. She had brown eyes and freckles and was too tall by half.

"'Langhanke?' Who can pronounce it?" Astor describes the process of choosing her new name. "'Lucile?'—out of fashion. Wordsworth and all that."

But what would be better? Something famous already. Something with a sheen of elegance, a name already known, but also not known. Not really.

"'Astor?'—a famous name, a famous family, a sound of affluence to it. Also, being an A, it would figure high in alphabetical lists. The combination would look brief and well in marquee lights. Mary Astor—sounds good. That's your name, better get used to it!" she writes.

Her new persona wasn't her own invention, but the product of a committee. "The name was chosen by Jesse Lasky, Louella Parsons and Walter Wanger. Legalized for contracts, so there would never be the cumbersome 'also known as' for documents. Practiced as a signature for autographs, with big capitals, curly r's and a long-tailed y." Jesse Lasky was the head of Paramount Pictures, Walter Wanger was a producer, and Louella Parsons was a gossip columnist. This committee of three decided that of all the names this auburn-haired ingenue, daughter of schoolteachers from Quincy, Illinois, should adopt, the best one of all was "Astor."

Once the name was settled upon, "there was food on the table for a change." Mary Astor started out making sixty dollars a week, more than her father had ever dreamed of. "So instead of a diet of rice and coffee, and an occasional splurge at the Automat," she writes in her autobiography of her life in Hollywood, "we had steak. And oranges and grapes. And *Kartoffel* salad. And *kaffeekuchen* for breakfast."[2]

Like the family whose name she took for her own, Lucile Langhanke had roots in Germany. Statuesque and leggy, the budding actress was rechristened when she was fourteen. She writes about being paraded before panels of strangers, having a producer take hold of her chin with his hairy hand and move her head as he looked at her profile, before sliding the hand down her adolescent chest and demanding that she smile. She expected her father to take a swing at the man, but he didn't. Instead, his "subservient smile" was "glued to his face." Her mother toyed with a chain of amber beads, watching.[3]

The Langhankes were an early, and far less clever, iteration of Kris Jenner, matriarch of the Kardashian clan, a type of showbiz parent that would become more familiar as Hollywood grew. Mary's father quit his job teaching high school German when Lucile was just twelve to take her to Chicago, where she studied drama and started appearing in local theater productions. When she was fourteen, he decided to try her in New York. The family arrived in Manhattan in June 1920 with three hundred dollars to their name and moved into a dreary apartment on 110th Street. Mary would sit in a window, looking down at the kids playing in the street below, coiling her long hair around her fingers, imagining she was Rapunzel trapped in a tower.

Mary Astor, though not technically an Astor, was in some ways as Astor-like as any of the real ones. Her father, Otto Ludwig Wilhelm Langhanke, would have been right at home alongside William Waldorf Astor, who died the year before Langhanke brought his family to New York City. Mary describes him as "ambitious, intense, a great deal of Prussian pompousness, a longing for luxury, a deep appreciation of beauty, sentimental about music, Christmas trees and sunsets, cold in his family relationships. . . . He was a rebel, who rebelled against anything new, who got stuck in his own century." The only difference was that Will Astor had already had everything Otto longed for and endeavored to use his daughter to obtain: money, fine things, fame, access, importance.

"What 'Being Somebody' meant to him was vague," Mary Astor wrote of her father, and she grew up with the sense that she was a constant failure. "I actually felt that he had given up on me," she confessed, "that I would never be very bright or intelligent or Educated [sic], and getting me into the movies was the best he could do for me." She also grew up alone, with no siblings or playmates and only a couple of early, brief friendships—not unlike the many real Astor heirs whose lonely childhoods pepper this book. She didn't know how to play. She could imagine other worlds, and other stories, and lose herself in them— but playing? That was alien to her.

Between a controlling father with a very specific definition of success and a childhood of relative isolation, Lucile Langhanke—or, rather, the team of adults scheming to make her into the product she would become—could not have settled on a more apt stage persona: Astor. The only missing element was wealth. Instead of studying real estate law at Columbia in preparation for a life in the family counting-house, the girl who would become Mary Astor studied at the movies, spending every Friday evening staring into the flickering images of Mary Pickford, Norma Talmadge, and D. W. Griffith. Instead of reading uplifting histories and biographies of the great dynasties of Europe in preparation for a life of collecting, she read *Motion Picture Magazine*, *Shadowplay*, and *Picture Play*, cutting out pictures of her favorite movie stars and pasting them up on the walls of her room. Soon enough, though, the wealth would come. Mary Astor would go on to a decades-long career in Hollywood, surviving a career-rocking adultery scandal in 1936 to emerge on the other side to an Academy Award for Best Supporting Actress in 1941 and a star on the Hollywood Walk of Fame.

The parallels don't end at German origins or the role played by an overbearing father. At seventeen, Mary Astor was wooed by the famous older actor John Barrymore, and they even entered into a secret engagement. But as Will Astor was denied the right to marry the Italian girl he loved, the Langhankes intervened, splitting the couple apart. Living off the considerable income of their daughter's contracts, the stage parents bought a sprawling Moorish Revival mansion,

Moorcrest, in the hills above Hollywood, California. In a period when Mary's contracts were paying her $2,500 a week—about $43,000 in current dollars—her parents allotted her a weekly allowance of $5. Their financial enmeshment would continue into Mary's late twenties, when she would gain control over her own finances—only to have her parents sue her for support. Money warped relationships with stage Astors as much as it did with the New York Astors, as it turned out, being not only an avenue for splendor, but also a mechanism for control.

Mary wasn't the only Astor in Hollywood in the 1930s. By the time she found success there, the name "Astor" had become shorthand for anything fancy, anything plush. Though it still referred to the family—Vincent and his detested half-brother John Jacob VI on the one hand and the flowering viscounts in England on the other, with Nancy Astor in the House of Commons—it had also begun to decouple from them. "Astor" had begun to mean a place of meeting, a certain level of style, a public life of glamour. "Astor" meant elegance, but no longer the exclusive kind that Caroline Astor had kept so carefully shuttered away from the arrivistes and wannabes. As the New York Astors faded gently from the scene, they left behind their name, an indelible impression in the fabric of American culture, over which they no longer had control.

That's why the dog in the wildly successful *Thin Man* series of films of the 1930s and '40s—about charming and urbane Nick and Nora Charles, who solve crimes while sipping glamorous cocktails and wearing fantastic clothes meant to dazzle the eyes of Depression-era moviegoers—was named "Asta." The spelling was a play on the pseudo-sophisticated accent that came to be called "mid-Atlantic," for its imaginary origin in the Atlantic Ocean at some undefined midpoint between the East Coast of the United States and Great Britain. The mid-Atlantic accent was a pure fabrication of elocution experts in the age of the talkies, the one you hear in old Hollywood films and nowhere else. The wily and rambunctious terrier who attends on the Charleses in their adventures is called Asta as a wink, as both William Powell (as Nick Charles) and Myrna Loy (Nora Charles) speak in the cultivated tones that Hollywood demanded of them. But the name "Asta" is also meant to underscore the glamour of the setting and characters. Nick has retired from private detecting to manage his wealthy wife's railroads, he says, and their lifestyle is one of shopping, supper clubs, black-tie parties, and no real work. Of course, they would name their dog after an Astor.

And what about all the places? Hallett's Cove, in Queens, renamed itself Astoria in 1839, in an attempt to invite John Jacob Astor to invest there. He did not, and in fact, he never had any connection with that community, but there his name sits, all these generations later. There are Astorias all along the old fur trading routes in the interior of the country: in Illinois from 1837; in Missouri from 1844; in Oregon, from the infamous remnants of Fort Astoria, back in 1811; and then, backtracking, in South Dakota from 1900, named not for John Jacob Astor himself, but for the Astoria he left in Oregon—a copy of a copy of a copy. With each wave, the impression in the historical sand that was originally made in the shape of John Jacob Astor becomes softer, harder to define, until the name is divorced from the individual or family entirely.

As I write this now, my sons, Sebastian and Wyatt, are upstairs sweetly giggling in front of old episodes of *The Muppet Show*, and the two old curmudgeons in the balcony cracking wise about how badly the show is going—"I liked their last joke. So long as it was their *last* joke! Ah ha ha ha ha!"—are named Statler and Waldorf. Did you know the grouchy Waldorf had a wife named Astoria? An Astoria also makes glancing appearances as a minor character in *Harry Potter*, on Tony

Bennett albums, in a comic book series called *Cerebus the Aardvark*. Astoria hotels still stand in Denmark, in Russia, in Budapest. The German football club in Walldorf named itself FC Astoria Walldorf. How many copies is that?

In New York City, you cannot walk a block without tripping over an Astor. Some are obvious: the great hall in the Stephen A. Schwarzman Building of the New York Public Library, where so much of this book was researched and written, was named Astor Hall in Brooke's honor. At the Metropolitan Museum of Art, the Astor Chinese Garden Court contains a re-creation of a Ming Dynasty–style courtyard, complete with softly bubbling fountain. And when you ride the subway, you can take the BMT Astoria Line to the Astoria Boulevard Station. You can picnic in Astoria Park, in Queens. Or live in the Astor Court Building, on the Upper West Side, a lovely 1915 co-op building developed by Vincent Astor, where a cheerful and sunny one-bedroom apartment recently sold for just under a million dollars. Or settle uptown on Astor Row, the elegant block of row houses on 130th Street between Fifth and Lenox Avenues, first built in the early 1880s as spec houses by William Backhouse Astor Jr., on land John Jacob Astor had originally bought for ten thousand dollars.

In some respects, we all already live in Astoria, in that we walk every day through spaces that were owned or leased or imagined or willed into being by this family who lived the American self-made myth that we have all imbibed for so long. The immigrant who arrived with nothing (he did not; remember the flutes), who saw a world in the process of its remaking (it was already made), who leached value from the labor of all the successive waves of our arrivals and our dreams. Does the name "Astor" mean "avarice"? Maybe. But thought of another way, it means less what one family has done or valued or made or spent, for as we have shown, "Astor" has also come to mean other, unexpected stories, stories of the self-determination of people trying to carve out lives they felt they deserved to have. Like teenage Lucile Langhanke, who took the connotations of wealth and establishment and class that still cling to the name "Astor" and decided that, by rights, they belonged to her, too.

The old New York of Brooke Astor and Gloria Vanderbilt lunching in polite mutual indifference at Mortimer's while social strivers look on from slightly less preferred tables has faded away, but the long shadow of the Astor-dominated Gilded Age hasn't disappeared entirely. In many respects, we are all living in a Second Gilded Age. Instead of couture Venetian princess costumes from Paris worn in private ballrooms designed to hold four hundred people, we now see the ultra-rich in bespoke space suits riding on privately funded rockets. The yachts owned by the Astors and the Vanderbilts are modest compared to the superyachts of today. And those who really want to flaunt their wealth will have a second yacht to house "the toys"—the helicopter, submarine, and assorted sailboats and launches they may rarely even use. We still subscribe to the national myth that vast fortunes are available to anyone with the right skill, insight, and gumption to voyage into the wilderness—though, the "wilderness" is now located on the blockchain or in an AI chatbot. And every day, young people in their teens and twenties still flood into New York City, waiting tables (like I did) or working retail (like Katherine Howe did), starting the hustle and idea and vision that will one day, they hope, make their fortunes.

Most of them take the subway.

The Astor Place subway station opened in 1904, underneath the square that bears its name, site of the 1849 theater riots that saw bullets blowing through shoulders and legs of men and women gathered at the front gates of the grand Astor town houses on Lafayette Place. Today it's a local stop on the 6 Line, the way to get to the East Village and

St. Mark's Place and Greenwich Village, a fairyland for people who want to visit record stores and vintage clothing shops that sell cheap silver jewelry and T-shirts that read, "New York Fucking City."

When you step out of the 6 train—standing clear of the doors, please—Astor Place feels much like any other subway station in the city: stifling hot in the summertime, cool and damp with blackening slush in the winter. The station swells with city dwellers shuffling by, their earbuds in place, looking into the carefully calibrated middle distance that avoids both collisions and eye contact as they stream out through the turnstiles and the emergency exit doors everyone uses, whether there's an emergency or not. When the express trains rattle by on the interior tracks at Astor Place, their wheels beat a rhythm that is not so very different from a heartbeat—*lug-lug-lug-lug-lug-lug-lug-lug*. In other stations, the passing express trains don't make this exact heartbeat sound—they squeal, they rush, they rattle, but they don't beat.

There's no real incentive to loiter in the Astor Place station—better to be on your way to whatever appointment brought you downtown. But if you linger, just for a few minutes, throbbing in the passing heartbeat of the city, and look carefully at the original subway tile walls patterned in mosaic, you'll see them—ceramic plaques of beavers, standing on their hind legs, clutching a tree, their teeth bared as they try to remake the world according to their will, alive with the possibility of something not yet to be. They are the last remnants of the bloody and brutal wilderness fortune a young German immigrant clawed into existence all those many years ago—the first dream of Astoria.

Acknowledgments

The idea to focus on the Astors was Katherine Howe's, after we completed *Vanderbilt*, our first book together, and I am grateful for her remarkable talent and patience and dedication. I am indebted to my literary agent, Luke Janklow, and his assistant, Claire Dippel, as well as Jonathan Burnham, Emily Griffin, Leslie Cohen, Katie O'Callaghan, Robin Bilardello, Nancy Singer, and everyone at HarperCollins. I'm also so thankful for Shimrit Sheetrit, Charlie Moore, and Jessica Ciancimino, as well as Carole Cooper and Jay Sures at UTA. Many thanks to Annette de la Renta, and George Chauncey for their time and advice, to Benjamin Maisani for his patience and support, and to Gabi Suau and Jeorjeth Piedrahita, for their dedication and kindness.

I would like to thank first and foremost Anderson Cooper, whose brilliance, good humor, curiosity, and skill continue to amaze me. I'm grateful also to my agent, Suzanne Gluck at WME, and to everyone at Harper who has worked so hard to make this book a reality, especially Jonathan Burnham, Emily Griffin, Leslie Cohen, Katie O'Callaghan, Robin Bilardello, and Nancy Singer. My particular thanks to Melanie C. Locay and the staff at the Center for Research in the Humanities at the New York Public Library for giving me research support and workspace for lo these many years; to the Patricia D. Klingenstein Library at the New-York Historical Society, the Cornell University

Law library, the New York Public Library Manuscripts and Archives Division, Orme Wilson, Hal Leonard Inc., the Songwriters Guild of America, the Authors' Guild, and especially to Louis Hyman, the best research assistant, partner, chef, sounding board, and on-site historian I could have dreamed of. My thanks also to Charles Howe for interrupting this manuscript at prescribed moments to play *Treasure Island*, and to the wonderful Annalise Wolf and the staff of Harborlight Montessori for playing pirates with him in my stead while this book wended its way to completion. Finally, I am grateful to the readers of *Vanderbilt* for spurring us to tackle another American story.

Notes

Introduction

1. Justin Kaplan, *When the Astors Owned New York* (New York: Penguin, 2006), 31.
2. Kaplan, *When the Astors Owned New York*, 31.
3. Excerpt from Donna M. Lucey, *Archie and Amelie: Love and Madness in the Gilded Age*, https://www.penguinrandomhouse.ca/books/104293 /archie-and-amelie-by-donna-m-lucey/9780307351456/excerpt.
4. John D. Gates, *The Astor Family* (New York: Doubleday, 1981), 4.

Chapter 1: New York, 1784

1. Eric Jay Dolin, *Fur, Fortune, and Empire: The Epic History of the Fur Trade in America* (New York: W. W. Norton, 2010), 189.
2. Dolin, *Fur, Fortune, and Empire*, 181.
3. Dolin, *Fur, Fortune, and Empire*, 189.
4. Dolin, *Fur, Fortune, and Empire*, 189.
5. Dolin, *Fur, Fortune, and Empire*, 189.
6. Dolin, *Fur, Fortune, and Empire*, 189.
7. Gus Lubin, Michael B. Kelley, and Rob Wile, "Meet the 24 Robber Barons Who Once Ruled America," *Business Insider*, March 20, 2012.
8. Rachel B. Juen and Fort St. Joseph Archaeological Project, "Fur Trade 01: Beaver: Mainstay of the Trade," Fort St. Joseph Archaeological Project, Western Michigan University, https://scholarworks.wmich.edu/cgi/viewcontent .cgi?article=1028&context=fortstjoseph.
9. Virginia Cowles, *The Astors* (New York: Knopf, 1979), 16.
10. "How to Skin a Beaver—Fred Eichler," YouTube, n.d., https://www.youtube.com /watch?v=PtcneeevIzI&ab_channel=FredEichler.
11. Cowles, *The Astors*, 16.
12. Cowles, *The Astors*, 20.
13. Lucy Kavaler, *The Astors: An American Legend* (New York: Dodd, Mead and Company, 1966), 3.

14. Michael Astor, *Tribal Feeling* (London: John Murray, 1963), 9.
15. Peter Stark, *Astoria: Astor and Jefferson's Lost Pacific Empire* (New York: HarperCollins, 2015), 9.
16. Stark, *Astoria*, 9.
17. Gates, *The Astor Family*, 3.
18. Stark, *Astoria*, 9.
19. Kavaler, *The Astors*, 4.
20. Kavaler, *The Astors*, 4.
21. Kavaler, *The Astors*, 4.
22. Stark, *Astoria*, 10–11.
23. Stark, *Astoria*, 11.
24. Stark, *Astoria*, 11.
25. Kavaler, *The Astors*, 5.
26. Stark, *Astoria*, 13.
27. Stark, *Astoria*, 13.
28. Kavaler, *The Astors*, 5.
29. Stark, *Astoria*, 13.
30. Kavaler, *The Astors*, 7.
31. Kavaler, *The Astors*, 9.
32. The Inflation Calculator, https://westegg.com/inflation/infl.cgi?money =250000&first=1800&final=2021. This and subsequent modern-day dollar equivalents given in this book are from https://westegg.com/inflation.
33. Kavaler, *The Astors*, 10.
34. Kavaler, *The Astors*, 11.
35. Kavaler, *The Astors*, 11.

Chapter 2: Astoria, 1810

1. Cowles, *The Astors*, 53.
2. Dolin, *Fur, Fortune, and Empire*, 202.
3. Thomas Jefferson to John Jacob Astor (April 13, 1808), in Thomas Jefferson, *The Writings of Thomas Jefferson*, 11:28, quoted in Dolin, *Fur, Fortune, and Empire*, 204.
4. Dolin, *Fur, Fortune, and Empire*, 204–5.
5. Dolin, *Fur, Fortune, and Empire*, 205.
6. Dolin, *Fur, Fortune, and Empire*, 205.
7. Stark, *Astoria*, 28.
8. Stark, *Astoria*, 28.
9. Stark, *Astoria*, 27.
10. Stark, *Astoria*, 29.
11. Dolin, *Fur, Fortune, and Empire*, 207.
12. Dolin, *Fur, Fortune, and Empire*, 208.

13. Alexander Ross, *Adventures of the First Settlers on the Oregon or Columbia River, Being a Narrative of the Expedition Fitted Out by John Jacob Astor to Establish the "Pacific Fur Company"* (London: Smith, Elder and Company, 1849), 55, quoted in Dolin, *Fur, Fortune, and Empire*, 209.

14. Dolin, *Fur, Fortune, and Empire*, 209.

15. Kavaler, *The Astors*, 14.

16. Kavaler, *The Astors*, 14.

17. Kavaler, *The Astors*, 14; and Dolin, *Fur, Fortune, and Empire*, 210.

18. Kavaler, *The Astors*, 15.

19. Dolin, *Fur, Fortune, and Empire*, 219.

20. Kavaler, *The Astors*, 15.

21. Dolin, *Fur, Fortune, and Empire*, 227.

22. Kavaler, *The Astors*, 16.

23. Cowles, *The Astors*, 47.

24. Cowles, *The Astors*, 48.

25. Cowles, *The Astors*, 48.

26. Cowles, *The Astors*, 52.

27. Cowles, *The Astors*, 52; and Drizly app.

28. Quoted in Cowles, *The Astors*, 52.

29. Quoted in Cowles, *The Astors*, 48.

30. Kavaler, *The Astors*, 17.

31. Cowles, *The Astors*, 52.

32. Kavaler, *The Astors*, 18.

33. Kavaler, *The Astors*, 22.

34. Stark, *Astoria*, 12.

35. Kavaler, *The Astors*, 20.

36. Kavaler, *The Astors*, 7.

37. Kavaler, *The Astors*, 27.

38. Kavaler, *The Astors*, 28.

39. Kavaler, *The Astors*, 25.

40. Kavaler, *The Astors*, 30.

41. Cowles, *The Astors*, 33.

42. Quoted in Cowles, *The Astors*, 60.

43. David Sinclair, *Dynasty: The Astors and Their Times* (New York: Beaufort Books, 1984), 129.

44. Sinclair, *Dynasty*, 129.

45. Sinclair, *Dynasty*, 129–30.

46. Kavaler, *The Astors*, 31.

47. Gates, *The Astor Family*, 3.

48. James Fox, *Five Sisters: The Langhornes of Virginia* (New York: Simon and Schuster, 2000), 86.

Chapter 3: Massacre Opera House, 1849

1. Kavaler, *The Astors*, 32.
2. Kavaler, *The Astors*, 32.
3. Kavaler, *The Astors*, 34.
4. Kavaler, *The Astors*, 34.
5. Sinclair, *Dynasty*, 132.
6. Kavaler, *The Astors*, 35; and Sinclair, *Dynasty*, 133.
7. Kavaler, *The Astors*, 35
8. Sinclair, *Dynasty*, 133.
9. Sinclair, *Dynasty*, 133.
10. Sinclair, *Dynasty*, 133–34.
11. Kavaler, *The Astors*, 37.
12. Quoted in Kavaler, *The Astors*, 38.
13. Quoted in Cowles, *The Astors*, 66.
14. Sinclair, *Dynasty*, 158.
15. Sinclair, *Dynasty*, 135.
16. Kavaler, *The Astors*, 40.
17. Kavaler, *The Astors*, 42.
18. Kavaler, *The Astors*, 43.
19. Kavaler, *The Astors*, 43.
20. Kavaler, *The Astors*, 44.
21. Kavaler, *The Astors*, 51.
22. Thomas Butler Gunn, *The Physiology of New York Boarding-Houses* (New York: Mason Brothers, 1857), 32–33.
23. Kavaler, *The Astors*, 54.
24. "Funeral of John Jacob Astor," *Cleveland Plain Dealer*, vol. 14, issue 89, April 10, 1848, Gale Document Number GALE|GT3004911292.
25. "Attempt to Extort $50,000 from William B. Astor," *Boston Globe*, vol. 17, issue 221, March 20, 1849, Gale Document Number GALE|GT3008313709.
26. "Holt's Hotel—1831," New York Historic Hotels, Geographic Guide, n.d., https://www.geographicguide.com/united-states/nyc/antique/hotels/holts -hotel.htm.
27. N. T. Hubbard, *Autobiography of N. T. Hubbard, with personal reminiscences of New York City from 1789 to 1875* (New York: J. F. Trow and Son, 1875), 117–18.
28. H. M. Ranney, publisher, *Account of the Terrific and Fatal Riot at the New-York Astor Place Opera House, on the Night of May 19th, 1849; with the quarrels of Forrest and Macready, including all the causes which led to that awful tragedy! Wherein an infuriated mob was quelled by the public authorities and military, with its mournful termination in the sudden death or mutilation of more than fifty citizens, with full and authentic particulars* (New York: H. M. Ranney, 1849), 15.
29. Ranney, *Account of the Terrific and Fatal Riot*, 15.

30. Ranney, *Account of the Terrific and Fatal Riot*, 15.
31. Ranney, *Account of the Terrific and Fatal Riot*, 16.
32. Ranney, *Account of the Terrific and Fatal Riot*, 16.
33. Ranney, *Account of the Terrific and Fatal Riot*, 17.
34. Ranney, *Account of the Terrific and Fatal Riot*, 17.
35. Ranney, *Account of the Terrific and Fatal Riot*, 18.
36. Ranney, *Account of the Terrific and Fatal Riot*, 19.
37. Ranney, *Account of the Terrific and Fatal Riot*, 20.
38. Ranney, *Account of the Terrific and Fatal Riot*, 20.
39. Ranney, *Account of the Terrific and Fatal Riot*, 20.
40. Ranney, *Account of the Terrific and Fatal Riot*, 5.
41. Ranney, *Account of the Terrific and Fatal Riot*, 6.
42. Ranney, *Account of the Terrific and Fatal Riot*, 6.
43. Ranney, *Account of the Terrific and Fatal Riot*, 25.
44. Ranney, *Account of the Terrific and Fatal Riot*, 6.
45. Ranney, *Account of the Terrific and Fatal Riot*, 24.
46. Ranney, *Account of the Terrific and Fatal Riot*, 6.
47. Ranney, *Account of the Terrific and Fatal Riot*, 6.
48. Ranney, *Account of the Terrific and Fatal Riot*, 32.

Chapter 4: 840 Fifth Avenue, 1908

1. "Hailing the History of New York's Yellow Cabs," *Weekend Edition Sunday*, NPR, July 8, 2007, https://www.npr.org/2007/07/08/11804573/hailing-the-history-of-new-yorks-yellow-cabs.
2. Over the years, Rebecca Insley-Casper's given birth year in census records creeps from 1872 to 1875 to 1880. In the *Delineator* article, she refers to herself as a "girl."
3. Rebecca, in her later years, published as R. Insley-Casper, with widely distributed bylines. She was also socially active enough for her marriage in England to be mentioned in the New York newspapers and for her involvement with the Woman's Press Club and other women's organizations to achieve notice in the society press, including, at one point, mention of her hosting a luncheon at which Eleanor Roosevelt was present. By the age of fifty, Insley-Casper was widowed and living in a rental apartment in a respectable building on East Ninety-Third Street, and still writing.
4. One of the members on the *Delineator* masthead was novelist Theodore Dreiser. Another was Sarah Field Splint, who, shortly after this interview, would sit with Alva Erskine Smith Vanderbilt Belmont and make notes toward her never-published memoir.
5. We are taking some narrative liberties here. We don't know for a fact that Rebecca took a cab to her interview. Metered cabs were introduced only in 1907

but were immediately successful. Rebecca was a respectable upper-middle-class journalist. She might have taken the subway, but our guess is that she would have wanted to make a good impression arriving at Mrs. Astor's house. We also don't know for certain what day the interview took place. We're hypothesizing late summer. The interview appeared in the October 7 edition of the *Delineator*, and it would have taken some time to edit and print it.

6. Eric Homberger, *Mrs. Astor's New York: Money and Social Power in a Gilded Age* (New Haven, Conn.: Yale University Press, 2002), 221.

7. Homberger, *Mrs. Astor's New York*, 221.

8. Kaplan, *When the Astors Owned New York*, 30.

9. Homberger, *Mrs. Astor's New York*, 224.

10. Greg King, *A Season of Splendor: The Court of Mrs. Astor in the Gilded Age* (Hoboken, N.J.: John Wiley and Sons, 2009), 29.

11. "Out-Doors Sports; the Kentucky Races. Spring Meeting of the Louisville Jockey Club Contest Between the East and the West the Derby Won by Vagrant Parole Nowhere. Pools on To-Day's Races," *New York Times*, May 16, 1876, https://www.nytimes.com/1876/05/16/archives/outdoor-sports-the-kentucky-races-spring-meeting-of-the-louisville.html.

12. King, *A Season of Splendor*, 30.

13. King, *A Season of Splendor*, 31.

14. King, *A Season of Splendor*, 31.

15. Edith Wharton, *The Age of Innocence*, ebook, Project Gutenberg, https://www.gutenberg.org/files/541/541-h/541-h.htm.

16. Cleveland Amory, *Who Killed Society?* (New York: Harper, 1960), 118.

17. King, *A Season of Splendor*, 36.

18. King, *A Season of Splendor*, 37.

19. King, *A Season of Splendor*, 37.

20. King, *A Season of Splendor*, 38.

21. King, *A Season of Splendor*, 38.

22. King, *A Season of Splendor*, 370.

23. Sven Beckert, *The Monied Metropolis: New York City and the Consolidation of the American Bourgeoisie, 1850–1896* (Cambridge, UK: Cambridge University Press, 2001), 1–2.

24. King, *A Season of Splendor*, 372.

25. King, *A Season of Splendor*, 372.

26. King, *A Season of Splendor*, 374.

27. King, *A Season of Splendor*, 375.

28. King, *A Season of Splendor*, 375.

29. King, *A Season of Splendor*, 376.

30. Anne Ewbank, "The Gilded-Age Dinner Party that Featured 7 Courses and 32 Horses," Gastro Obscura, Atlas Obscura, October 23, 2017, https://www.atlasobscura.com/articles/dinner-horseback-horse-king.

31. King, *A Season of Splendor*, 19–20.
32. King, *A Season of Splendor*, 36.
33. Kaplan, *When the Astors Owned New York*, 31.
34. Kaplan, *When the Astors Owned New York*, 31.
35. "Mrs. William Astor Is Critically Ill," *New York Times*, October 30, 1908, https://timesmachine.nytimes.com/timesmachine/1908/10/30/104811750 .html?pageNumber=1.
36. "Mrs. William Astor Is Critically Ill."
37. Kaplan, *When the Astors Owned New York*, 148.
38. Kaplan, *When the Astors Owned New York*, 149.
39. 1920 U.S. Census and 1907 Indianapolis city directory, ancestry.com. https:// www.ancestry.com/discoveryui-content/view/45974448:6061?tid =&pid=&queryId=a511ab003afe62c1379716f95ab1c7b1&_phsrc=uee274& _phstart=successSource and https://www.ancestry.com/discoveryui-content /view/635568128:2469?tid=&pid=&queryId=faade61ab0df91689 c4208660b808a0d&_phsrc=uee271&_phstart=successSource.

Chapter 5: Waldorf-Astoria, 1928

1. This quote and this entire account come from Horace Smith, *Crooks of the Waldorf, Being the Story of Joe Smith, Master Detective* (New York: Macaulay and Company, 1929).
2. Smith, *Crooks of the Waldorf*, 12
3. Kaplan, *When the Astors Owned New York*, 73.
4. Kaplan, *When the Astors Owned New York*, 73.
5. Kaplan, *When the Astors Owned New York*, 74.
6. Kaplan, *When the Astors Owned New York*, 75.
7. Kaplan, *When the Astors Owned New York*, 75.
8. Kaplan, *When the Astors Owned New York*, 75.
9. Kaplan, *When the Astors Owned New York*, 76.
10. Albin Pasteur Dearing, *The Elegant Inn* (Secaucus, N.J.: Lyle Stuart, 1986), 19.
11. Kaplan, *When the Astors Owned New York*, 77–78.
12. *Town Topics*, vol. 29, issue 11, March 16, 1893, p. 1.
13. "The Astor Tramp Guilty," *New York Times*, December 11, 1894, https:// timesmachine.nytimes.com/timesmachine/1894/12/11/106844013. html?pageNumber=7.
14. "Why He Went into Mrs. Astor's House," *New York Times*, November 19, 1894, https://timesmachine.nytimes.com/timesmachine/1894/11/19/106879769 .html?pageNumber=8.
15. "The Astor Tramp Is Free," *New York Times*, November 20, 1894, https:// timesmachine.nytimes.com/timesmachine/1894/11/20/106879985.html?page Number=8.

16. "The Astor Tramp Is Free."
17. "The Astor Tramp's Woes," *New York Times*, November 22, 1894, https://nyti
    .ms/3BHl4Ul .
18. "The Astor Tramp's Woes."
19. "The Astor Tramp Guilty."
20. https://nyti.ms/3pOh6GN.
21. https://nyti.ms/3pOh6GN.
22. Kaplan, *When the Astors Owned New York*, 79.
23. Kaplan, *When the Astors Owned New York*, 85.
24. Kaplan, *When the Astors Owned New York*, 79.
25. *Town Topics*, vol. 38, issue 19, November 11, 1897, p. 1.
26. Kavaler, *The Astors*, 137.
27. Quoted in Kaplan, *When the Astors Owned New York*, 80.
28. Kaplan, *When the Astors Owned New York*, 89.
29. Alison Baird, "If You're on the Outside, You're In: The Infamous Red Velvet
    Rope Culture at Studio 54" (bachelor of arts thesis, College of Arts and
    Sciences, Georgetown University, April 15, 2019), https://repository.library
    .georgetown.edu/handle/10822/1061156.
30. Dearing, *The Elegant Inn*, 228.
31. https://www.nytimes.com/1929/10/31/archives/leaseholds-listed-record-of
    -site-for-the-new-waldorfastoria-is.html.

Chapter 6: Hever Castle, 1916

1. "1880 New York City Weather Extremes," Table, New York City Weather
   in 1880, Extreme Weather Watch, https://www.extremeweatherwatch.com
   /cities/new-york/year-1880.
2. Kaplan, *When the Astors Owned New York*, 42.
3. Kaplan, *When the Astors Owned New York*, 29.
4. Kaplan, *When the Astors Owned New York*, 37.
5. Fox, *Five Sisters*, 87.
6. Kaplan, *When the Astors Owned New York*, 38.
7. Quoted in Kaplan, *When the Astors Owned New York*, 34.
8. Astor, *Tribal Feeling*, 8.
9. Kaplan, *When the Astors Owned New York*, 35–36.
10. Kaplan, *When the Astors Owned New York*, 38.
11. Jeremy Lewis, *David Astor: A Life in Print* (London: Jonathan Cape, 2016), 2.
12. Kaplan, *When the Astors Owned New York*, 36.
13. Kaplan, *When the Astors Owned New York*, 36.
14. Kaplan, *When the Astors Owned New York*, 40.
15. Kaplan, *When the Astors Owned New York*, 40.

16. Kaplan, *When the Astors Owned New York*, 41.
17. Kaplan, *When the Astors Owned New York*, 41.
18. Kaplan, *When the Astors Owned New York*, 40.
19. Quoted in Kaplan, *When the Astors Owned New York*, 40.
20. Kaplan, *When the Astors Owned New York*, 34–35.
21. Kaplan, *When the Astors Owned New York*, 42.
22. Lewis, *David Astor*, 3.
23. Kaplan, *When the Astors Owned New York*, 43.
24. Kaplan, *When the Astors Owned New York*, 112.
25. Kaplan, *When the Astors Owned New York*, 32.
26. Kaplan, *When the Astors Owned New York*, 44.
27. Lewis, *David Astor*, 2.
28. Kaplan, *When the Astors Owned New York*, 45.
29. Kaplan, *When the Astors Owned New York*, 45.
30. Kaplan, *When the Astors Owned New York*, 46.
31. "Mr. Astor Not Dead," *New York Times*, July 13, 1892, https://timesmachine
    .nytimes.com/timesmachine/1892/07/13/104097305.html?pageNumber=1.
32. Lewis, *David Astor*, 3.
33. Kaplan, *When the Astors Owned New York*, 124.
34. Kaplan, *When the Astors Owned New York*, 125.
35. Kaplan, *When the Astors Owned New York*, 127.
36. Lewis, *David Astor*, 3.
37. Amory, *Who Killed Society?*, 475.
38. Kaplan, *When the Astors Owned New York*, 116–17.
39. Kaplan, *When the Astors Owned New York*, 117.
40. Kaplan, *When the Astors Owned New York*, 48.
41. Kaplan, *When the Astors Owned New York*, 113.
42. Pauline Spender-Clay quoted in Kaplan, *When the Astors Owned New York*, 114.
43. Kaplan, *When the Astors Owned New York*, 118.
44. Lewis, *David Astor*, 3.
45. Kaplan, *When the Astors Owned New York*, 121.
46. Kaplan, *When the Astors Owned New York*, 139.
47. Kaplan, *When the Astors Owned New York*, 142.
48. Kaplan, *When the Astors Owned New York*, 49.
49. Kaplan, *When the Astors Owned New York*, 49.
50. Kaplan, *When the Astors Owned New York*, 54.
51. Maurice Collis, *Nancy Astor: An Informal Biography* (London: Faber and Faber,
    1960), 25.
52. Collis, *Nancy Astor*, 28–29.
53. Collis, *Nancy Astor*, 29.
54. Kaplan, *When the Astors Owned New York*, 129.

55. Kaplan, *When the Astors Owned New York*, 161.
56. Collis, *Nancy Astor*, 11.
57. Kaplan, *When the Astors Owned New York*, 163.
58. Collis, *Nancy Astor*, 16.
59. Kaplan, *When the Astors Owned New York*, 164.
60. Kaplan, *When the Astors Owned New York*, 165.
61. Kaplan, *When the Astors Owned New York*, 168.
62. Kaplan, *When the Astors Owned New York*, 168.
63. Kaplan, *When the Astors Owned New York*, 168.
64. Kaplan, *When the Astors Owned New York*, 169.
65. Amory, *Who Killed Society?*, 475.
66. Lewis, *David Astor*, 4.

Chapter 7: Rokeby, 1875

1. Lately Thomas, *The Astor Orphans: A Pride of Lions* (Albany, N.Y.: Washington Park Press, 1999), 41.
2. Thomas, *The Astor Orphans*, 11.
3. Thomas, *The Astor Orphans*, 13.
4. Thomas, *The Astor Orphans*, 12.
5. Thomas, *The Astor Orphans*, 13.
6. Thomas, *The Astor Orphans*, 21.
7. "La Bergerie"/"Rokeby," Wikimapia, n.d., http://wikimapia.org/6578657/La-Bergerie-Rokeby.
8. Thomas, *The Astor Orphans*, 14.
9. Thomas, *The Astor Orphans*, 15.
10. Thomas, *The Astor Orphans*, 15.
11. Thomas, *The Astor Orphans*, 16.
12. Thomas, *The Astor Orphans*, 17.
13. Thomas, *The Astor Orphans*, 17.
14. Thomas, *The Astor Orphans*, 18.
15. Thomas, *The Astor Orphans*, 19.
16. Thomas, *The Astor Orphans*, 22.
17. Thomas, *The Astor Orphans*, 22.
18. Thomas, *The Astor Orphans*, 23.
19. Thomas, *The Astor Orphans*, 23.
20. Thomas, *The Astor Orphans*, 24.
21. Thomas, *The Astor Orphans*, 26.
22. Thomas, *The Astor Orphans*, 30.
23. Thomas, *The Astor Orphans*, 36.
24. Thomas, *The Astor Orphans*, 37.
25. Lucey, *Archie and Amelie*, 49.

26. Thomas, *The Astor Orphans*, 39.
27. Thomas, *The Astor Orphans*, 40.
28. "Miss Amelie Rives to Marry," *New York Times*, June 3, 1888, https://times machine.nytimes.com/timesmachine/1888/06/03/109316800.html?page Number=11.
29. https://nyti.ms/3In9Zvq.
30. Thomas, *The Astor Orphans*, 43.
31. Walter Scott, *Rokeby* (Edinburgh: Ballantyne, 1813), 206–7.
32. Thomas, *The Astor Orphans*, 43.
33. Thomas, *The Astor Orphans*, 43.
34. Melinda J. Gough, "Tasso's Enchantress, Tasso's Captive Woman." *Renaissance Quarterly* 54, no. 2 (2001): 523–52.
35. Thomas, *The Astor Orphans*, 44.
36. Thomas, *The Astor Orphans*, 44.
37. Thomas, *The Astor Orphans*, 45.
38. Thomas, *The Astor Orphans*, 50.
39. Thomas, *The Astor Orphans*, 104.
40. Thomas, *The Astor Orphans*, 104.
41. Thomas, *The Astor Orphans*, 105.
42. Thomas, *The Astor Orphans*, 105.
43. Thomas, *The Astor Orphans*, 106.
44. Thomas, *The Astor Orphans*, 106.
45. Thomas, *The Astor Orphans*, 142.
46. Thomas, *The Astor Orphans*, 145.
47. https://encyclopediavirginia.org/entries/chaloner-john-armstrong-1862–1935.
48. Rokeby, n.d., https://www.eventsatrokeby.com/rokeby.
49. Penelope Green, "The House Inherited Them," *New York Times*, July 21, 2010, https://www.nytimes.com/2010/07/22/garden/22hudson.html.
50. Green, "The House Inherited Them."
51. Alexandra Aldrich, *The Astor Orphan: A Memoir* (New York: Echo, 2013), 10.

Chapter 8: Halifax, April 15, 1912

1. Mandi Bierly, "*'Mythbusters'* Settles *'Titanic'* Debate! The Answer . . ." *Entertainment Weekly*, October 8, 2012, https://ew.com/article/2012/10/08 /mythbusters-titanic-debate-jack-die/.
2. "Let's settle the jack door debate once and for all." Reddit, n.d., https:// old.reddit.com/r/titanic/comments/uaei55/lets_settle_the_jack_door _debate_once_and_for_all/
3. Quinn Keaney, "Yet Another Theory About Rose and Jack on That Door in Titanic Is Here to F*ck You Up." PopSugar, November 23, 2017, https://www .popsugar.com/entertainment/Titanic-Theory-Jack-Doesnt-Exist-43479718.

4. "How Col. Astor Died to Let Woman Live," *New York Times*, April 19, 1912, https://timesmachine.nytimes.com/timesmachine/1912/04/19/100530748.html?pageNumber=7.

5. "Bodies of Astor and Straus Found," *New York Times*, April 27, 1912, https://timesmachine.nytimes.com/timesmachine/1912/04/27/100531460.html?pageNumber=1.

6. "Why So Few?" question posed in "Titanic: Frequently Asked Questions," Maritime Museum of the Atlantic, n.d.,https://maritimemuseum.novascotia.ca/what-see-do/titanics-halifax-connection/frequently-asked-questions#5.

7. Two separate cruise ships marked the centenary of the *Titanic*'s sinking in April 2012 by traveling to the site of the wreck and throwing wreaths into the water. See https://www.cnn.com/2012/04/15/world/europe/titanic-anniversary.

8. Daniel Allen Butler, *"Unsinkable": The Full Story of the RMS* Titanic (Cambridge, Mass.: Da Capo, 2002), 29.

9. Quoted in Sinclair, *Dynasty*, 199.

10. Kavaler *The Astors*, 126–27.

11. Kavaler, *The Astors*, 127.

12. Sinclair, *Dynasty*, 198.

13. Sinclair, *Dynasty*, 199.

14. Fox, *Five Sisters*, 72.

15. Elizabeth Drexel Lehr, *"King Lehr" and the Gilded Age* (1935; repr. Bedford, Mass.: Applewood Books, 2005), 163.

16. Kavaler, *The Astors*, 131.

17. Kavaler, *The Astors*, 132.

18. Lehr, *"King Lehr" and the Gilded Age*, 164.

19. Kavaler, *The Astors*, 142.

20. Butler, *"Unsinkable,"* 28.

21. Butler, *"Unsinkable,"* 28.

22. Butler, *"Unsinkable,"* 27.

23. Walter Lord, *A Night to Remember* (New York: St. Martin's Griffin, 1955), 1.

24. Lord, *A Night to Remember*, 67.

25. Lord, *A Night to Remember*, 67.

26. Lord, *A Night to Remember*, 67.

27. Lord, *A Night to Remember*, 67.

28. Lord, *A Night to Remember*, 72.

29. Lord, *A Night to Remember*, 73.

30. Lord, *A Night to Remember*, 82.

31. Lord, *A Night to Remember*, 82.

32. Lord, *A Night to Remember*, 89–90.

33. Lord, *A Night to Remember*, 92.

34. Kavaler, *The Astors*, 130.

35. Butler, *"Unsinkable,"* 28.

Chapter 9: Blackwell's Island, 1910

1. Karl Marx and Friedrich Engels, *Manifesto of the Communist Party* (1848), PDF, https://archive.org/details/communistmanifestomarxengels/page/n31/mode/2up.

2. A portion of this notorious building survives today in the form of the Octagon, a structure on the National Register of Historic Places that is incorporated into a sprawling twenty-first-century apartment complex. In the spring of 2022, this building, the site of so many generations of misery and despair, offered a café space with Keurig coffee and vending machines selling potato chips.

3. "Bar Harbor's Social Season Promises to Last Until the Snow Flies—Col. Astor a Host at Many Dinners," *New York Times*, September 4, 1910, https://timesmachine.nytimes.com/timesmachine/1910/09/04/105089609.pdf.

4. "John Jacob Astor," Find a Grave, https://www.findagrave.com/memorial/152137273/john-jacob-astor.

5. Peter Megargee Brown and Walter L. Stratton, eds., *Riot of The Century: The New York City Draft Riots of July 1863* (New York: Trustees of the Riot Relief Fund, c. 2005), 2.

6. Adrian Cook. *The Armies of the Streets: The New York City Draft Riots of 1863* (Lexington: University Press of Kentucky, 1974), 8.

7. Cook, *The Armies of the Streets*, 9.

8. Cook, *The Armies of the Streets*, 7.

9. Cook, *The Armies of the Streets*, 6–7.

10. Cook, *The Armies of the Streets*, 6.

11. Cook, *The Armies of the Streets*, 11.

12. Quoted in Cook, *The Armies of the Streets*, 11.

13. Cook, *The Armies of the Streets*, 12.

14. *New York Herald*, February 2 and July 6, 1856, quoted in Cook, *The Armies of the Streets*, 13.

15. Cook, *The Armies of the Streets*, 13.

16. "Squatter Settlement, 1855, Now Central Park," issued 1870–1879, New York Public Library Digital Collections, https://digitalcollections.nypl.org/items/510d47e1–2cb0–a3d9–e040–e00a18064a99.

17. Cook, *The Armies of the Streets*, 14.

18. Cook, *The Armies of the Streets*, 14.

19. Cook, *The Armies of the Streets*, 14.

20. Farida B. Ahmad, Jodi, A. Cisewski, and Robert N. Anderson, "Provisional Mortality Data—United States, 2021," *Morbidity and Mortality Weekly Report*, 71, no. 17 (April 29, 2022): 597–600, https://pubmed.ncbi.nlm.nih.gov/35482572; calculations by author.

21. Cook, *The Armies of the Streets*, 16.

22. Cook, *The Armies of the Streets*, 17.

23. Cook, *The Armies of the Streets*, 59.

24. Iver Bernstein, *The New York City Draft Riots: Their Significance for American Society and Politics in the Age of the Civil War* (New York: Oxford University Press, 1990), 3.

25. Bernstein, *The New York City Draft Riots*, 4.

26. Bernstein, *The New York City Draft Riots*, 5.

27. Bernstein, *The New York City Draft Riots*, 6.

28. David M. Barnes, *The Draft Riots in New York, July, 1863: The Metropolitan Police, Their Services During Riot Week, Their Honorable Record* (New York: Baker and Godwin, 1863), 5.

29. Barnes, *The Draft Riots in New York, July, 1863*, 6.

30. Barnes, *The Draft Riots in New York, July, 1863*, 6.

31. Barnes, *The Draft Riots in New York, July, 1863*, 50.

32. Barnes, *The Draft Riots in New York, July, 1863*, 81.

33. Bernstein, *The New York City Draft Riots*, 3.

34. Cook, *The Armies of the Streets*, 20.

35. Cook, *The Armies of the Streets*, 31.

Chapter 10: Mrs. Astor's Bar, 1910 to 1966

1. William R. Taylor, ed., *Inventing Times Square: Commerce and Culture at the Crossroads of the World* (Baltimore, Md.: Johns Hopkins University Press, 1996), 317.

2. Taylor, ed., *Inventing Times Square*, 318.

3. William McGowan, "The Chickens and the Bulls: The Rise and Incredible Fall of a Vicious Extortion Ring that Preyed on Prominent Gay Men in the 1960s, *Slate*, July 11, 2012, https://slate.com/human-interest/2012/07/the-chickens-and-the-bulls-the-rise-and-incredible-fall-of-a-vicious-extortion-ring-that-preyed-on-prominent-gay-men-in-the-1960s.html.

4. George Chauncey, *Gay New York: Gender, Urban Culture, and the Making of the Gay Male World, 1890–1940* (New York: Basic Books, 1994), 350.

5. Chauncey, *Gay New York*, 214.

6. Taylor, ed., *Inventing Times Square*, 317.

7. Taylor, ed., *Inventing Times Square*, 319.

8. Chauncey, *Gay New York*, 201.

9. Chauncey, *Gay New York*, 147.

10. Taylor, ed., *Inventing Times Square*, 321.

11. Taylor, ed., *Inventing Times Square*, 324.

12. Chauncey, *Gay New York*, 351.

13. Chauncey, *Gay New York*, 350.

14. Chauncey, *Gay New York*, 350.

15. Paul Forbes, "Mrs. Astor's Bar," *Drum* 20 (1966): 11.

16. Forbes, "Mrs. Astor's Bar," 11.

17. Forbes, "Mrs. Astor's Bar," 11–12.

18. Allan Berube, *Coming Out Under Fire: The History of Gay Men and Women in World War Two* (New York: Free Press, 1990), 114–15.

19. Berube, *Coming Out Under Fire*, 115.

20. Steve Estes, "The Greatest Generation," in Steve Estes, *Ask and Tell: Gay and Lesbian Veterans Speak Out* (Chapel Hill: University of North Carolina Press, 2007).

21. Berube, *Coming Out Under Fire*, 118.

22. Berube, *Coming Out Under Fire*, 120.

23. Berube, *Coming Out Under Fire*, 120.

24. William McGowan, "The Chickens and the Bulls: The Rise and Incredible Fall of a Vicious Extortion Ring that Preyed on Prominent Gay Men in the 1960s *Slate*, July 11, 2012, https://slate.com/human-interest/2012/07/the-chickens -and-the-bulls-the-rise-and-incredible-fall-of-a-vicious-extortion-ring-that -preyed-on-prominent-gay-men-in-the-1960s.html.

25. McGowan, "The Chickens and the Bulls."

26. McGowan, "The Chickens and the Bulls."

27. McGowan, "The Chickens and the Bulls."

28. McGowan, "The Chickens and the Bulls."

29. McCandlish Phillips, "Astor Furnishings Are Going, Going . . ." *New York Times*, October 4, 1966, https://nyti.ms/3MHbjff.

30. "Astor to Auction: Well, You Name It," *New York Times*, September 19, 1966, https://timesmachine.nytimes.com/timesmachine/1966/09/19/90224387.html ?pageNumber=45.

Chapter 11: Ferncliff, 1952

1. https://nyti.ms/43d8w2.

2. Astor Family Papers. Manuscripts and Archives Division, New York Public Library. Astor, Lenox, and Tilden Foundations. Box 4 (MssCol 141).

3. Kavaler, *The Astors*, 171.

4. Kavaler, *The Astors*, 171.

5. Kavaler, *The Astors*, 172.

6. John Richardson, "The Battle for Mrs. Astor," *Vanity Fair*, October 2008.

7. Kavaler, *The Astors*, 172.

8. Kaplan, *When the Astors Owned New York*, 154.

9. "Sport: Down to the Sea," *Time*, February 6, 1928, https://content.time.com /time/subscriber/article/0,33009,731503,00.html.

10. Glenway Wescott Collection, Beinecke Library, Yale University, New Haven, Connecticut.

11. "Part II: Vincent, the Astor Who Gave Away the Money," New York Social Diary, n.d., WaybackMachine, https://web.archive.org/web/20130512034627/http://www.newyorksocialdiary.com/node/317873/print.

12. Eve Brown, *Champagne Cholly: The Life and Times of Maury Paul* (New York: E. P. Dutton and Company, 1947), 70.

13. David Patrick Columbia, "Part II: Vincent, the Astor Who Gave Away All the Money," New York Social Diary, https://web.archive.org/web/20130512034627/http://www.newyorksocialdiary.com/node/317873/print.

14. "Astor Home for Children," Wikipedia, n.d., https://en.wikipedia.org/wiki/Astor_Home_for_Children.

15. Kavaler, *The Astors*, 177.

16. Kavaler, *The Astors*, 177.

17. "Vincent Astor Dies in His Home," *New York Times*, February 4, 1959, https://timesmachine.nytimes.com/timesmachine/1959/02/04/89115584.html?pageNumber=1.

18. Kavaler, *The Astors*, 179.

19. Brown, *Champagne Cholly*, 98.

20. "Nourmahal," Naval History and Heritage Command, n.d., https://www.history.navy.mil/research/histories/ship-histories/danfs/n/nourmahal.html#:~:text=Nourmahal%20(PG%2D72)%2C,ownership%20by%20the%20Coast%20Guard.

21. Erin Marquis, "Jeff Bezos's $500-Million Yacht Hits the Open Ocean for the First Time," Jalopnik, February 17, 2023, https://jalopnik.com/jeff-bezos-500-million-yacht-hits-the-open-ocean-for-t-1850128708.

22. Kavaler, *The Astors*, 183.

23. "Astor Yacht Nourmahal Also a Floating Laboratory," *New York Times*, February 12, 1933, https://nyti.ms/3Wf6OM2.

24. "Part II: Vincent, the Astor Who Gave Away the Money."

25. USS *Nourmahal* photograph album, Manuscript and Archives Division, New York Public Library.

26. "Sport: Down to the Sea," *Time*, February 6, 1928, https://content.time.com/time/subscriber/article/0,33009,731503,00.html.

27. Kavaler, *The Astors*, 180.

28. Log of the USS *Nourmahal*, Archives and Manuscripts Division, New York Public Library.

29. Sans Souci, Havana. n.d., https://jstor.org/stable/community.11899021.

30. Log of the USS *Nourmahal*, Astor Family Papers. Manuscripts and Archives Division, New York Public Library. Astor, Lenox, and Tilden Foundations. Box 4 (MssCol 141).

31. "The Galapagos Affair," Galapagos Island, n.d., https://www.galapagosisland.net/galapagos-islands/the-galapagos-affair/.

32. Log of the USS *Nourmahal,* Astor Family Papers. Manuscripts and Archives Division, New York Public Library. Astor, Lenox, and Tilden Foundations. Box 4 (MssCol 141).

33. Kavaler, *The Astors,* 184.

34. Kavaler, *The Astors,* 184–85.

35. Kavaler, *The Astors,* 186.

36. Kavaler, *The Astors,* 187.

37. Kavaler, *The Astors,* 187.

38. David Patrick Columbia, "The Life in the House and the House in the Life of Mrs. Astor," New York Social Diary, January 28, 2022, https://www.newyork socialdiary.com/the-life-in-the-house-and-the-house-in-the-life-of-mrs-astor/.

39. Richardson, "The Battle for Mrs. Astor."

40. Brooke Astor, *Footprints: An Autobiography* (New York: Doubleday, 1980), 262.

41. Astor, *Footprints,* 262.

42. Astor, *Footprints,* 263.

43. Astor, *Footprints,* 265.

44. Astor, *Footprints,* 266.

45. Steve Fishman, "Mrs. Astor's Baby," New York, November 9, 2007, https://nymag.com/news/features/40662/.

46. Astor, *Footprints,* 269.

47. Astor, *Footprints,* 270.

48. Author interview with Annette de la Renta, March 6, 2023.

49. Fishman, "Mrs. Astor's Baby."

50. Meryl Gordon, *Mrs. Astor Regrets: The Hidden Betrayals of a Family Beyond Reproach* (New York: Mariner Books, 2008), 71.

51. Fishman, "Mrs. Astor's Baby."

52. Michael Wilson, "Lawyers Tried to Brighten Grim Courtroom Images of an Aged Thief," *New York Times,* December 21, 2009.

53. Astor, *Footprints, 304.*

54. Astor, *Footprints,* 303.

55. Astor, *Footprints,* 287–88.

56. Gordon, *Mrs. Astor Regrets,* 74.

57. Richardson, "The Battle for Mrs. Astor."

58. Alice Macycove Perdue and James W. Seymore. *In Brooke Astor's Court: An Insider's Story* (CreateSpace Independent Publishing Platform, 2014), 48–49.

59. John Eligon, "Fight for Astor Estate Mirrors Battle 50 Years Ago," *New York Times,* April 25, 2009, https://www.nytimes.com/2009/04/26/nyregion/26 astor.html.

60. Astor, *Footprints,* 325.

61. Eligon, "Fight for Astor Estate Mirrors Battle 50 Years Ago."

62. Kavaler, *The Astors,* 198.

Chapter 12: The Last Astor, 2013

1. Russ Buettner, "Astor's Son Was Contrite Ahead of Release from Prison," *New York Times*, August 29, 2013, https://www.nytimes.com/2013/08/30/nyregion/astors-son-was-contrite-ahead-of-release-from-prison.html.

2. Robert D. McFadden, "Anthony D. Marshall, Astor Son Who Was Convicted in Swindle, Dies at 90," *New York Times*, December 1, 2014, https://www.nytimes.com/2014/12/02/nyregion/anthony-d-marshall-son-of-brooke-astor-convicted-in-swindle-dies-at-90.html.

3. Russ Buettner, "Brooke Astor's Son Is Paroled," *New York Times*, August 22, 2013, https://www.nytimes.com/2013/08/23/nyregion/brooke-astors-son-to-be-paroled.html.

4. "Regrets? He's had a few," *Daily Mail* August 30, 2013, https://www.dailymail.co.uk/news/article-2406511/Astor-heir-Anthony-Marshall-swindled-millions-dollars-ailing-mother-tells-parole-board-hes-sorry.html.

5. Gordon, *Mrs. Astor Regrets*, 196.

6. Todd Venezia, "'Evil' Son Sees Astor in the Hospital," *New York Post*, July 29, 2006, https://nypost.com/2006/07/29evil-son-sees-astor-in-hospital/.

7. Stefanie Cohen, "Astor's Hayseed Daughter-in-Law Left Her First Husband with Just . . . $578.50," *New York Post*, August 2, 2006, https://nypost.com/2006/08/02/astors-hayseed-daughter-in-law-left-her-first-hubby-with-just-578-50/?utm_source=url_sitebuttons&utm_medium=site%20buttons&utm_campaign=site%20buttons.

8. Fishman, "Mrs. Astor's Baby."

9. Fishman, "Mrs. Astor's Baby."

10. Fishman, "Mrs. Astor's Baby."

11. Fishman, "Mrs. Astor's Baby."

12. Julia Marsh, "Disinherited Astor Grandson: I'd Do It Again," *New York Post*, June 10, 2015, https://nypost.com/2015/06/10/disinherited-astor-grandson-id-do-it-again/.

13. Russ Buettner, "Appeals Exhausted, Astor Case Ends as Son Is Sent to Jail," *New York Times*, June 21, 2013, https://www.nytimes.com/2013/06/22/nyregion/astors-son-his-appeals-exhausted-goes-to-prison.html.

14. Fishman, "Mrs. Astor's Baby."

15. Fishman, "Mrs. Astor's Baby."

16. McFadden, "Anthony D. Marshall, Astor Son Who Was Convicted in Swindle, Dies at 90."

17. Wilson, "Lawyers Tried to Brighten Grim Courtroom Image of an Aged Thief."

18. Astor, *Footprints*, 24.

19. Frances Kiernan, *The Last Mrs. Astor: A New York Story* (New York: W. W. Norton and Company, 2008), 60.
20. Wilson, "Lawyers Tried to Brighten Grim Courtroom Image of an Aged Thief."
21. Astor, *Footprints*, 152.
22. Astor, *Footprints*, 152.
23. Astor, *Footprints*, 155.
24. Astor, *Footprints*, 204.
25. Gordon, *Mrs. Astor Regrets*, 51.
26. Author interview with Annette de la Renta.
27. Gordon, *Mrs. Astor Regrets*, 62.
28. Gordon, *Mrs. Astor Regrets*, 62.
29. Author interview with Annette de la Renta.
30. Kiernan, *The Last Mrs. Astor*, 258.
31. Perdue and Seymore, *In Brooke Astor's Court*, 171.
32. Astor, *Footprints*, 305.
33. Marilyn Berger, "Brooke Astor, 105, Aristocrat of the People, Dies," *New York Times*, August 14, 2007.
34. Gordon, *Mrs. Astor Regrets*, 102.
35. Gordon, *Mrs. Astor Regrets*, 286.
36. Gordon, *Mrs. Astor Regrets*, 286.
37. Geraldine Fabrikant, "Brooke Astor Has a Year's Worth of Giving Left," *New York Times*, December 18, 1996, https://www.nytimes.com/1996/12/18/nyregion/brooke-astor-has-a-year-s-worth-of-giving-left.html.
38. Author interview with Annette de la Renta.
39. Richardson, "The Battle for Mrs. Astor."
40. Gordon, *Mrs. Astor Regrets*, 143.
41. "Howard M Fillit, MD," profile, Mount Sinai, https://profiles.mountsinai.org/howard-m-fillit.
42. Gordon, *Mrs. Astor Regrets*, 221.
43. Gordon, *Mrs. Astor Regrets*, 286.
44. Meryl Gordon, "The New Astor Court," *Vanity Fair*, September 2009, https://www.vanityfair.com/news/2009/09/astor-trial200909.
45. "I don't know what's the matter," Anthony D. Marshall to Dr. Howard Fillit, December 26, 2000, Supreme Court of the State of New York, Index no. 500095/06, quoted in Gordon, Mrs. Astor Regrets, 221.
46. Gordon, *Mrs. Astor Regrets*, 126.
47. Gordon, "The New Astor Court."
48. Gordon, Mrs. Astor Regrets, 128.
49. Gordon, *Mrs. Astor Regrets*, 130.
50. Gordon, *Mrs. Astor Regrets*, 131.

51. Christopher Mason, "The Cherished Remainders of a Luxe Life," *New York Times*, August 15, 2012, https://www.nytimes.com/2012/08/16/garden /sothebys-auctions-brooke-astors-treasures.html.

52. Leah Bourne, "#Throwback Thursday: Brooke Astor Celebrated Her 100th Birthday at the Historic Rockefeller Estate," SC, May 16, 2013, https://style caster.com/throwback-thursday-brooke-astor-celebrated-her-100th-birthday -at-the-rockefeller-estate/.

53. Post Staff, "Video Shows Astor's 100th Birthday," *New York Post*, May 8, 2009, https://nypost.com/2009/05/08/video-shows-astors-100th-birthday/.

54. Emily Rueb, "A Lavish Celebration, Now Evidence," *New York Times*, May 8, 2009, https://www.nytimes.com/video/nyregion/1194840094476/a-lavish -celebration-now-evidence.html.

55. Alice Macycove Perdue and James W. Seymore, *In Brooke Astor's Court: An Insider's Story* (CreateSpace Independent Publishing Platform, 2014), 102.

56. Author interview with Annette de la Renta.

57. Perdue and Seymore, *In Brooke Astor's Court*, 103.

58. Gordon, *Mrs. Astor Regrets*, 155.

59. Gordon, *Mrs. Astor Regrets*, 155.

60. Gordon, *Mrs. Astor Regrets*, 156.

61. Gordon, *Mrs. Astor Regrets*, 155.

62. Purdue and Seymore, *In Brooke Astor's Court*, 101.

63. Richardson, "The Battle for Mrs. Astor."

64. Fisher, "Mrs. Astor's Baby."

65. Gordon, *Mrs. Astor Regrets*, 158.

66. Gordon, *Mrs. Astor Regrets*, 158.

67. Vicky Ward, "In Mrs. Astor's Shadow," *Vanity Fair*, December 2006, https:// archive.vanityfair.com/article/2006/12/in-mrs-astors-shadow.

68. Fisher, "Mrs. Astor's Baby."

69. Richardson, "The Battle for Mrs. Astor."

70. Gordon, *Mrs. Astor Regrets*, 162.

71. Gordon, "The New Astor Court."

72. Gordon, *Mrs. Astor Regrets*, 162.

73. Gordon, *Mrs. Astor Regrets*, 166.

74. Gordon, *Mrs. Astor Regrets*, 185.

75. Gordon, *Mrs. Astor Regrets*, 168.

76. Kiernan, *The Last Mrs. Astor*, 282.

77. Marsh, "Disinherited Astor Grandson: I'd Do It Again."

78. Gordon, "The New Astor Court."

79. Ward, "In Mrs. Astor's Shadow."

80. McFadden, "Anthony D. Marshall, Astor Son Who Was Convicted in Swindle, Dies at 90."

81. Gordon, *Mrs. Astor Regrets*, 232.
82. Gordon, *Mrs. Astor Regrets*, 245.
83. Fisher, "Mrs. Astor's Baby."
84. Gordon, "The New Astor Court."
85. Kiernan, *The Last Mrs. Astor*, 297.
86. John Eligon, "Prosecutor in Brooke Astor Case Points Finger at a Daughter-in-Law," *New York Times*, April 27, 2009.
87. Gordon, "The New Astor Court."
88. John Eligon, "Brooke Astor's Son Guilty in Scheme to Defraud Her," *New York Times*, October 8, 2009, https://www.nytimes.com/2009/10/09/nyregion /09astor.html.
89. Gordon, "The New Astor Court."
90. Gordon, "The New Astor Court."
91. Gordon, "The New Astor Court."
92. Eligon, "Prosecutor in Brooke Astor Case Points Finger at a Daughter-in-Law."
93. Wilson, "Lawyers Tried to Brighten Grim Courtroom Image of an Aged Thief."
94. Eligon, "Brooke Astor's Son Guilty in Scheme to Defraud Her."
95. Eligon, "Brooke Astor's Son Guilty in Scheme to Defraud Her."
96. Eligon, "Brooke Astor's Son Guilty in Scheme to Defraud Her."
97. Eligon, "Brooke Astor's Son Guilty in Scheme to Defraud Her."
98. Eligon, "Brooke Astor's Son Guilty in Scheme to Defraud Her."
99. McFadden, "Anthony D. Marshall, Astor Son Who Was Convicted in Swindle, Dies at 90."
100. Buettner, "Appeals Exhausted, Astor Case Ends as Son Is Sent to Jail."
101. Buettner, "Appeals Exhausted, Astor Case Ends as Son Is Sent to Jail."
102. Post Staff, "Anthony Marshall Surrenders, Sent to Prison in Astor Theft Case," *New York Post*, June 21, 2013, https://nypost.com/2013/06/21/anthony -marshall-surrenders-sent-to-prison-in-astor-theft-case/.
103. Post Staff, "Anthony Marshall Surrenders."
104. Michael Schwirtz, "Anthony Marshall, Brooke Astor's Son, Experienced 'Atrocious' Treatment at Rikers, His Family Says," *New York Times*, December 17, 2015, https://www.nytimes.com/2015/12/18/nyregion /anthony-marshall-brooke-astors-son-experienced-atrocious-treatment-at -rikers-his-family-says.html.
105. McFadden, "Anthony D. Marshall, Astor Son Who Was Convicted in Swindle, Dies at 90."
106. Deborah L. Jacobs, "Anthony Marshall, Brooke Astor's Son, Receives Get-Out-of-Jail Card," *Forbes*, August 22, 2013, https://www.forbes.com/sites /deborahljacobs/2013/08/22/anthony-marshall-brooke-astors-son-receives -get-out-of-jail-card/?sh=322e25955c91.

107. Russ Buettner, "Brooke Astor's Son Is Paroled," *New York Times*, August 22, 2013, https://www.nytimes.com/2013/08/23/nyregion/brooke-astors-son -to-be-paroled.html.

108. Amory, *Who Killed Society?*, 468.

Epilogue

1. Mary Astor, *A Life on Film*, New York: Delacorte Press, 1971, 1.

2. Astor, *A Life on Film*.

3. Astor, *A Life on Film*, 2.

BIBLIOGRAPHY

Aldrich, Alexandra. *The Astor Orphan: A Memoir.* New York: Ecco, 2013.

Amory, Cleveland. *Who Killed Society?* New York: Harper, 1960.

Astor, Brooke. *Footprints: An Autobiography.* New York: Doubleday, 1980.

Astor, John Jacob, IV. *A Journey in Other Worlds: A Romance of the Future.* London: Longmans, Green, and Company, 1894.

Astor, Mary. *A Life on Film.* New York: Delacorte Press, 1971.

Astor, Michael. *Tribal Feeling.* London: John Murray, 1963.

Barnes, David M. *The Draft Riots in New York, July, 1863: The Metropolitan Police, Their Services During Riot Week, Their Honorable Record.* New York: Baker and Godwin, 1863.

Barratt, Nick. *Lost Voices from the* Titanic*: The Definitive Oral History.* New York: Palgrave Macmillan, 2010.

Beckert, Sven. *The Monied Metropolis: New York City and the Consolidation of the American Bourgeoisie, 1850–1896.* Cambridge, Mass.: Harvard University Press, 2001.

Bernstein, Iver. *The New York City Draft Riots: Their Significance for American Society and Politics in the Age of the Civil War.* New York: Oxford University Press, 1990.

Berube, Allan. *Coming Out Under Fire: The History of Gay Men and Women in World War Two.* New York: Free Press, 1990.

Brown, Eve. *Champagne Cholly: The Life and Times of Maury Paul.* New York: E. P. Dutton and Company, 1947.

Brown, Peter Megargee, and Walter L. Stratton, eds. *Riot of the Century: The New York City Draft Riots of July 1863.* New York: Trustees of the Riot Relief Fund, c. 2005.

Burrows, Edwin G., and Mike Wallace. *Gotham: A History of New York City to 1898.* Oxford: Oxford University Press, 1999.

Butler, Daniel Allen. *"Unsinkable": The Full Story of the RMS* Titanic. Cambridge, Mass.: Da Capo, 1998.

Carnes, Mark C. *Past Imperfect: History According to the Movies.* New York: Henry Holt Reference, 1995.

Chauncey, George. *Gay New York: Gender, Urban Culture, and the Gay Male World, 1890–1940*. New York: Basic Books, 1994.

Collis, Maurice. *Nancy Astor: An Informal Biography*. London: Faber and Faber, 1960.

Cook, Adrian. *The Armies of the Streets: The New York City Draft Riots of 1863*. Lexington: University Press of Kentucky, 1974.

Cowles, Virginia. *The Astors*. New York: Knopf, 1979.

Crockett, Albert Stevens. *Peacocks on Parade: A Narrative of a Unique Period in American Social History and Its Most Colorful Figures*. New York: Sears Publishing Company, 1931.

Dearing, Albin Pasteur. *The Elegant Inn: The Waldorf-Astoria Hotel, 1893–1929*. Secaucus, N.J.: Lyle Stuart, 1986.

Dolin, Eric Jay. *Fur, Fortune, and Empire: The Epic History of the Fur Trade in America*. New York: W. W. Norton, 2010.

Estes, Steve. "The Greatest Generation." In *Ask and Tell: Gay and Lesbian Veterans Speak Out*. Chapel Hill: University of North Carolina Press, 2007.

Fox, James. *Five Sisters: The Langhornes of Virginia*. New York: Simon and Schuster Paperbacks, 2000.

Freeland, David. *American Hotel: The Waldorf-Astoria and the Making of a Century*. New Brunswick, N.J.: Rutgers University Press, 2021.

Gates, John D. *The Astor Family*. New York: Doubleday, 1981.

Gordon, Meryl. *Mrs. Astor Regrets: The Hidden Betrayals of a Family Beyond Reproach*. New York: Mariner Books, 2008.

Grigg, John. *Nancy Astor*. London: Sidgwick and Jackson, 1980.

Gunn, Thomas Butler. *The Physiology of New York Boarding-Houses*. New York: Mason Brothers, 1857.

Homberger, Eric. *Mrs. Astor's New York: Money and Social Power in a Gilded Age*. New Haven, Conn.: Yale University Press, 2002.

Hone, Philip. *The Diary of Philip Hone, 1828–1851*. Edited by Allan Nevins. New York: Dodd, Mead and Company, 1927.

Hubbard, N. T. *Autobiography of N. T. Hubbard, with Personal Reminiscences of New York City from 1789 to 1875*. New York: J. F. Trow and Son, 1875.

Kavaler, Lucy. *The Astors: An American Legend*. New York: Dodd, Mead and Company, 1966.

Kiernan, Frances. *The Last Mrs. Astor: A New York Story*. New York: W. W. Norton and Company, 2008.

Lehr, Elizabeth Drexel. *"King Lehr" and the Gilded Age*. 1935; repr. Bedford, Mass.: Applewood Books, 2005.

Lewis, Jeremy. *David Astor: A Life in Print*. London: Jonathan Cape, 2016.

Lord, Walter. *A Night to Remember*. New York: St. Martin's Griffin, 1955.

Lucey, Donna M. *Archie and Amelie: Love and Madness in the Gilded Age.* New York: Harmony, 2006.

McCarthy, James Remington, with John Rutherford. *Peacock Alley: The Romance of the Waldorf-Astoria.* New York: Harper, 1931.

Morehouse, Ward, III. *The Waldorf-Astoria: America's Gilded Dream.* New York: M. Evans and Company, 1991.

Peiss, Kathy. *Cheap Amusements: Working Women and Leisure in Turn-of-the-Century New York.* Philadelphia, Penn.: Temple University Press, 1986.

Perdue, Alice Macycove, and James W. Seymore. *In Brooke Astor's Court: An Insider's Story.* CreateSpace Independent Publishing Platform, 2014.

Ranney, H. M. *Account of the Terrific and Fatal Riot at the New-York Astor Place Opera House, on the Night of May 19th, 1849; with the quarrels of Forrest and Macready, including all the causes which led to that awful tragedy! Wherein an infuriated mob was quelled by the public authorities and military, with its mournful termination in the sudden death or mutilation of more than fifty citizens, with full and authentic particulars.* New York: H. M. Ranney, 1849.

Schecter, Barnet. *The Devil's Own Work: The Civil War Draft Riots and the Fight to Reconstruct America.* New York: Walker and Company, 2005.

Sinclair, David. *Dynasty: The Astors and Their Times.* New York: Beaufort Books, 1984.

Smith, Horace Herbert. *Crooks of the Waldorf.* New York: Macaulay Company, 1929.

Stark, Peter. *Astoria: Astor and Jefferson's Lost Pacific Empire.* New York: Harper-Collins, 2015.

Taylor, William R., ed. *Inventing Times Square: Commerce and Culture at the Crossroads of the World.* Baltimore, Md.: Johns Hopkins University Press, 1996.

Terrell, John Upton. *Furs by Astor.* New York: William Morrow and Company, 1963.

Thomas, Lately. *The Astor Orphans: A Pride of Lions.* Albany, N.Y.: Washington Park Press, 1999.

Trachtenberg, Alan. *The Incorporation of America: Culture and Society in the Gilded Age.* New York: HarperCollins, 1982.

Voorsanger, Catherine Hoover, and John K. Howat, eds. *Art and the Empire City: New York, 1825–1861.* New York: The Metropolitan Museum of Art; and New Haven, Conn.: Yale University Press, 2001.

ARCHIVAL SOURCES

Astor Family Papers. New-York Historical Society.

Astor Family Papers. Special Collections. New York Public Library.

Citizens' Association of New York. *Report of the Council of Hygiene and Public Health of the Citizens' Association of New York upon the Sanitary Condition of the City.* New York, 1865.

New York, New York, U.S., Almshouse Ledgers, 1758–1952 [online database]. Lehi,
    Utah: Ancestry.com Operations, 2021. Original data: *Almshouse Ledgers*. New
    York: New York City Department of Records and Information Services.

William Waldorf Astor Papers. Library of Congress. Washington, D.C.

Boston Globe

New York Daily News

New York Herald

New York Herald Tribune

New York Magazine

New York Post

New York Times

Town Topics

Vanity Fair

INDEX

About the Authors

Anderson Cooper is an anchor at CNN and a correspondent for CBS's *60 Minutes*. He has won twenty Emmys and numerous other major journalism awards. Cooper is also the author of three number one *New York Times* bestsellers: *The Rainbow Comes and Goes*, *Dispatches from the Edge*, and *Vanderbilt* (coauthored by Katherine Howe). He lives in New York with his two sons.

Katherine Howe is a novelist and a historian of America. She is the author of the *New York Times* bestsellers *The Physick Book of Deliverance Dane* and *The House of Velvet and Glass*, and the young adult novels *Conversion* and *The Appearance of Annie van Sinderen*, and was the editor of *The Penguin Book of Witches*. She lives with her family in New England.